Paperwork

Fiction and Mass Mediacy in the Paper Age

KEVIN MCLAUGHLIN

PENN

University of Pennsylvania Press

Philadelphia

Copyright © 2005 University of Pennsylvania Press
All rights reserved
Printed in the United States of America on acid-free paper

10 9 8 7 6 5 4 3 2 1

Published by
University of Pennsylvania Press
Philadelphia, Pennsylvania 19104–4011

Library of Congress Cataloging-in-Publication Data

McLaughlin, Kevin, 1959–
    Paperwork : fiction and mass mediacy in the Paper Age / Kevin McLaughlin.
       p.   cm. — (Critical authors & issues)
    Includes bibliographical references (p.) and index.
    ISBN 0-8122-3888-5 (cloth : alk. paper)
    1. English fiction—19th century—History and criticism. 2. Capitalism and literature—
English-speaking countries—History—19th century. 3. Literature publishing—English-
speaking countries—History—19th century. 4. Mass media—English-speaking countries—
History—19th century. 5. American fiction—19th century—History and criticism.
6. Economics and literature—English-speaking countries. 7. Paper money—English-
speaking countries. 8. Economics in literature. 9. Money in literature. I. Title. II. Series

PR868.C25 M37   2005
823'.8093553—dc22

                                                                          2005042242

Pour Ourida et pour nos filles

Contents

Frequently Cited Texts

Frequently cited texts appear in parentheses by the following abbreviations:

MC   Edgar Allan Poe, "The Man of the Crowd," *Tales of Mystery and Imagination*

MRM   Edgar Allan Poe, "The Murders in the Rue Morgue," *Tales of Mystery and Imagination*

GB   Edgar Allan Poe, "The Gold Bug," *Tales of Mystery and Imagination*

TI   Robert Louis Stevenson, *Treasure Island*

BI   Robert Louis Stevenson, "The Bottle Imp," *South Sea Tales*

BF   Robert Louis Stevenson, *The Beach of Falésa*

BH   Charles Dickens, *Bleak House*

GE   Charles Dickens, *Great Expectations*

TMC   Thomas Hardy, *The Mayor of Casterbridge*

RN   Thomas Hardy, *The Return of the Native*

Introduction: Apparitions of Paper

> *Time of sunniest stillness;—shall we call it, what all men thought it, the new Age of Gold? Call it at least, of Paper; which in many ways is the succedaneum of Gold. Bank-paper, wherewith you can still buy when there is no gold left; Book-paper, splendent with Theories, Philosophies, Sensibilities,—beautiful art, not only revealing Thought, but also of so beautifully hiding from us the want of Thought! Paper is made from the rags of things that did once exist.*
>
> —*Thomas Carlyle,* The French Revolution *(1837)*

> *Paper—product no less marvelous than the impression for which it serves as a basis.*
>
> —*Honoré de Balzac,* Lost Illusions *(1837)*

"The Paper Age"

"The Paper Age" is the phrase coined by Thomas Carlyle in 1837 to describe the monetary and literary inflation of the French Revolution—an age of mass-produced "Bank-paper" and "Book-paper."[1] Carlyle's metaphor draws on the concept of the material support, the technical term adopted in the nineteenth century to name the substance charged with the bearing of impressions. Dictionaries tell us that this sense of support was derived from a metaphysical context in which the word had been used interchangeably with the Scholastic concept of the *substratum*, the fundamental substance bearing a particular quality or mode.[2] Carlyle's metaphor seems very much to turn on this derivation: with mass-produced paper and with the conditions of mass mediacy for which it stands, he claims, the support itself loses substance ("Bank-paper" has no "Gold"; "Book-paper" no "Thought"). According to this historical narrative, loss of substance in the mass media prefigures the appearance of what Carlyle does not hesitate to call "the masses," a social and political medium equally lacking in substance.[3] Such are the "waste multitudes" that rise up in *The French Revolution* as the ghostly support of "an inarticulate cry" (36).[4] In their "winged raggedness" these masses become the medium

of the message born by the emergence of the mass media: the announcement of a society without substance, a paper society (36). Yet,
how can paper stand for such a loss? How can a substance represent a
condition excluding substantiality? The problem with the metaphor is
that paper as a material support cannot be identified simply with the
insubstantiality of mass mediacy diagnosed by Carlyle. The spreading
condition needs a material support to bear the loss of substantial presentation in the traditional sense conveyed by the logic of metaphor.[5]

Carlyle's phrase is nevertheless suggestive, not only because it demonstrates the need to reconsider the status of the material support in the
mass media, but also because it points to the particular substance—
paper—that provides the basis for reflection on the mass media in much
popular fiction appearing around the time of his historical essay. Rather
than becoming a metaphor, however, paper in some of this fiction seems
to display the "marvelous" quality attributed to the support in the phrase
cited above from Balzac. In these works paper exhibits the elusive status
compared to language or linguistic "impressions" in the first part of *Lost
Illusions*. By associating paper with language in a novel dealing with the
emergence of the mass media in the nineteenth century, Balzac makes
a connection that would become critical a century later in Walter Benjamin's effort to interpret the impact of mass mediacy on traditional
concepts of historical and aesthetic experience. The loss of substantial
presentation in the mass media—what Benjamin describes as the "decline
of the aura"—is repeatedly compared to occurrences in language in his
writings of the later 1930s.[6] For Benjamin, as for Balzac, linguistic experience proves exemplary for the encounter with mass mediacy. The critical perspective elaborated by Benjamin serves as the point of departure
for the readings of paper proposed in this book. What emerges in the
chapters that follow is an account of paper in some works of Anglo-
American fiction of the nineteenth century as something other than a
metaphor for mass mediacy. The material support in these works becomes subject to the "decline of the aura": the "withdrawal," as Benjamin puts it, of the "here and now" of the traditional work of art into the
dispersing or distracting (*zerstreuende*) movement of the mass media.[7]

There are, strictly speaking, no metaphors for mass mediacy—no metaphors for conditions under which the principle of self-consistent substantiality as such is suspended. This is the thesis we will pursue: mass
mediacy does not present itself in the form of self-contained images. The
thesis becomes especially challenging when it comes to the question of art
and the mass media. For, in a manner that may appear paradoxical from
a traditional aesthetic point of view, this quality of the mass media, we will
contend, is implied in a certain concept of the work of art, specifically, in
the concept of the work of art as a medium that is not self-contained. This

concept of the aesthetic medium was the subject of Benjamin's early dissertation on the German Romantic theory of the absolute dependence of the work of art on critical activity (*Kritik*).[8] We will be coming back to this point. What needs to be emphasized at the start is that mass mediacy for Benjamin, like aesthetic mediacy for the German Romantics, manifests itself only through the critical involvement of subjects—subjects that precisely by becoming involved also cease to remain self-contained. This mode of involvement in the mass media is described by Benjamin's often-cited comments on the "distracted public" (*zerstreutes Publikum*) in his essay on the work of art in the age of technical reproducibility. In this sense, the withdrawal of the mass media from substantial self-presentation involves the activity of a subject, even when the subject in question happens to be a collective, as it is in Benjamin's later writings on mass culture. Paper in the literary works that will concern us in this book is the site of such withdrawing interactions. On a broad historical level, one might even argue, as I will suggest below, that this action is detectable with regard to the substance paper itself in the West—the material that arrived in Europe from China in the twelfth century and that came to be called "paper" by way of comparison to *papyrus*. For paper is of course not the same thing as papyrus and the fact that the former became identified with the latter has had enormous consequences for the media culture that began to emerge in medieval Europe when the name *paper* was applied. In this sense paper never is completely itself, in the West at least. The oriental import refuses to become assimilated to a Western media discourse informed by the principle of the relative durability of material supports for writing, a discourse the German Egyptologist Jan Assmann has recently traced to what he calls the *Steinkultur* of Ancient Egypt and in particular to the fundamental "digraphic" distinction in this influential ancient culture between enduring hieroglyphic inscription in stone and ephemeral cursive writing on papyrus.[9]

This Western discourse on the media founders on paper. Indeed it is precisely this collapse of the representational and metaphorical system of classical media theory that Carlyle's metaphor seeks to arrest, unsuccessfully as it turns out. The metaphor he employs to this end proves a case in point, as we will see if we look at it more closely. The paper of "Paper Age"—the "book paper" as well as the "bank paper"—is a monetary metaphor, and more specifically, a metaphor of counterfeit money. Carlyle's paper metaphor would stand for something that passes itself off falsely as standing for some other thing. The paper of *The French Revolution* is, in short, a metaphor for something patently fake: something, that is, like the French Revolutionary *assignat*, the paper money that was in fact printed on the first mass-produced paper in the 1790s.[10] This Revolutionary paper money—according to Carlyle, counterfeit money since it pretended falsely to stand for the estimated value of the property confiscated from the Church—becomes in his account the metaphor for the false pretense or fraud of the French Revolution as a whole. Yet this counterfeit money metaphor is based on the very substance that withdraws when it becomes money, that is to say paper. Carlyle's paper money metaphor involves a sort of *trompe l'œil*: it substitutes the substance paper for its disappearance. This substitution, the paper money metaphor, is very much in keeping with the traditional metaphorical logic of money—the one thing, it is supposed, that can be substituted for all others on the basis of the fiction or principle of the comparability and thus of the fundamental likeness of all things (what the political economists call exchange-value).

Money in this sense is an ideal *and* a real thing—it is a real substance, and it stands for an ideal element making all things comparable.[11] Paper money, still traditionally speaking, is also ideal and real, but with an important difference. It is ideal, not in standing for the ideal element rendering all things comparable, but rather in referring to the real thing that is in fact both real and ideal—what Marx called the money commodity (we might want to think of it as gold). And paper money is real, not in appearing as a substance that is also ideal (like gold), but, on the contrary, in *not appearing* as a substantial thing. This is the peculiarity of paper money (Marx would say it is the peculiarity—as he puts, it the "sensuously supersensuous" character—of money as such): it *must* appear as an insubstantial thing.[12] This might seem impossible. Surely *something* must appear, something must present itself, when paper money appears. And yet the thing that appears in this case must not be identifiable at any point with the substance that appears, with the substance paper. For, unlike the substance of the money commodity—according to the traditional, as it were, pre-Marxian view—the paper of paper money does not really exist as a substance. It exists only at the point of referring to some real and ideal thing; it is only a thing (if we can still call it a thing) at the point where it recedes as a substance. Until it recedes the paper of paper money is not money. Thus even in this rather traditional context—even before the disappearance of convertibility or of the gold standard, for instance, as a specific monetary institution—the paper of paper money is virtual: it does not present itself in the substantial form, in the "here and now," as Benjamin would say, of paper, but rather in the withdrawal of paper.[13]

Because the metaphorical counterfeit money of Carlyle's essay, including the metaphorical *assignat*, is based on the substitution of the substance paper for its disappearance, the paper of the "Paper Age" is not really paper money but rather a paper money metaphor. By way of such a metaphor Carlyle seeks to contain mass cultural forces—forces he reductively identifies with, and projects onto, the Revolution in France—by apprehending them as a self-consistent substance (paper). The *trompe l'œil* of the paper money metaphor in Carlyle's narrative of the French Revolution thus encourages, or admonishes, readers to keep their eyes fixed squarely on the very kind of self-consistent and reliably representational medium that breaks down under conditions of mass mediacy: when the economic and literary media that traditionally express the political interests of the nation-state start to correspond with the emergence of mass collective.[14] Such are the points of breakdown that we will be exploring in the treatment given paper by some leading works of popular fiction published in English during the decades following the appearance of Carlyle's also quite popular historical essay—the period when Anglo-American literary mass culture entered what might well be called its paper age. The handling of paper in these works marks a series of encounters with the specific conditions of mass mediacy repressed by Carlyle's defensive metaphor. Such encounters provoke reflection on the limits of a view of aesthetic and economic exchange that remains within the phenomenological horizon of self-consistent subjects and objects. The effects of mass mediacy at issue in the treatment of paper in this fiction reveal the fundamental inadequacy of a traditional perspective on subjectivity to the workings of the mass media. Throughout the chapters that follow, the subject emerges again and again as the support for a movement that exceeds subjective limits. As we will see, this is a matter not only of character or individual writer but also of what might be called a national literary subject. For, the challenge posed by the mass media to subjectivity also puts in question the literary historical category of the isomorphic national literary movement in this particular field.

The broad literary historical argument implied by the main chapters of this study is that two of the most important developments in narrative fiction in English during this period—the emergence of the American "romance" or short story on the one hand, and of Victorian novel on the other—can be understood as interrelated attempts to exploit the loss of self-control enacted by the distracting or dispersing force Benjamin attributes to the mass media.[15] Along these lines we will start with Poe, Stevenson, and Melville and then move on to Dickens and Hardy. As has already been suggested, the very premise of the argument being made about fiction and mass mediacy in this period dictates that we engage in detailed readings of specific, though not self-contained, works by the writers in question. This critical method alone can show how exposure to an aesthetic medium turns out to involve readers in the distracting movement of the mass media. Paper will have a fundamental bearing on each case: not metaphors of paper, but rather a metaphorical failure drawing the subject into the force field of a medium—a mass medium—that suspends self-presentation. What confronts us as we engage in this paperwork is exposure, overexposure even, to mass mediacy as displayed on a distracted subject.

The approach we will be taking to paper provides a supplement and an alternative to much materialist research on literature and culture, specifically, to recent developments in print history or the history of the book on the one hand and studies of communication technology on the other. Print or book history is relevant to this project in that it provides an account of the emergence of a material support ephemeral enough to suggest to some nineteenth-century writers a point at which the materiality of the support might be understood to dissolve, at least as a self-contained or self-consistent material thing. In the fiction we will consider, such a point of dissolution is repeatedly associated with the withdrawal of the material support in the act of reading. Our concern in this sense will be with an action and an interaction that has remained largely in the margins of materialist print and book history.[16] By taking up the psychic and even physical engagement of the human subject in a mass medium, this project also touches on questions being pursued in contemporary studies of communication technology, in particular those focusing on the challenge posed by new media to traditional concepts of subjective agency. But, in contrast to much of this work, our aim will be to trace a movement marked by a singularly declining agency that does not simply become mechanical in the sense of carrying out a command or conveying information.[17] The readings of paper in this study will be carried out, therefore, at the limits of both materialist print history and materialist studies of the new media.[18] Before we turn to these readings, however, some philosophical and historical background is in order.

The Philosophy of Paper

The exposure to paperwork that concerns us in what follows is the subject of some recent remarks by Jacques Derrida. These remarks reenact a scene similar to those encountered in the nineteenth-century fiction we will be considering. They also suggest a philosophical context for an approach to paper as a material support along the lines of Benjamin's later studies of mass mediacy. Derrida's comments come in an interview recently published under the title of "Le papier ou moi."[19] In response to questions put to him on paper for a special issue of a media journal, Derrida writes of "an epoch in the history of technics and in the history of humanity" delimited by the "hegemony" of paper.[20] Paper is associated in passing with the mass media and indeed the interview itself has subsequently been collected, under the heading of "*Papier journal*," with a series of writings that initially appeared in newspapers. Paper here, however, is not a metaphor. It does not stand for a historical phenomenon in the usual sense, a period, for instance, that has come to a close with the advent of essentially new electronic forms of technical support often identified with virtuality.[21] On the contrary, the paper in question is already virtual—at the start of the interview, for example, it comes to Derrida as something that did not properly present itself as a subject in his work. And it comes to him at this moment, appearing on the very support that bears its name, not precisely as paper but rather as an "impression" of it, an impression Derrida now gets of the subject of paper in his work: "To see coming all these questions on paper, I have the impression (*impression*, what a word already) that I have never had any other *subject*."[22] Thus at this moment—at the moment of the interview—paper does not present itself to the now self-conscious subject (Derrida) but instead makes an impression on the subject. The subject, that is, turns into a support for an impression. At this point, we might say, paper becomes the *subject* and vice versa. This is the sense in which (the subject) Derrida may be said "never to have had any other subject," the sense in short of "Le papier ou moi."[23] The subject of the interview, more precisely the subject of the scene with which it opens, is not paper or the subject (Derrida) but something between the two, or better, some intermediary event leaving an impression of paper, an apparition of paper. Paper appears to enter into the subject, as it were, not in presenting itself in the manner of a self-consistent substance, but in withdrawing.

The paper, then, is a point of departure. The impression it leaves unsettles not just the conventional historical view according to which paper becomes the metaphor or code-word for a previrtual medium, but also the conventional philosophical perspective from which paper becomes a metaphor for the mind or the subject. For, although it is never explicitly mentioned in this passage, the conventional metaphor in question is Locke's image of the mind as a sheet of "white paper."[24] In this implicit sense, the impression Derrida gets in the scene may well be of the role of paper as a point of departure for the deconstructive project, a project that may be said never to have had any subject other than the refusal of the psychological metaphor of the subject as a simple, that is to say, actual or substantially self-consistent sheet of paper. As Derrida goes on to make more explicit, the apparition of paper in this scene marks the return of the subject that was one of the chief preoccupations of his early work on Freud's search for a metaphor for the human psyche that would be adequate to psychoanalytic theory of the unconscious. Freud for his part, we should note, never mentions Locke's comparison of the mind to a sheet of "white paper." This is remarkable considering the psychoanalyst's well-documented tendency to draw on writing materials in his attempts to describe the human psyche. The omission stands out in particular in the 1925 "Note on the Mystic Writing Pad," an essay that seems to take issue precisely with Locke's simile. While suggestive of the mind's capacity for preserving memory traces, Freud argues in his "Note," the metaphor of paper fails to account for the "limitless receptivity" of the human psyche, a receptivity Freud compares to the erasability of a writing slate. The problem with paper is that "the receptive capacity of the writing-surface is soon exhausted. The sheet is filled with writing, there is no room on it for any more notes, and I find myself obliged to bring another sheet into use, that has not been written on."[25]

Some forty years after its appearance, Freud's "note" was taken up by Derrida in his groundbreaking "Freud and the Scene of Writing." In his essay, Derrida retraces what he calls the "double system" that Freud saw represented in the "mystic writing pad"—the manner in which the simultaneous psychic demands for receptivity and preservation, perception and memory, were combined in the little device that had recently "come on the market" consisting of a dark slab covered by a piece of wax paper and a protective sheet of transparent celluloid. Like the human perceptual apparatus, the pad is both infinitely receptive—marks made by pressing a stylus on the surface of the pad can be erased by lifting the wax paper and the celluloid sheet—and at the same time preservative—the traces of the erased marks are conserved, and remain legible, in the underlying slab. Derrida's reading of Freud aims to uncover a possibility broached but not explicitly considered in the "Note," namely, that the description of the resemblance Freud perceives between the mystic writing pad and the psychic apparatus is ill-suited to the traditional, and for Derrida fundamental, philosophical distinction between writing materials and the human psyche.

According to Derrida, Freud's comparison of the mind to the mystic writing pad, bears witness to the finitude of what has been traditionally thought of, and what Freud in spite of his description continues to think of, as the "spontaneity" of the tracings of human memory: "Freud, like Plato, thus continues to oppose hypomnemic writing and writing *en tei psychei* itself woven of traces, empirical memories of a present truth outside of time."[26] What Freud represses, even while outlining in his note on the mystic writing pad, is the proposition that "the machine—and, consequently, representation—is death and finitude *within* the psyche."[27] This repression occurs in Freud's text as a sketch of a materialized psyche—that of the mystic writing pad as a nonpsychic metaphor of the psyche—is effaced and in its place a figure of a more traditional psyche appears: the psyche, for example, of the "I" who emerges in the last lines of the "Note" to delineate the two-handed operation of writing on and effacing the mystic writing pad: "If we imagine one hand writing upon the surface of the Mystic Writing-Pad while another periodically raises its covering sheet from the wax slab, we shall have a concrete representation of the way in which I tried to picture the functioning of the perceptual apparatus of our mind."[28] This concluding sketch in Freud's "Note"—that of an "I" seeking to produce an image of how it was trying to represent to itself the functioning of the human psyche—doubles the operation it seeks to represent with the metaphor of the mystic writing pad. The effacement of the sketch of the psychic apparatus as a mystic writing pad and the appearance in its place of the image of the subject trying to represent itself conforms to the process of inscription and reinscription made materially possible by the device of the writing pad.

This is "the scene of writing" staged by Freud's "Note." The psychoanalyst's paper, or rather the removal of this paper, becomes the stage for Derrida's depiction of the Freudian "scene of writing." If, like the mystic writing pad, Freud's machine "does not run by itself," neither does Derrida's: these machines become stages or supports for a scene only through the involvement of a participant, in this case of a writer, who must also be removed. For, the "subject" of this scene cannot be identified simply with what we usually think of as a writer (Freud, Derrida, or someone writing on Derrida's essay on Freud), any more than it can be simply identified with an independent writing apparatus (the mystic writing pad, Freud's "Note," or Derrida's "Freud and the Scene of Writing"). Instead of a subject, the "scene of writing," as Derrida writes of Freud's "Note," stages "a *system* of rapports" (between Freud and the device of the mystic writing pad, Derrida and Freud's "Note on the Mystic Writing Pad," a writer and Derrida's "Freud and the Scene of Writing"). But the key rapport is one of a psyche that is not self-contained to dynamic writing material or support that is not simply a self-present *aide-mémoire*. If this scene is in part one of psychic exteriorization—a spatialization of the mind in the figure of an inorganic graphic support—it is also, again reciprocally, one of the interiorization of the inorganic matter of the writing machine in the psyche (what Derrida calls "death and finitude *within* the psyche").

It is noteworthy that in Freud's analysis of the mystic writing pad paper plays the role of the kind of enduring graphic support to which it has been traditionally opposed in Western culture. By way of contrast with such materials as stone and later on parchment, paper has customarily been seen as an ephemeral bearer of writing. The appearance of paper in Freud's "Note" is brief but telling: "I can choose a writing-surface which will preserve intact any note made upon it (*die ihr anvertraute Notiz*) for an indefinite length of time—for instance, a sheet of paper which I can write upon in ink. I am then in possession of a 'permanent memory-trace.'"[29] Paper here, then, is the durable material to which one entrusts a "Note" (*Notiz*), such as, for example, the "Note (*Notiz*) on the Mystic Writing Pad."[30] In this way, Freud may be seen to try to preserve his note from the hazards to which writing on a real mystic writing pad is exposed, the energetic process of effacement and reinscription that his paper goes on to describe and that Derrida's reception of the paper enacts. If the attempt at preserving this description "intact" may not entirely succeed, the manner in which the "Note" is taken up in Derrida's writing seems to provide another illustration of the operation sketched in Freud's essay. For Derrida does not analyze the role of paper as such in his 1966 "Freud and the Scene of Writing." In that essay, paper remains a preliminary and ephemeral figure in Freud's discussion of the psychic apparatus. Derrida's remarks on the mystic writing pad reappear some thirty years later in his *Mal d'archive: une impression freudienne*. A block citation from the earlier essay is followed by a reflection on the potential significance of newer, especially electronic, archival machines for the Freudian search for a material model of the psychic apparatus. There is in this "Freudian impression," however, no explicit trace of paper, the material support to which Freud entrusts his "*Notiz.*"[31] But in the interview that appeared in 1997 in the journal *Cahiers de médiologie*, Freud's paper resurfaces.[32] Taking up again the invaluable "Note," Derrida writes:

> The pedagogical or illustrative recourse to the technical device of the "Mystic Writing-Pad" poses all sorts of problems to which I cannot return here, but the putting to work of paper there, properly speaking, remains striking. Freud puts himself on paper, to be sure, as support and surface of inscription, place for the retention of marks—but he attempts simultaneously to free himself from it. He wants to clear its limit. He uses paper, but as if he wanted to place himself beyond the paper principle. . . . Paper here is already "reduced" or "retired," withdrawn/recessed [*en retrait*] (the paper, properly speaking, if one can still say this, but can we speak here of paper *itself*, of the "thing itself" named "paper" or only of its *figures*? and has not "withdrawal" (*retrait*) always been the mode of being, the very movement of what we call "paper"? Would not the essential trait [*trait*] of paper be the withdrawal [*retrait*] of what is effaced and retires *under* what a supposed support is supposed to support, receive or accept? Is not paper always and forever in the process of "disappearing" and do we not mourn this departed one in the very moment that we entrust it with the nostalgic signs of this mourning and make it disappear under ink, tears and the sweat of this work, a work of writing that is always a work of mourning and bodily loss? *What is* paper, itself, properly speaking?[33]

Reading the "Note" again, Derrida takes conscious note this time of the role of paper: paper is here, he suggests, put to work in order to go beyond its limit, beyond the limit of the principle of limited graphic receptivity for which it is supposed to be the metaphor. It is precisely with this aim in mind in fact that Freud seeks to move beyond the figure of paper as a graphic support to the peculiar apparatus of the mystic writing pad. And yet this movement beyond is itself put on paper. The movement beyond in this sense would "reduce" paper to the status of an enduring material support that is of limited receptivity. And this reduction would in turn amount to the "withdrawal" of paper from the movement that would exceed its finitude. Not entirely, however, from the scene of writing since, as we have just seen, paper is the stage on which the movement is put. Paper here is split: it is both a finite material support and a stage on which this finitude is exceeded. Paper is, then, the exterior surface, the material in the world, that repeatedly withdraws from what it is to support—a surface that is, as Derrida suggests, "recessing" or "retiring" (*en retrait*).

The limit represented by paper in this scene of writing is traced by Derrida in the context of Freud's search for a material model of psychic writing. It is traced, as we have noted, on and beyond Freud's paper (the "beyond" here being precisely that hazardous space from which Freud seeks to preserve his "Note"—a space of death and finitude represented *within* the Freudian text itself in figures of various writing materials). The impression left on Derrida by the "questions on paper" put to him in the interview some thirty years after the appearance of "Freud and the Scene of Writing" is thus of a certain finitude, the finitude marked by the subject of paper in his work. In this sense the subject of the interview, like the subject of all genuine interviews, is death—the interview announces, as Derrida might say, the future disappearance of its subject. It is in this sense that the end of paper's "hegemony" is said to have accelerated during a period that "coincides, roughly speaking, with that of my 'generation': a lifetime."[34] But the death in question is one to which the material presence of the substance paper is inadequate. Paper shrinks from this death.[35] The impression left on Derrida, then, is of this shrinkage or withdrawal of the material support—what he calls the "subject" of paper (*le papier ou le moi*)—as the material limit and the material condition of possibility for "the scene of writing" and for his writing in particular. We will be tracing a parallel limit marked by figures of paper in works of nineteenth-century fiction. In the works studied here, as in the "scene of writing" just delineated, paper operates both as a stage for the literary medium and as its limit—*le point mort*, so to speak, in the movement of the literary medium.[36]

Paper and History

Paper is a historical, as well as a philosophical, subject. Indeed, the history of paper corresponds in some ways to the philosophy of paper sketched by Derrida. Before going on to develop the parallel between Derrida's remarks on paper as a material support and Benjamin's media theory, let us respond to the question left suspended in the passage from Derrida that we just analyzed: "*What is* paper, itself, properly speaking?" A good place to begin addressing this question is with the word *paper: paper* derives from the Greek *papuros.* Paper, however, is not the same thing as papyrus.[37] Historians tell us that the substance called paper had its beginnings in ancient China. In 105 A.D., it is said, Ts'ai Lun invented a technique for making this material from "mulberry and other barks, fish nets, hemp, and rags."[38] Westerners, at least since Marco Polo, have been fascinated by the ceremonial value of this substance among the Chinese. In the definitive twentieth-century history of paper, Dard Hunter puts it with remarkable precision: "The fibrous substance called paper is regarded in a vastly different light in the Orient from what it is in the Occident, for in the Far East it has a spiritual significance that overshadows its practical use, while in the Western world the purposes for which paper is intended are purely practical and utilitarian."[39] A good example of this "spiritual significance," one to which Hunter devotes considerable attention, is the paper *spirit-money* that came to be placed in the tombs of the dead shortly after the invention of paper and well before—by some five centuries in fact—paper became officially used as legal tender in the Celestial Empire.[40] Thus, perhaps due to its frailty as a medium, as some have speculated—due, in other words, to its status as a sign of the transient mediacy of human life— paper in China was credited with a special potentiality to take on spiritual value. Over time the ritual burning of this paper money and of all sorts of worldly objects constructed in paper—vehicles, animals, clothing and so on—became common at Chinese burials.[41] References to this practice can be found throughout the literature of this period.[42] In a seventh-century text, to take just one instance, the sage, Jen-ts'ien, instructs his student, Wen-Pen: "things used by spirits and by men differ; only gold and silk can circulate among both; but it is better if they are imitations. Gold imitated by spreading a layer of yellow color on a sheet of tin and paper presented in place of silk and other materials are the most highly valued."[43] Without being able to enter completely into the perspective from which such "imitations" are valuable, or even to comprehend fully the meaning of the word that "imitations" translates in this passage, we must limit ourselves to pointing out that the ritual incineration or "transformation" (*houa*) of paper is, it seems, just one manifestation of the wealth of "paper symbolism and paper worship" found in a Chinese culture where, as Jen-ts'ien appears to say, the spirits want worldly semblance.[44]

The greeting given the Chinese invention when it first came on the market in Europe in the twelfth or the thirteenth century was, however, hardly ceremonious. The identification of the foreign substance with the Arabs and Jews responsible for introducing it into an anxiously Christian Europe did not help.[45] But this appearance was marked in another way as well. For when the word paper—stemming, as we noted, from papyrus—was applied, the frail substance elaborately venerated in China became abruptly relegated to the inferior role played by papyrus in a Western civilization that had its origins in the reverence of stone as the enduring material support of inscription. The very name paper, in other words, assimilated the "Oriental" import to a Western tradition that Jan Assmann has recently called "digraphism." The origin of this digraphic discourse, Assmann argues, is to be found in Ancient Egyptian "stone culture" (*Steinkultur*). According to his account, Ancient Egypt consisted of two linguistic cultures that existed side-by-side. On the one hand, there was the everyday language of the street and the marketplace and, on the other, the sacred language of eternity. Such "diglossia" permeated Ancient Egypt. With respect to architecture, for example, the Greek chronicler Hecataeus reported that the ancient Egyptians referred to the buildings in which they lived as "shelters" (*katalyseis*) while calling the graves in which they were buried "eternal houses" (*aidioi oikoi*). This distinction operated throughout the architectural vocabulary of ancient Egypt—between the merely functional buildings like residences, which were usually made of clay, and monumental structures like graves, temples, steles, statues, pyramids, obelisks, and so on, which were made of stone. Scholarship in this area has stressed that the dichotomy between the everyday and the eternal in ancient Egyptian "stone culture" was especially evident in its writing practices and, more specifically, in a distinction between the diverse graphic supports to which they corresponded.[46] Referring to Hecataeus's account, Assmann observes, for instance:

through the Egyptian writing system runs the same boundary that Hecataeus recognized in Egyptian architecture—the one separating the monumental from the functional. The monumental writing of hieroglyphs, as opposed to other pictographic systems, faithfully preserved its original iconicity over three and a half millennia. . . . With this writing stone 'monuments' were inscribed. For everyday purposes, by contrast, one did not of course use stone but more portable materials like papyrus, pieces of clay or limestone, wood, leather and so on. Employed for these was cursive writing, which deviated from the realistic pictorial quality of hieroglyphs, distilling from them only certain distinguishing features.[47]

This "digraphism" of ancient Egypt left a profound impression on classical antiquity and in turn on the Western tradition as such, as has been especially shown with respect to the hieroglyph.[48] Thus in a sense Assmann and other archeologists of the ancient communicative media have been attempting to demonstrate recently what Hegel believed before them: everything from the schemata in Plato and the Aristotelian categories to the emergence of the principle of canonization in art, they argue, can be traced to the monumental language of Egyptian stone culture.[49]

Perhaps more than associations with the Orient or the Judeo-Arab world, then, it is the legacy of hieroglyphic "stone culture" of Ancient Egypt in the Occident that accounts for what André Blum in his classic account has called the "prejudice against paper" in the European Middle Ages.[50] There were of course paper advocates during the medieval and early-modern periods, but the image of paper was largely the same on both sides. This was a basic conflict over the role of the material support in the communication of writing and images, but the status of the supports themselves was not in question. On the one hand, there were those who saw the advantages of paper in a culture based on practical, efficient and abundant media of communication and, on the other, those who regarded this relatively perishable substance as a threat to the enduring basis of the culture. So, without disagreeing about the quality of paper as a graphic support, the Englishman Thomas Churchyard could sing its praises as a useful disseminator of information and the German Benedictine Johannes Trithemius could warn about its ephemerality as a bearer of sacred scripture.[51] In this sense, the arguments for and against paper throughout the European Middle Ages and Renaissance demonstrate the ongoing hold of Egyptian digraphism on the image of paper in the West.[52]

With the industrialization of papermaking at the end of the eighteenth century, the medieval and early modern conflict over paper became more acute, and more fundamentally challenging to traditional views of the matter. Mass-produced paper first appeared from Nicolas Louis Robert's machine "in an endless web" during the 1790s in France.[53] The remarkable machine was first put to work in fact printing *assignats,* the highly inflationary and short-lived paper money emitted by the Revolutionary government (Figure 1).[54] In the hands of the English satirists who, in spite of their appeals to practicality, failed to appreciate the economic feasibility of such a paper money experiment, the *assignats* became the signs of the Revolution's mystification, a Revolutionary spirit-money that was to have been passed off on the credulous masses. The idea of paper as the counterfeit currency of a fraudulent Revolutionary promised land fit in well with a satirical perspective informed by Western digraphism. The metaphor of paper in Carlyle's phrase "the Paper Age"—the metaphor of an age marked by the economic and aesthetic hyperinflation of "bank-paper" and "book-paper," according to Carlyle—marks an intersection between digraphism and a broad discourse of value to be found throughout the literature of the nineteenth century. To the English imagination during this time, or at least to a dominant strain in it, paper appeared as a figure of what was anxiously identified with the destructive and illegitimate forces of the French and American Revolutions rather than with the civilizing and legitimate "financial revolution" of modern England's own origins.[55] From this perspective, nothing represented the fundamental ephemerality of paper more than the notorious *assignat.* The revolutionary paper currency was seen as the very sign of the instability, the evanescence and, as Burke put it, the "fictitiousness" of the French Revolution itself.[56] The line of thought followed by Burke and Carlyle can be traced back in English satirical writing to Pope, as we will see below in our reading of Poe and Stevenson, but it draws on a much older image of paper that derives from the digraphism of Ancient Egypt.

A search of nineteenth-century materials on paper turns up an 1829 treatise on machine-made paper by a certain John Murray entitled *Practical Remarks on Modern Paper.* Murray's little treatise reveals the persistence of the legacy of Egyptian digraphism in the nineteenth century,

Figure 1. Sheet of assignats. Courtesy of the Hay Library, Brown University.

the period that concerns us here, and also the way this legacy was arriving at a crisis in the century after the appearance of mass-produced paper. A seemingly evanescent publication (indeed there are no original editions in any of the major research libraries I have consulted), Murray's text has recently been brought out by a small artisanal press in an expensive edition printed on hand-made paper. As his title indicates, Murray's concern is with the practical problem posed by the greater material frailty of industrially produced paper. For, making paper with Robert's machine required the use of acidic materials (mainly alum and rosin) that could bind and fill in the spaces between the more finely ground cotton fiber. The problem was that these interstitial "sizing" agents were precisely what caused paper to decompose more rapidly.[57] In other words, what held mass-produced paper together in its weave was also the source of its more rapid disintegration. Murray gives "testimony in favor of hand-made paper, over that manufactured by machinery," but he is not "hostile to the diffusion of mechanical aids."[58] On the contrary, his "practical remarks" are offered as a disinterested, scientific contribution toward making mass-produced, "modern" paper with the material endurance of stone. Mass-produced paper, Murray proclaims, must be made into a material worthy of bearing the "tangible symbols [that] could only have come originally from heaven."[59] It must be made, in other words, in the image of the original medium of the divine "legacy"—the tablets that Moses brought down from Mount Sinai. Mass-produced paper must be made, then, in the image of stone, for the tablets were, as Murray emphasizes, "tables of stone, written with the finger of God."[60] The engraved tables were in fact made, he goes on to specify, of "Hebrew or graphic granite"[61]: "granite is a primitive rock, and may be emphatically and truly termed the foundation-stone of the globe,—admirably emblematic of the permanence and stability of the words of the law. . . . [The characters "graven on the tables"] were therefore an integrant part of the stone, and identified with it."[62] Murray associates the durability of Mosaic law with stone and, as he makes explicit elsewhere in this passage, with the hieroglyphs like those on the Rosetta Stone that had recently been deciphered by Champollion (in 1822). This linking of stone, hieroglyph and the Decalogue is in keeping with the traditional association of Moses with Egypt and the Egyptian art of writing (the Moses who "was brought up in all the wisdom and sciences of the Egyptians"; Acts 7:22).

But within this tradition the precise character of the original medium has been of course the source of endless speculation and disagreement.[63] Writing of the same Biblical passages almost a century before Murray, for instance, the English cleric William Warburton went to great lengths in his *Divine Legation of Moses* to insist on the specifically nonhieroglyphic character of the writing "graven in the tables." Warburton argued that the iconic quality conventionally attributed to the hieroglyph would have been at odds with the prohibition on divine images. "All hieroglyphic writing was absolutely forbidden by the second commandment," Warburton reasoned, "hieroglyphics being . . . the greatest source of [the Egyptians'] idolatry and superstitions."[64] Thus, according to Warburton, "to cut off . . . all occasion of danger from symbolic images, Moses, as I suppose, altered the shapes of the Egyptian letters, and reduced them into something like those simple forms in which we now find them."[65] For Warburton, we might say, Moses broke with the digraphism associated with ancient Egypt when he obeyed the aniconic commandment and "altered the shapes of the Egyptian letters." As Kant recognized in his *Critique of Judgment*, it is precisely this, for Warburton and other Enlightenment thinkers, nonhieroglyphic character of the second commandment that makes it an example of sublimity and allows it to become, as Kant says, "a representation of the infinite."[66] Indeed, Kant's familiarity with these eighteenth-century debates over the Egyptian sources of the Decalogue and in particular over the kind of writing that was "graven in the tables"[67] may well have contributed to his sense of the reflexive, sublime character of the second commandment: that the aniconic commandment prohibiting divine representations must be communicated in a medium that is itself aniconic.[68]

We need not trace in detail the lines of influence that lead from the Enlightenment debates over Moses's Egyptianness to the appearance of the aniconic sublime in Kant's aesthetics. These brief suggestions seem enough to indicate that, due to the ongoing importance of the discourse of Western digraphism, Murray's practical project for making more durable mass-produced paper can become something more than a merely practical matter. Such a project raises questions and presents ideological conflicts about the status of the material support in communication. Murray's comments illustrate superbly what might be called the metaphysical innocence of modern practicality when it comes to communicative material. It is indeed precisely such innocence that the literary works studied here explore and attempt to foreground in their handling of paper.[69] In Murray's case the metaphor he employs to describe a material model for modern paper (that of Moses's stone tablets) carries him to, and in fact beyond, the limits of traditional digraphism. The metaphysical implications of his practical proposal to reform the material medium seem to undercut the straightforward practicality of his message. For, while Murray's project aims merely to propose techniques for making of paper a more durable material support for writing, the language he tries simply to use to make this point ends up projecting him beyond the traditional understanding of paper—beyond the paper principle.

Murray's treatise is of course nothing more, or less, than a piece of nineteenth-century ephemera by an obscure writer on an esoteric subject. And yet is it not precisely this ephemerality that Murray's proposal would abolish? Still, as one reads the expensive limited edition of his treatise recently printed on hand-made paper in the rarified surroundings of the reading room in the Houghton Library (Harvard University's special collections archive), one cannot help getting the impression that the little text has gone beyond the strictly practical purposes for which Murray claims it was intended.[70] Perhaps Murray's treatise can be found here and in this form because it is of surpassing "historical interest," say for the history of the craft of papermaking (this is the point made by the publishers of this edition). But our reading of the passage above attributes to it something more than "historical interest," something more like literary or philosophical significance. Yet again: is not such a reading—of this text and every other text on paper—implied by Murray's selection of the Tablets of the Law as the model for mass-produced paper?

Virtuality and Materiality in Benjamin's Media Theory

There is a parallel between the "subject" of paper in the philosophical and historical contexts just outlined and the "subject" of the mass media in Benjamin. This parallel requires that we refine a point made earlier. We began by asserting that, for Benjamin, the involvement of subjects in the mass media is implicit in the concept of aesthetic mediacy explicated in his study of the German Romantics. In both cases, we noted, the subject is taken up in a medium that resists substantial self-presentation. Yet, with aesthetic media and with the mass media, Benjamin repeatedly insists, it is a matter of singular encounters with a certain materiality— a withdrawing materiality. At issue, as Benjamin says, is an *immediate* experience of *mediacy*. In the last section of this chapter, we will explore this point in Benjamin's discussion of aesthetic mediacy in German Romanticism. First, however, let us try to specify how this materiality or "immediacy" enters into his approach to art under the conditions of technical reproducibility peculiar to the mass media. Especially apt for our purposes is Benjamin's account of the impact in the nineteenth century of the invention of photography on the traditional concept of the work of art since it is here that the question of a withdrawing material support becomes most poignant.

Like Freud in his "Note on the Mystic Writing Pad," Benjamin is concerned in his reflections on photography with an inorganic mechanism of inscription as a model for what has traditionally been considered an organic process—in Freud's case the mystic writing pad as a metaphor for the human psyche, in Benjamin's the photographic apparatus as a model for aesthetic experience. A fine example of the latter comes in *The Arcades Project* when Benjamin cites the following passage from Félix Nadar's description of his photographic work in the Paris catacombs:

> With each new camera setup, we had to test our exposure time empirically; certain of the plates were found to require up to eighteen minutes.—Remember, we were still, at that time, using collodion emulsion on glass negatives. . . . I had judged it advisable to animate (*animer*) some of these scenes by the use of a human figure—less from considerations of picturesqueness than in order to give a sense of scale, a precaution too often neglected by explorers in this medium and with sometimes disconcerting consequences. For these eighteen minutes of exposure time, I found it difficult to obtain from a human being the absolute, inorganic immobility (*l'immobilité absolue, inorganique*) I required. I tried to get round this difficulty by means of mannequins, which I dressed in workman's clothes and positioned in the scene (*mise en scène*) with as little awkwardness as possible; this business did nothing but complicate our task.[71]

Let us try to retrace what happens in the scene. For the purpose of scale and proportion, the animate human figure is placed before the camera: only to discover, however, that such a figure cannot in fact be adequately placed by this apparatus which is, it turns out, not on the human scale, if by human we understand (as Nadar seems to at first) that which is animate. The scene simply cannot be animated. In other words, the problem of scale and proportion here is not the size of the human figure, but its organic mobility. For a human figure to enter this scene it must attain what Nadar's living subjects failed to achieve (in spite of his efforts apparently) and what they by definition had to fail to achieve: "absolute, inorganic immobility." That is to say: death. Death is the scale here, and not just any death: human death, the transformation of the human body from the animate into the inanimate. If the latter is suggested by the huge piles of human skeletons that appear in many of Nadar's photographs of the catacombs, the former might have been represented by living subjects who would have "animated" the scene (Figure 2). Perhaps this was Nadar's idea: to have the photographic apparatus, this marvelous machine that had recently been brought on the market, "see" the scene the way he did—as the juxtaposition of human death and life. But the scale of life is excluded from the perspective of the photographic apparatus—it "sees" only death. The human figure enters its field of vision only at the point of death, and since the human subjects Nadar introduces into this scene were unable to provide the semblance of death, even in the service of attempting to animate the scene, Nadar furnishes it himself.

Benjamin seems to be taking up this passage from Nadar again when he observes in "On Some Motifs in Baudelaire": "What was inevitably

Figure 2. Félix Nadar, *The Paris Sewers*. Musée nationale de la photographie, Paris.

felt to be inhuman, one might even say deadly, in daguerrotypy was the (prolonged) gazing into the camera (*Apparat*), since the camera (*Apparat*) records (*aufnehmen*) the human image without returning our gaze."[72] This is what Nadar portrays in the passage above, and perhaps what he is compelled by the camera to portray through the use of the presumably inanimate human figures that he nevertheless describes with the somewhat ambiguous French word *mannequins*[73]: the deadly gazing into a camera (*Hereinblicken in den Apparat*), a sort of gazing to death. Of fundamental import for Benjamin is that, from the perspective of the camera, the process described here is all take and no give. This is the crisis of reciprocation or restitution in aesthetics that Benjamin calls the "the decline of the aura."[74] Nadar expects the camera to look as he does, in effect to return or reproduce (*wiedergeben*) the gaze of a living subject— his and that of those figures he places before the camera. At this point Nadar appears to follow the law of reciprocation governing auratic experience, according to Benjamin: in return for the "transposition" (*Übertragung*) of the living relations between humans (of reciprocity) to the relations between humans and it, the camera is supposed to give back in kind. But the camera does not recognize the auratic and so it does not reciprocate: it gives back the gaze neither of the living subjects placed before it nor of the living artist who wants to animate its scene. Nadar views the camera as an inanimate graphic machine that can in fact "see" the scene the way he wants to see it: animated. But the camera carries him beyond this vision to one that his initial attempts to animate the scene were designed to repress, namely, that of the death that stared blankly out from the catacombs' every recess. In this sense the machine is indeed a model for Nadar's vision. But, again, not exactly the machine itself, for "the machine does not run by itself." It depends upon the involvement of a receptive participant in its workings. The subject of this scene of photography, if it still is one, cannot be entirely identified with the photographer Nadar or with the photographic apparatus; it is rather a "system of rapports," as Derrida says, into which both are drawn.

Moreover, in order for this scene of writing to be enacted as such, the system of rapports requires a support—it must be on something. In Nadar's passage the glass plates play this role of support, and indeed, as we have seen, in a manner that upstages the leading role that would traditionally be played by the artist-photographer. Yet, if in order to become a support for the photographic marks, the glass plates imperiously demand "absolute, inorganic immobility," once they become supports, the plates recede or retire under marks that now have an infinitely dynamic potentiality to exceed them. By becoming a material support, the plates disappear. This is due, as Benjamin precisely formulates it, both to the camera itself—to the peculiar character of its marking—as well as to its

Hilfsmittel, its supplementary "devices" or "resources," which include lowerings and liftings, enlargements and reductions, and so on—all of which in the end are determined and made possible by the finitude of a receding material support. In this sense, like paper in Derrida's gloss on Freud's "Note," the glass plates withdraw from the movement that exceeds their finitude. And, as with Freud's paper, while this movement beyond has the effect of reducing the material support to the status of a durable bearer of marks that is of limited receptivity, the movement as such needs the material support—or, more precisely, the withdrawal of the support—in order, not to carry itself out (for it cannot do this by itself), but to be carried out. The movement needs the receding support, in other words, to become possible—to exist in the mode of potentiality.[75] Like the support in the scene of photography, the figure of paper as support in the scenes of writing in the literary works analyzed in this study is *le point mort* in at least two senses: it is the point at which the graphic apparatus demands "absolute, inorganic immobility" and also the point at which movement starts to exist purely as potentiality. From this perspective, Nadar's passage stages *le point mort* of the photographic medium's virtuality.

The "Critical Fact": Aesthetics and Mass Mediacy in Benjamin

The idea of a virtual medium that draws the subject into a scene of writing like the one described by Benjamin's citation of Nadar is ill suited to the traditional concept of the work of art as a self-contained medium of subjective reflection. Not, however, to the concept of the work of art as medium that emerges in Benjamin's dissertation on German Romanticism. It would be more accurate to say that the absorption of the subject in photography, and by extension in the mass media, reiterates and reveals the action traced in the early study of the German Romantic concept of the aesthetic medium, in the same way that film and now the newer electronic media are, as Benjamin would say, "virtually implied" in photography.[76] The analysis of aesthetic mediacy in Romanticism is part of Benjamin's radical rethinking of the status of mediacy in communication as such. It is this critique that leads him to develop a theory of the virtual power of communicative media, a theory of the conservation of communicative energy, as it were. Such an approach to the question involved Benjamin in the broader debates of his day extending from the natural and the social sciences to the human and "cultural" sciences over what his contemporary, Emile Meyerson, called principles of conservation—principles determining persistence in time.[77] The Cartesian conservation principles of classical political economy, to take an example touched upon in our analysis of Carlyle at the outset, were subject to much criticism and revision in debates about political economy in the nineteenth century. Much of this criticism and revision, and certainly its most influential strain, was carried out as part of an effort to elaborate a theory of conservation in economic exchange based on potentiality or virtuality, that is to say, on the basis of the Leibnizian and, more directly, Kantian theory of infinite divisibility that led to the emergence of the theory of the conservation of energy in natural science during this period.[78]

As the occurrence of the word *virtual* at key points in his writing clearly indicates and as his many allusions to contemporary scientific theory suggest, Benjamin's aesthetic theory is related to, although by no means identical with, these developments in other fields of inquiry.[79] The importance of such a context in this work can be suggested briefly by sketching Benjamin's approach to the category of aesthetic "content" (*Gehalt*), a category that is fundamental to the emergence of Idealist aesthetics in the later eighteenth- and early nineteenth-century German philosophy. First of all, we should note that until the end of the eighteenth century, *Gehalt* described the amount of precious metal (gold or silver) contained in a coin (J. L. Frisch in his 1741 *Teutsch-lateinisches Wörterbuch* gives *valor* as the Latin equivalent of *Gehalt*). The application of the term to aesthetics in the late eighteenth century is registered in Grimms' dictionary. Under the general signification of *Gehalt* we find: "content (*Gehalt*) of coins . . . what they contain of pure silver, gold or what of real value they hold in themselves." The Grimms identify the extension of this meaning of *Gehalt* to aesthetics with Schiller, and in particular with the 1781 preface to *The Robbers* and the phrase "*ein gewisser Gehalt von Geisteskraft*" (a certain amount of spiritual or mental power)—an amount necessary, according to Schiller, for the adequate comprehension of his play.[80] Following Schiller and adapting this metaphor to aesthetic theory, Hegel employs the term *Gehalt* to describe the essential substance or kernel of truth in the work of art. As such, *Gehalt* defines what is essential in art for philosophy according to Hegel. In an illuminating essay on this topic, Lukács identifies what he calls the "priority of content (*Gehalt*)" in Hegel's understanding of the "dialectical interaction of form and content." In a Hegelian turn of his own, Lukács coins the term *Gehaltsästhetik*, claiming that this focus on the substantial content of the work of art is itself the "hidden and fruitful kernel" of Hegel's aesthetics. Only from such an understanding of *Gehalt*, Lukács argues, will a genuinely historical aesthetic theory grow.[81]

By contrast, for Benjamin aesthetic "content" is a matter, not of extraction and purification, but of divisibility.[82] From his perspective, the work of art communicates itself as a medium of divisible "content"—its "communicability," Benjamin might say, derives from its "divisibility" (in

German: its *Mitteilbarkeit* derives from *Teilbarkeit*). This is part of the constellation Benjamin seeks to make readable in his manipulation of the German root word *Teil* (part) in an early essay on language that is closely related to his study of Romanticism—for example, the relation of communicability (*Mitteilbarkeit*) to judgment (*Urteil* as in *Urteilskraft*).[83] Such a stress on divisibility is in keeping with the broader understanding of matter as potentiality in the tradition of *Naturphilosophie* and, not surprisingly, there are some very concrete signs of Benjamin's interest in such a broader scientific context throughout his writings—allusions, not only to Leibniz and Kant, but also to the contemporary work of Bertrand Russell, Henri Bergson, Arthur Stanley Eddington and Emile Meyerson. Yet even more significant than these references to the philosophy of science is the way Benjamin's critical vocabulary works with the language of force, power, and energy—right up to his late observations in the *Arcades Project* on the dialectical image as a force-field: "The fore- and after-history of a historical phenomenon show up the phenomenon itself on the strength of its dialectical presentation. What is more: every dialectically presented historical circumstance polarizes itself and becomes a force field in which the confrontation between its fore- and after-history is played out. It becomes such a field insofar as the present instant interpenetrates it. And thus the historical evidence polarizes itself into fore- and after-history always anew, never in the same way."[84] The energetic character of Benjamin's critical language is perhaps most evident in the conditionality of his key terms.[85] "Translatability," "reproducibility," "legibility," "cognizability," "communicability," and, in the study of Romanticism, "criticizability" are all examples of this stress on potentiality. These terms are part of a discourse of virtuality that is to be contrasted with the Hegelian-dialectical concept of aesthetic content.

The difference this virtuality makes when it comes to a theory of the aesthetic medium becomes clear in Benjamin's early study of German Romanticism. The Romantics, he contends, radically reinterpreted the question of the aesthetic content, and they did so in particular by re-thinking the status of the work of art as medium. Their decisive philosophical contribution starts with the attempt to think through Kantian reflective judgment in relation, not to the Cartesian ego, but to the work of art and, more specifically, to the infinite possibility of aesthetic form manifested in a certain non-subjective mode of reflection. "Intellectual intuition is thinking that produces its object," Benjamin begins, "reflection in the Romantics' sense, however, is thinking that produces its form."[86] What is more, if reflection produces form, form for the Romantics is, as Benjamin says, the "possibility of reflection in the work."[87] The first point then is in itself not controversial: in keeping with Kantian aesthetic principles, Romantic reflection produces a theory of art, and of criticism, as a medium of possibility.[88] Benjamin now goes on, however, to make a distinction by contrasting Romantic reflection with the more Cartesian interpretation of reflection offered by Fichte.[89] Fichte serves as an example of the Hegelian approach to aesthetic content mentioned above. With the Cartesian ego, as inflected by a theory of dialectical self-positing, reflection occurs as a single, realized action. It is a fait accompli—what Fichte also calls an "actual deed" (*eine Tathandlung*), adopting what had been at the time a juridical term that distinguished between a completed or real act as opposed to one that was merely intended or potential.[90] Thus, while Fichte starts by taking up the topic of Kantian reflective judgment, reflection is then immediately subordinated to dialectical self-positing of the ego in his work.[91] As Benjamin puts it, "reflection is not the method of Fichtean philosophy; this is, rather, to be seen in dialectical positing (*dialektischen Setzens*). . . . For what in Fichte occurs in only a 'single' case . . . takes place, according to the Romantic intuition, incessantly, and first of all constitutes not the object but the form, the infinite and purely methodical character of true thinking."[92] In contrast with the *fait accompli* of dialectical self-positing, Romantic reflection on the work, that is to say, critique, is an incomplete act; its mode is the imperfect. Moreover, critique for the Romantics, Benjamin insists, is not the expression of the subject, or of the *sensus communis* of a collective; it is neither subjective nor social "opinion," "impressions," etc. It is also not the identification of the idea of beauty in the work, or the divining of the "immediate inspired emotion" of the author.[93] Instead, critique is the potentially endless, nonsubjective completion—the representation or dramatization (*Darstellung*)—of the work.

The completion of the work is performed by the subject, but the performance, Benjamin insists, is "objective": "[the subject] represents [or dramatizes] an objective moment in the work."[94] The work of art as medium is dramatized by such non-subjective performances. This stress on the non-subjective character of aesthetic mediacy is what distinguishes the Romantic theory of art from the dialectical, and ultimately Hegelian, self-positing of Fichte. The difference between Romantic reflection and dialectical self-positing comes down to the fact that the latter embraces a theory of subjective immediacy—the immediacy of self-consciousness. "Fichte looks for and finds," Benjamins says, "an attitude of mind in which self-consciousness is already immediately present. . . . In the absolute 'I' the infinity of reflection is overcome."[95] Instead of *destroying* the infinity of reflection through the dialectical positing of self-consciousness, the Romantic theory of aesthetic form *multiplies* reflection through non-subjective, or what Benjamin calls "objective moments" of critique. For the Romantics, we might say, aesthetic mediacy needs the non-subjective support of the subject; it requires that the subject become the objective support for a medium that exceeds subjective limitation (the immediacy of self-consciousness). The peculiar virtuality of the aesthetic medium demands a critical performance—this is what the Romantics call "the critizability of the work"—but this performance cannot be identified with the subject.

The consequences of this insistence on nonsubjective critical potentiality, on "criticizability," are clear in the Romantic approach to the classically subjective aesthetic question of evaluating or judging works of art. Benjamin enumerates three such consequences. We can leave aside the second and third—the principle of the "impossibility of a positive scale of values" and that of the "uncritizability" of inferior works—in order to focus on the first, from which the other two derive, namely, "the principle of the *mediacy of judgment.*" Here is Benjamin's explanation:

The first principle . . . affirms that the judgment of a work must never be explicit, but rather must always be implicit in the fact of its Romantic critique (that is, its reflection). For the value of a work depends solely on whether it makes its immanent critique possible or not. If this is possible—if there is present in the work a reflection that can unfold itself, absolutize itself, and resolve itself in the medium of art—then it is a work of art. The mere criticizability of a work demonstrates on its own the positive value judgment made concerning it; and this judgment can be rendered not through an isolated inquiry but only by the fact of critique itself, because there is no other standard, no other criterion for the presence of a reflection than the possibility of its fruitful unfolding, which is called criticism.[96]

The concept of the "critical fact" is fundamental to the theory of aesthetic mediacy that Benjamin draws out of the Romantics. And, in keeping with the conservation principles outlined earlier, the virtuality of the aesthetic medium dictates that the "critical fact" itself be fundamentally divisible—split between the fore- and after-history of the work's critical completion. A peculiar mode of Kantian reflective judgment, the "critical fact" is not a matter of measuring up to a "standard": it does not identify the idea of beauty in the work. But it also not a matter, strictly speaking, of the subject, since it does not divine the "immediate inspired emotion" of the author, nor even represent the expression of subjective or collective "opinion." The "critical fact" is a judgment of value—it conserves Kantian judgment—but it is radically nonsubjective. It is the "objective moment" on which the infinite divisibility of the aesthetic medium depends. Benjamin cites Friedrich Schlegel: "A true judgment of art . . . is always a critical fact, if I may speak this way. But it is also only a fact, and, for just this reason, to wish to motivate it is a vain endeavor, for the motive itself would then have to contain a new fact or a closer determination of the first fact."[97] Critical facts are, in other words, fundamentally mediate and, Schlegel insists, subject to the principle of divisibility. They are also, for this reason, fundamentally a matter of potentiality, as Benjamin, for his part, suggests at the end of his study: "In the final account this assessment of [Romantic] criticism rests on the completely positive evaluation of its medium, prose. The legitimation of criticism—which counterposes criticism as the objective instance of all poetic production, depends upon its prosaic nature." The program for the coming philosophy of art prepared by the Romantics, Benjamin appears to say matter of factly here, is critical prose. Benjamin's study of Romanticism, we might add, aims to dramatize nothing more or less than this critical fact. It attempts to support a virtual theory of aesthetic mediacy that defies the classic aesthetic categories based on substantial self-presence, whether of the work of art or of the subject.

This is the double sense in which for Benjamin the subject becomes involved in the aesthetic mediacy of the Romantics. The virtuality of the aesthetic medium relies on the support of the subject to exceed the limits of the classic concept of the work as self-contained substance, and it draws the subject into a movement that exceeds subjective limitation. By dramatizing the subjective enactment of, and subjective absorption in, a medium that defies self-presentation, Benjamin's critique of German Romanticism brings out a theory of aesthetic mediacy that, as he might say, "virtually implies" the quality of mass mediacy that preoccupies him in later writings. The readings we will be pursuing in the chapters that follow also work on this connection between aesthetic mediacy and mass mediacy. In this work paper becomes a crux, in part due to the historical and philosophical contexts we have outlined. Specifically how this occurs, however, is a matter of singular, and absorbing, encounters with works of fiction, for which there are no substitutes. We will be especially concerned with the ways in which such encounters involve what Benjamin calls the "distracted" collective in his famous essay, "The Work of Art in the Age of Its Technical Reproducibility." While this collective haunts so many of the recent critical attempts to conceptualize the impact of the mass media on the public sphere, its radical strangeness has not been fully recognized.[98] The reason for this is that what Benjamin discerns in the encounter with the mass media is a collective that cannot be recognized, if by recognition we mean the self-conscious perception that is the defining experience of the traditional subject.[99] In this sense, the collective that emerges from the encounter with the mass media resembles the one that serves as the point of departure for Benjamin's theory of the novel—the literary genre marked by the breakdown of "transmissible experience."[100] For Benjamin the novel is not ironic but barbaric: it is the narrative mode peculiar to the experiential poverty of the information age.[101]

This study attempts to clarify and to elaborate on this point in

Benjamin's work—the "zero point," as he might call it—where the mass media intersects with his theory of the novel.[102] Fiction appearing in English during the nineteenth century provides an especially dynamic field for this endeavor. The emergence of an unruly and decentralized America and of the problem of American literature under the conditions of mass mediacy had an extraordinary impact on literary writing in English. Moreover, the sense of England itself as a national collective came under the great pressure exerted by the accelerated pace of capitalism in the British Empire.[103] These developments, taken together, tended to make popular fiction in English especially resistant to assimilation into a self-identical national literary subject. In what follows we will try to trace this resistance as it surfaces at a fleeting empirical moment of exposure to the mass media—a moment like one that occurs while reading. Historical accounts of technology or of material culture hesitate before such a threshold. For this reason, a historical account of the dissemination of mass-produced paper in the nineteenth century followed by an analysis of metaphors of paper in the literature of the period would be inadequate. The most challenging aspects of the mass media confronting the traditional individual and collective subject emerge at dynamic and highly divisible moments of reading—what Benjamin somewhat cryptically associated with the springing up of a "dialectical image."[104] At such moments, we might say, the mass media becomes "criticizable." In this sense, the following chapters approach the mass mediacy of the nineteenth century by way of literary criticism. The genre may seem outmoded in this context—overtaken by forces separating it from the traditional aesthetic categories of self-contained work, on the one hand, and self-conscious author or critic, on the other. But then again, as Benjamin suggests, this separation was characteristic of a certain concept of criticism from the start.

Chapter 1

Distraction in America: Paper, Money, Poe

Mass Movements: "The Man of the Crowd"

At the beginning of "The Man of the Crowd" (1840) the narrator is in the state of mind against which Poe's tales are directed. He is subject to that mode of distracted receptivity to "worldly interests" that the ideal short story would absorb into an "hour of perusal" during which "the soul of the reader is at the writer's control," a period of "no external or extrinsic influences—resulting from weariness or interruption."[1] It is thus fitting that this narrator is reading, not a novel, which is the immediate target of the critical remarks just cited, but a newspaper: "With a cigar in my mouth and a newspaper in my lap, I had been amusing myself for the greater part of the afternoon, now in poring over the advertisements, now in observing the promiscuous company in the room, and now in peering through the smoky panes into the street."[2] This state of distracted amusement is rapidly converted into one of absorption in the tale. With the lighting of the lamps, the narrator reports, "I gave up, at length, all care of things within the hotel, and became absorbed in contemplation of the scene without" (MC 108). What follows in this passage, as "observations" proceed from a "generalizing turn" to particular "details" of the types identified in the crowd, is the very portrait of Cartesian absorption:

were it not for the analogous instance of human beings passing on in the street below, as observed from a window. In this case I do not fail to say that I see the men themselves, just as I say that I see the wax; and yet what do I see from the window beyond hats and cloaks that might cover artificial machines, whose motions might be determined by springs? But I judge that there are human beings from these appearances, and thus I comprehend, by the faculty of judgment alone which is in the mind, what I believed I saw with my eyes.[3]

Like the "I" of this passage from the *Metaphysical Meditations*, Poe's narrator takes in a street scene in order to absorb himself in a stabilizing process of self-consciousness. In the passage from Descartes, doubtful sense-perceptions of hats and coats are overcome by the certitude of the thinking or "judging" subject, a subject that secures itself and its objects or representations through a process of reflexivity.[4] In the absence of such a process, man threatens to become a specter, a counterfeit man (*un homme feint*)—in Descartes's Latin, an *automaton*—a machine, not in the Cartesian sense of an end-oriented, purposeful mechanism (like the human body), but in the post-Romantic sense of a merely mechanical, inorganic apparatus.[5] The process of self-securing reflexivity is already underway when the narrator of "The Man of the Crowd" introduces himself in the tale: "Not long ago, about the closing in of an evening in autumn, I sat at the large bow window of the D— Coffee House in London. For some months I had been ill in health, but was now convalescent, and, with returning strength, found myself in one of those happy moods which are so precisely the converse of *ennui*" (MC 108). Thus the narrator's distracted receptivity becomes an occasion for self-recovery, convalescence. And this is precisely the action set in motion as the narrator, like the Cartesian "I," gazes out the window at the men passing in the street.

This process is of course brought to a halt by the appearance of "the man of the crowd." And yet the narrator also describes this interruption in terms of absorption: the "countenance" of the strange man "at once arrested and absorbed my whole attention" (MC 112). The absorption is now, however, of a different order. For, whereas taking in the crowd followed the Cartesian model of self-securing reflexivity, each "glance" reflecting back to the narrator the "returning strength" of his "peculiar mental state" (MC 108; 111), the man of the crowd refuses to be taken in. What is so absorbing in this figure, what makes the narrator "aroused, startled, fascinated," is a sense of overwhelming narrative possibility: "'How wild a history,' I said to myself, 'is written within that bosom!'" (MC 112). The man of the crowd promises, then, the kind of absorption for which Poe's stories aim—the absorption of a reader whose "soul . . . is at the writer's control," a reader who knows no "external or extrinsic influences." But even if the shift in absorption to the arresting possibility of what might be written within the bosom of the stranger does indeed seem to seize control of the narrator's (and the reader's) soul, this does not entirely block out impressions "of the scene without." Indeed what the narrator picks up unreflectively, mechanically even, while he is trying to take in the man of the crowd are precisely the "worldly interests" of the London streets that were the focus of the newspaper writing of the early Dickens, writing that Poe of course followed closely.[6] It is as if Poe's narrator, eyes fixed on the strange man, were led through a series of street scenes from the sketches Dickens wrote under the pseudonym of Boz for the London newspapers of the 1830s: from the "densely filled" cross street, the square "overflowing with life," the "busy bazaar" and the crowd "thronging the doors" of the theater to the "noisome quarter" at the "verge of the city" with its "tall, antique, worm-eaten, wooden tenements" and to "one of the palaces of the fiend, Gin" (MC 113–15).

Poe's narrator seems, in other words, to track the man of the crowd through the topoi of Dickens's newspaper writing, that is to say, through the writing that was explicitly devoted to the very mundane distractions Poe's magazine tales were designed to screen out.[7] For, in contrast to Poe, Dickens in his journalism and serial fiction encouraged his readers openly to pay attention to the interruptions of the world in the reception of his writing, even suggesting how this writing, far from striving for the self-contained "totality" recommended by Poe, might be seen to infiltrate the world it sought to describe.[8]

Distracting Dickensian scenes, then, make a certain impression on Poe's narrator while he is concentrating on the bizarre flânerie of the man of the crowd. Yet the very subject of this effort of concentration— the effort in a sense to discern the presence, the "here and now" or the "aura," of the *man* in the crowd—becomes a source of distraction. For, the man of the crowd is, it turns out, more like a machine than a man, a copy machine in fact (he retraces his steps, the narrator retraces them, the reader retraces, and so on). In this sense, the encounter with him is marked by the "crisis of reciprocity" characteristic of what Benjamin calls "the decline of the aura" in the age of mass media. Repeatedly in Poe's tale the man of the crowd fails to return the narrator's gaze: "Never once turning his head to look back, he did not observe me" (MC 113); "At no moment did he see that I watched him" (MC 114); and finally, "I grew wearied unto death, and, stopping fully in front of the wanderer, gazed at him steadfastly in the face. He noticed me not, but resumed his solemn walk, while I, ceasing to follow, remained absorbed in contemplation" (MC 116). Like the deadly gazing into the camera in the passage Benjamin cites from Nadar, which we analyzed in the preceding chapter, the narrator's steadfast gaze here is taken up—absorbed—in the "vacant stare" of a machine (MC 114).[9] "What is involved here," Benjamin observes of the lyric poetry of Poe's great follower, Baudelaire, "is that the expectation aroused by the look of the human eye is not fulfilled. Baudelaire describes eyes of which one is inclined to say that they have lost their ability to look."[10] The man of the crowd has the effect of a machine that takes us in when, following the narrator, we take it for a man. In the end, absorption in the man of the crowd constitutes receptivity to, rather than rejection of, the distracting machinery of mass movement and of mass mediacy—machinery precisely marked at the beginning of the tale by the narrator's newspaper.

Read All About It: "The Murders in the Rue Morgue"

Poe's detective stories also begin in a sense with the image of the newspaper as a medium of distracting receptivity. In "The Murders in the Rue

Morgue" (1841), Dupin and the narrator become aware of the murders of Madame and Mademoiselle L'Espanaye while "looking over an evening edition of the *Gazette des Tribunaux*" (MRM 418). The readers of the tale are made to follow this lead as the narrator simply transcribes, paragraph by paragraph, the newspaper article detailing the facts of the case. These paragraphs, the narrator reports, "arrested our attention" and their transcription is designed to have the same effect on the readers. Yet it is this very absorption that distracts us from what is significant, as Dupin's initial reaction to the newspaper account suggests:

> To look at a star by glances—to view it in a side-long way, by turning towards it the exterior portions of the *retina* (more susceptible of feeble impressions of light than the interior), is to behold the star distinctly—is to have the best appreciation of its lustre—a lustre which grows dim just in proportion as we turn our vision *fully* upon it. . . . it is possible to make even Venus herself vanish from the firmament by a scrutiny too sustained, too concentrated, or too direct. (MRM 426)

Things, we learn, are overlooked through concentration, and not only by the police. While absorbed in the perusal of the newspaper article, the tale's narrator and now, in turn, its readers receive, without knowing it, impressions of the character of the crime. As Dupin instructs the narrator, "there *was* something to be observed" in the newspaper (MRM 429), something that could form the basis of a syllogism: since, according to the newspaper, "the denizens of the five great divisions of Europe could recognize nothing familiar" (MRM 429) in the "shrill voice" that issued from the room in which the murders were committed, and since, presumably according to Aristotle, man is the animal of meaningful speech, then the "shrill voice" must not have been human.[11] What distracts the narrator, and again the readers, is the very possibility that this unintelligible voice could have been human, that this inhuman act could have been carried out by a human and, more broadly, that the fundamental distinction between the non-human and the human could have been suspended in this case. This is the fear on which the tale plays, after all. There is, for example, the blurring of this distinction in the story of the sailor and the Ourang-Outang: captured by the sailor during "an excursion of pleasure," the animal is sharing lodgings with the sailor in Paris when, upon returning from yet another act of bestial self-indulgence (a "sailors' frolic on the night"), the sailor discovers "the beast occupying his own bedroom" and with "razor in hand, and fully lathered, . . . sitting before a looking-glass, attempting the operation of shaving, in which it had no doubt previously watched its master through the keyhole of the closet" (MRM 441–42). The confusion of man and beast continues as the latter, having murdered the women, shows itself to have a moral conscience: it is "conscious of having deserved punishment" (MRM 443).

If these details play on the readers' anxieties about the distinction between the human and the nonhuman, Dupin seems to draw on similar fears exhibited by the narrator. "If now," Dupin is reported by the narrator to have told him,

you have properly reflected upon the odd disorder of the chamber, we have gone so far as to combine the ideas of an agility astounding, a strength superhuman, a ferocity brutal, a butchery without motive, a *grotesquerie* in horror absolutely alien from humanity, and a voice foreign in tone to the ears of men of many nations, and devoid of all distinct or intelligible syllabification. What result, then, has ensued? What impression have I made upon your fancy?"

I felt a creeping of the flesh as Dupin asked me the question. "A madman," I said, "has done this deed—some raving maniac, escaped from a neighbouring *Maison de Santé.*"

"In some respects," he replied, "your idea is not irrelevant." (MRM 423)

The anxiety called forth by Dupin's dramatic questioning distracts the narrator. Absorbed by the beastly possibility, his flesh creeps and he leaps to the conclusion that this is a case of the human crossing over into the non-human—of a mania that transforms a man into "a madman." The mania here is of course the narrator's and, as Dupin suggests, this "idea [of mania] is not irrelevant," since it is precisely such an idea that leads the narrator astray. Or rather, it is the "impression" Dupin makes on the narrator's "fancy"—an impression that provokes an idea of mania in the workings of this mechanical faculty—that is distracting.[12] Dupin distracts the narrator. But he also replaces the impression of mania—the idea in the narrator's "fancy" that a human could act with a madness "absolutely alien from humanity"—and puts in its place a more rational, more humane impression. For, this endeavor seems to call for another support. Instead of making his own human bearing into the medium of the humane impression (as he does when he poses the absorbing questions that give the narrator the inhumane impression that man could become manic enough to commit the crime), Dupin reaches for a piece of paper. "Glance at this little sketch I have here traced upon this paper," he directs the narrator. "It is a *fac-simile* drawing of what has been described in one portion of the testimony as 'dark bruises, and deep indentations of finger-nails,' upon the throat of Mademoiselle L'Espanaye, and in another (by Messrs Dumas and Etienne), as a 'series of livid spots, evidently, the impression of fingers'" (MRM 437). Once again, there *was* something in the newspaper. In order to concentrate on it, however, a support is needed—a support that bears closer scrutiny. A sheet of paper placed around the throat of the victim enables Dupin to take an impression of the marks left by the Ourang-Outang's stranglehold. Like a photographic impression, this facsimile drawing freezes, and makes it possible to enlarge upon, the descriptions cited by Dupin from the *Gazette des Tribuneaux*: the "dark bruises, and deep indentations of finger-nails" and the "series of livid spots, evidently, the impression of fingers" on the victim's throat. With these prints in one hand and Cuvier's zoological account in the other, Dupin can definitively assign the death-grip to the non-human and substitute a more humane impression for the inhumane one he had just made with his questions.[13]

This two-handed operation is likewise at work in the narrator's portrayal of Dupin in "The Murders in the Rue Morgue": the inhumane impression made by the detective's apparent madness—what the narrator initially allows may "perhaps" be the "result" of his "diseased intelligence" (MRM 415)—is replaced in the reading of the tale by the seemingly humane impression made by his ratiocinative solution to the troubling crime. Both cases, that of the elusive murderer in the Rue Morgue as well as that of the mysterious Dupin, call for concentration and require for this a material support capable of becoming the medium of an impression (of the murderer and of Dupin). Like Dupin's reflections, the literary medium of the tale cannot do without paper. For the tale to make its impression—to exercise its absorbing effects—it needs a material support: it must be drawn into an "outside" world, the public world, in this case the mass medium of the serial press, that cannot be simply external to it. In this sense, as with "the man of the crowd," Dupin marks the encounter between Poe's literary work and the materiality of the mass media.[14] "The Murders in the Rue Morgue" demonstrates the process by which Dupin and Poe convert the distractions both of the newspaper in the story and of the serial press in which the story appears into a medium of unifying impressions. These impressions serve to integrate the humanity of the individual and the collective. But the tale also shows that this process unfolds as a series of "effects" produced by "mental features" that can never appear "in themselves" (MRM 397). And because these unifying "effects"—of the detective as well as of the tale—depend upon an appearance in a world that, as Poe puts it, "destroys" the "unity of impression," the impression must occur on a peculiar kind of material support, specifically, one that withdraws from the world and suspends its disarray.[15] Concentration demands a material support to bear the loss of worldly distraction. For, only on the basis of such a support can "the affairs of the world" be avoided and the semblance of unity be seen to emerge. The world must become a stage for an appearance liberated from "worldly interests."

Poe went on correcting the newspaper in an attempt to convert the worldly distractions of the serial press into the unifying form of his fiction in a second Dupin story, "The Mystery of Marie Rogêt" (1842–43). The results were mixed: the sequel to "The Murders in the Rue Morgue," drawn from journalistic accounts of a real murder in the world, turns on the collation and comparison of conflicting information taken from newspapers and incorporated into the tale. But at this time Poe also pursued his aesthetic project in the other major sphere where the distractions of "worldly interest" are connected to paper—that of economic life and in particular monetary exchange. In "The Gold Bug" (1843) Poe suggests that the very medium of "worldly interest," paper money, can become the basis of an appearance that breaks free of "the affairs of the world."

Money in America

As Marc Shell has impressively shown, Poe's "The Gold Bug" contributes to the debates between the "paper-money men" and the "gold bugs" in the aftermath of Andrew Jackson's failed attempt to establish a national bank of the United States at the end of the 1830s.[16] Rather than take sides, though, Poe's tale explores the grounds for the debate and extends the reflection on paper we just considered in "The Murders in the Rue Morgue" to the controversies over money and national identity in America. By turning to the distraction of monetary exchange based on paper, Poe implicitly adopts the parallel suggested by Carlyle's remarks on "Book-paper" and "Bank-paper" in *The French Revolution*. Yet "The Gold Bug" shows the American writer rejecting the well-established satirical tradition in British letters, from Alexander Pope and Edmund Burke to Thomas Love Peacock and Carlyle, that projects paper exchange onto some foolish foreign—revolutionary French or American—other in order ostensibly to protect British national identity from economic and aesthetic inflation but also, more covertly, to paper over the questionable financial origins of the modern British state itself.[17] Offering a counterpoint to the standard view expressed by Carlyle's derisory announcement of the "Paper Age," the treatment of paper in "The Gold Bug" gives a more positive account of semblance in collective life and associates it with America. In this sense, Poe's account hints at an alternative approach to paper money in American history and raises an aesthetic question that is of fundamental importance to America's sense of itself.[18]

As it happens, the proposition that America starts to be born when paper becomes a material support for economic exchange in the colonies was the thesis of a remarkably overlooked interpretation elaborated by the American historian Alexander Del Mar at the end of the nineteenth century. By approaching colonial American monetary history as a study in the politics of representation, Del Mar's interpretation of the role played by paper money in the origins of America suggests a historical parallel to the positive account of paper worked out aesthetically in Poe's "The Gold Bug."[19] Throughout the seventeenth and eighteenth centuries, Del Mar observes, the relationship between England and its American colonies was dominated by what the former considered the latter's illegitimate monetary schemes. An early culprit was the Massachusetts Bay Colony. Beginning in 1652, due to shortages of money, the Massachusetts Colonial Legislature authorized John Hull's mint in Boston to begin striking Pine Tree Shillings in denominations of 12, 6, and 3 pence (and in 1662 also of 2 pence). This practice continued through 1686, when the Pine Tree Shilling was suppressed by order of the King of England. As Del Mar notes, "upon being shown one of the Pine-tree shillings struck by the mint, [Charles II] became greatly offended at the assumption of the coinage prerogative by the Americans, a prerogative which, it must be remembered, he had already sold to the East India Company."[20] It was this suppression of the Pine Tree Shillings that led to the emergence of the first paper money in Massachusetts where in 1690 Colonial Bills of Credit were printed (Figure 3). These Bills in fact followed several unsuccessful attempts to introduce private promissory notes between 1686 and 1690.[21] Originally, these bills were not legal tender but promises to pay money issued by the Colony. In July of 1692, however, again because of the scarcity of English money, they were made legal tender by the legislature. These bills of credit circulated in the Colony until 1727 when, in the wake of the French experience of the Mississippi Bubble, the English government instituted, as Del Mar says, "that series of repressive measures which furnished the first distinctive provocation to the American Revolution."[22]

Del Mar's interpretation of the colonial paper money experiments as a political struggle over representation illustrates a point that the French economists Michel Aglietta and André Orléan have made recently on a more explicitly theoretical level: "monetary crises are always crises of sovereignty."[23] Charles II was thus not mistaken in regarding the colonial experiments as a threat to his authority. The colonists may not have had this intention. For them it may well have been merely a practical matter—the lack of money.[24] But by granting credit to one another in economic transactions on the basis of promissory notes and paper money guaranteed only by themselves, the colonists were starting to appear as a collective in their own right, as distinct from the right granted to them by the English crown. The colonists were, in short, asserting a right to appear as an autonomous collective and suspending the king's authority over the space of economic representation. The emergence in these monetary experiments of a collective that was a matter of nothing but appearance—the mere semblance of a collective—would prove unbearable

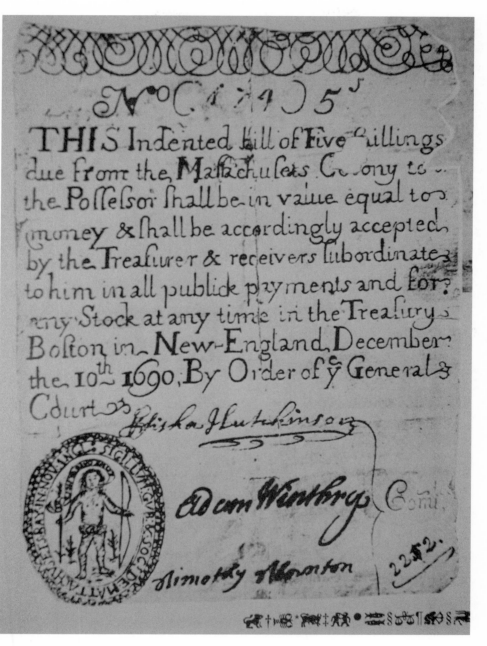

Figure 3. Massachusetts Bay Company bill of credit, 1690. Eric P. Newman, *The Early Paper Money of America,* 124.

to the renegade states that eventually became the United States. The need for more self-assurance was expressed after the American Revolution, not only in the repeated demands for a supposedly more substantial gold money, but also in the writing of United States economic historians in the nineteenth century who looked back with some embarrassment on the colonial paper money experiments.[25] The clearest example of this view is the work of nineteenth-century economic historian, Charles J. Bullock.[26] Based on a belief in the wholesomeness of the gold standard, Bullock denounced the pre-Revolutionary experiments, and especially those involving paper money, as a "curse" and as contributing to the "carnival of fraud and corruption" of the period (32 and 43). Bullock makes a similar point about the Continental Bills authorized by the Colonial Congress in 1775: "The paper money opened the door to the most shameful frauds upon all who were so unfortunate as to be in the position of creditors. Dishonest debtors were enabled to pay their debts in worthless currency" (69).[27] Even more forgiving nineteenth-century economic historians, such as Samuel Breck and Henry Phillips, Jr., looked with shame on the monetary practices of colonies and the insurgent United States.[28]

Twentieth-century economic historians like Richard A. Lester and John Kenneth Galbraith dismiss the disdain for paper expressed by their nineteenth-century precursors. But the more recent economic historians have been interested mainly in conferring legitimacy, from the vantage point of a full-blown credit economy, on the financial practices of the American colonists—Galbraith, for instance, writes with admiration of the "astonishing skill and prudence" of paper money experiments in the Middle Colonies.[29] In other words, the twentieth-century economists advocating paper money, like the nineteenth-century economists promulgating gold money, tend to discount or even overlook the way sovereignty is connected to representation in the paper money experiments. Del Mar's work stands out for its interpretation of the financial practices of the colonists as responses to a crisis of economic and political representation. This crisis precipitated the appearance of paper devices that challenged the sovereignty of the king and led to the American Revolution.[30] "Lexington and Concord," as Del Mar notes, "were trivial acts of resistance which chiefly concerned those who took part in them and which might have been forgiven; but the creation and circulation of bills of credit by revolutionary assemblies in Massachusetts and Philadelphia, were the acts of a whole people and coming as they did upon the heels of the strenuous efforts made by the Crown to suppress paper money in America, they constituted acts of defiance so contemptuous and insulting to the Crown that forgiveness was thereafter impossible."[31]

To the British authorities, the bills of credit were simply counterfeit.[32] But, as we have already indicated, there is plenty of evidence that the Americans themselves were not entirely ready to accept something so seemingly insubstantial as paper money as the basis of their collective existence. Many shared the sentiment informing the tradition of paper satires that emerged in the first half of the eighteenth century and continued well beyond that period.[33]

Yet evidence of a divergence from this tradition in American letters and of an awareness of the link between money and representation discerned by Del Mar in his historical writing can be found in the work of the colonial American poet Ebeneezer Cooke, in particular in his poem *Sot-Weed Redivivus* (1727).[34] In this work, Cooke fashions himself as a sort of wise fool or "sot" and offers his poem to the colonial reader as what he ambiguously calls "Waste Paper" (meaning both trash and "rough accounting book," according to the *Oxford English Dictionary*). With these "Home-spun Weeds" (l. 60), Cooke urges his colony (Maryland) to abandon its use of the besotting currency of "Indian Weed" (l. 106)—tobacco "secure in Bags"—in favor of "Paper made of Rags" (ll. 113–14). The relatively little attention paid to Cooke has, it seems, failed to note this aspect of his work. Perhaps because of the desire to find similarities to mainstream Augustan poetry that would legitimate Cooke, scholars of this work have not scrutinized the surface of the poet's "Waste Paper" intently enough to appreciate how the poem marks an important departure from the standard Augustan tendency to satirize paper from the supposedly secure ground of land and precious metal.[35] In the *Epistle to Lord Bathurst* (1733), for example, Cooke's English contemporary, Alexander Pope, writes of paper:

Blest paper-credit! last and best supply!
That lends Corruption lighter wings to fly!
Gold imp'd by thee, can compass hardest things,
Can pocket States, can fetch or carry Kings;
A single leaf shall waft an Army o'er,
Or ship off Senates to a distant Shore;
A leaf, like Sybil's, scatter to and fro
Our fates and fortunes, as the winds shall blow:
Pregnant with a thousand flits the Scrap unseen,
And silent sells a King or buys a Queen.

In direct contrast to Pope, Cooke's poet fools with the stock Augustan ridicule of the fraudulent deceptions of paper. After dramatizing the silly feudal preference of the Maryland Assemblymen for "Predial Tythes" (I. 113), Cooke turns to contemporary writers who also suffer from the feverish superstition against paper:

The Scribes likewise, and Pharisees,
Infected with the same Disease,
On Paper Money look a squint,
Care not to be made Folls in Print. (I. 115–18)

For the standard Augustan satire of paper, epitomized by Pope, Cooke substitutes an argument for, and indeed a poetic demonstration of, the real effectiveness of what may look like mere *tromperie*. By urging the abandonment of a "commodity currency" (see Einzig, 278–87) and by conflating the possibilities of paper money with its own literary presentation, the poem that appeared in the colony of Maryland foreshadows the work of the writer who would die just over a century later in what had become in the meantime the state of Maryland, Edgar Allan Poe.

The colonial poetry of Cooke and the historical writing of Del Mar provide examples of an alternative attitude in America toward paper as the material support for economic exchange. In each case, rather than a metaphor for mere insubstantiality or fraud, paper appears as a fragile material ground for real effects. To illustrate the influence of this aesthetic principle in an American context Shell has extended his interpretation of paper money in Poe to an analysis of an American genre of *trompe l'œil* paper money painting in the nineteenth century. In works such as Victor Dubreuil's *Don't Make a Move!* (Figure 4), Shell argues, some nineteenth-century American painters became interested in exploiting the play of surface and depth in a manner that related visual representation on the surface of a canvas with monetary representation of value on the surface of a bill. Of Dubreuil's painting, Shell observes, for example: "Dubreuil extends the monetary trompe l'oeil's representational house of mirrors a step further in his *Don't Make a Move!* Here a man with one eye closed points the barrel of a revolver at the viewer. A woman bank robber grabs trompe l'oeil paper money bills from the money drawer. You, the viewer, are absorbed into the painting as the teller in this pawnshop or moneychanger's stall. In the larger composition of *Don't Make a Move!* the pull ring on the money drawer answers to the gun's barrel or the looter's eye. This eye, or *oeil,* is the trompe l'oeil of the piece, figuring both the *eye* of the robber whose mate withdraws paper money from the drawer and also the *I* of the artist who draws his material from the visual realm."[36] In this way, Shell argues, the viewer is being cheated or fooled (*trompé*) when taking the surface of the painting for depth. The viewer feels really threatened by the gun, but the hole in the gun barrel is really nothing. While being tricked into believing there is depth, the viewer is distracted from seeing something taking place on the surface of the painting—the viewer is in *le point mort*, the dead spot, of the work. It is as if something were, rather incongruously, *in* the surface of the painting—as if three dimensions were folded or implied in two. The distracting "something" that takes place here is on the order of a referential illusion—the unfolding of three dimensions out of two. Yet in a sense when a two-dimensional surface is taken, as in the painting by Dubreuil, for three-dimensional depth, the real effect may be comparable to what happens when, for example, the Maryland colony takes itself to be real and authorizes itself to trade in paper. This may be what Cooke's poet-fool well foresaw—the coming to light, as he announces at the end of his poem, of "an Independent State" (l. 79). As it turned out, Cooke and his colonial readers were not merely kidding. Something similar is to be observed in the treatment of paper in Poe's fiction, as we will now see.[37]

Just Fooling: "The Gold Bug"

Everything begins in "The Gold Bug" with a "foolscap." Legrand, the narrator's friend, we are told, "drew from his waistcoat pocket a scrap of what I took to be very dirty foolscap, and made upon it a rough drawing with

Figure 4. Victor Dubreuil, *Don't Make a Move*, ca. 1900. Private collection.

the pen" (GB 74). The narrator, it seems, knows something now that he did not know when this event occurred. This is suggested in the choice of the word "foolscap," since the selection of this word appears to be informed by a knowledge of the very aspect of the paper to which the narrator was blind in the scene and about which now the reader is being kept in the dark. *The Oxford English Dictionary* informs us that "foolscap" means "1. A cap of fantastic shape, usually garnished with bells, formerly worn by fools or jesters . . . b. A dunce's cap"; "2. The device of a 'fool's cap' used as a watermark for paper"; "3. A long folio writing- or printing-paper, varying in size." The first sense of the word "foolscap" is self-explanatory, but for the second, and by metonymy the third, the dictionary's editor provides the following comment: "It has been asserted that the fool's cap mark was introduced by Sir John Spielman or Spilman, a German who built a paper-mill at Dartford in 1580; but we have failed to find any trustworthy authority for this statement."

The unauthenticated statement refers to the "Spilman" or "Spielman" of Thomas Churchyard's *A Sparke of Friendship and Warme Goodwill* (1588). Albeit untrustworthy, this identification of the "foolscap" mark with the subject of a poem in praise of paper turns out to be entirely fortuitous. For the foolscap in question in Poe's story is certainly worthy of praise: this "writing- or printing-paper" (sense 3) does indeed bear a "watermark" (sense 2) that leads Legrand to the buried treasure, while the narrator and now the reader are left wearing in a sense the "dunce's cap" (sense 1). Just as he was about to discard it as waste-paper, Legrand literally "perceived" (GB 93), as he later says, that it contained a sort of watermark: "a distinguishing mark or device impressed in the substance of a sheet of paper during manufacture, usually barely noticeable except when the sheet is held against strong light" (*Oxford English Dictionary*). Having discovered the value of this paper, Legrand "took from his coat-pocket a wallet, placed the paper carefully in it, and deposited both in a writing desk, which he locked" (GB 76). In fact, when he originally discovered the paper, Legrand tells the narrator, its value already registers, as we would say, unconsciously: he "deposited" it in his pocket "without being conscious of it" (GB 94). What comes to light in the substance of the paper's surface, as the narrator and we later learn, are the outlines of "death's-head" and then something else as we discover later in this passage from the tale that begins with Legrand narrating to the narrator:

there became visible, at the corner of the slip, diagonally opposite to the spot in which the death's-head was delineated, the figure of what I at first supposed to be a goat. A closer scrutiny, however satisfied me that it was intended for a kid. "Ha! ha!" said I, "to be sure I have no right to laugh at you—a million and a half of money is too serious a matter for mirth—but you are not about to establish a third link in your chain—you will not find any especial connection between your pirates and a goat—pirates, you know, have nothing to do with goats; they appertain to the farming interest." "But I have just said that the figure was *not* that of a goat." "Well, a kid then—pretty much the same thing." "Pretty much, but not altogether," said Legrand. "You may have heard of one *Captain* Kidd." I at once looked upon the figure of the animal as a kind of punning or hieroglyphical signature. I say signature; because its position upon the vellum suggested this idea. The death's-head at the corner diagonally opposite, had, in the same manner, the air of a stamp, or seal. (GB 96–97)

The "kid" appears, then, like a "foolscap," a watermark, and in fact the goat was, it seems, a common watermark in Renaissance Europe.[38] The narrator may well laugh derisively at Legrand here and throughout the story as a fool, but his friend is no more fooling than Captain Kidd was kidding. For, as is noted here, the Captain's "punning or hieroglyphic signature" or "seal" leads Legrand to real money. And, what is more, as the narrator will learn, Legrand has, partly in imitation of the foolery of the Captain (another meaning of "foolscap" perhaps), merely been making a fool of himself in order to kid the narrator in a rather serious, if somewhat paternalistic, manner. Explaining the gratuitous theatrics of swinging the gold bug to point to the treasure, Legrand reveals to the narrator: "Why, to be frank, I felt somewhat annoyed by your evident suspicions touching my sanity, and so resolved to punish you quietly, in my own way, by a little bit of sober mystification" (GB 107).

So, once again, the narrator knows something when he selects the word "foolscap" at the beginning of the tale, something that he did not know at the time of the event and something that he withholds from the reader now. And it is this withholding that brings us back to the historical context of the debates over paper versus gold money at the time. That this debate is clearly in evidence in the tale is already indicated by the importance of watermarks, which are used for the authentication of both literary and monetary paper. But this context can be made still clearer by referring to two related statements in the tale. The first one is made by Legrand's servant, Jupiter, who says of the gold bug: "I catch him wid a piece of paper" (GB 78); and the second is from the narrator who says of the treasure: "all was gold of antique date and of great variety. . . . There was no American money" (GB 91). Taken together these two statements would seem to suggest that treasure is old gold and American money is new paper. Indeed, such an interpretation is bolstered by the distinction made in the tale, one that I have deliberately glossed over up to now, between paper and parchment or vellum. When, for example, Legrand finds the map, he specifies that it was a "scrap of parchment, which I then supposed to be paper" (GB 94). This would seem to indicate a distinction between different kinds of graphic support that is analogous to the one made between different kinds of money—

parchment is to old gold as paper is to American paper money. This appears to lead to the following conclusion: the main point of the story is that treasure is to be distinguished from the gold bug as genuine parchment from counterfeit paper?

It is precisely this straightforward interpretation of the tale's meaning that Legrand's elaborate deception troubles. For this fiction fabricated by Legrand seems to have as its aim not so much the demonstration of the authenticity of the parchment by successfully arriving at its meaning and winning the treasure. Rather, Legrand's fiction seems designed to impress upon the narrator something else, hinted at by a second reading of the narrator's description of his second visit to Legrand on Sullivan's Island in the company of Jupiter:

Legrand had been awaiting us in eager expectation. He grasped my hand with a nervous *empressement* which alarmed me and strengthened the suspicions already entertained. His countenance was pale even to ghastliness, and his deep-set eyes glared with unnatural lustre. After some inquiries respecting his health, I asked him, not knowing what better to say, if he had yet obtained the *scarabaeus* from Lieutenant G——. "Oh, yes," he replied, colouring violently, "I got it from him the next morning. Nothing should tempt me to part with that *scarabaeus*. Do you know that Jupiter is quite right about it? "In what way," I asked, with a sad foreboding at heart. "In supposing it to be a bug of real gold." He said this with an air of profound seriousness, and I felt inexpressibly shocked. "The bug is to make my fortune," he continued, with a triumphant smile; "to reinstate me in my family possessions. Is it any wonder, then, that I prize it? Since Fortune has thought fit to bestow it upon me, I have only to use it properly, and I shall arrive at the gold of which it is the index." (GB 79–80)

Now of course, unbeknownst to the narrator, at this point Legrand knows that it is the "foolscap" and not the gold bug that is the point. He is acting in this exchange for the benefit of his friend. The theatrics have already begun: Legrand is fabricating or counterfeiting the authenticity of the gold-bug, or as Jupiter says "ghoul bug," and suggesting that the gold (bug) is not in fact the "index" of the gold (treasure)—the secret writing on the parchment is. And as a result of Legrand's fabrication, the narrator is made to repeat the error of being distracted by the gold bug in his first visit to Sullivan's Island when he fails to see that there *was* something in the paper after all.

What is more, this distraction by the gold bug has a double meaning in the tale, for the narrator is also distracted by the "gold bug" when he observes his friend, in an unfriendly manner, as an example of "Southern superstitions" and of "a mind disposed to lunacy" (GB 87). This is what the narrator seems to suspect in the passage just cited when Legrand alludes to Jupiter's ambiguous description of the bug as a "ghoul bug," which the narrator appears to interpret as meaning "ghost" and which

Legrand specifies as meaning "gold," but which of course, in keeping with Legrand's counterfeiting posture throughout, is in a certain sense neither simply a phantasm nor a weighty matter. Thus the narrator concludes that Legrand has been "infected" (GB 87) by the "gold bug" when in fact it is he, the narrator, whose mind is clouded by the gold bug. The narrator believes mistakenly that he is the doctor—he presents himself at the outset as Legrand's "physician" (GB 81)—while, in fact, he is the patient: he is being cured of the disease he attributes to Legrand who is truly administering the (counterfeit) antidote—the "sober mystification." The illness is a punishment, the narrator will learn, for treating Legrand like a lunatic instead of like a friend (GB 107). This is the point of Legrand's fabrication: the gold bug is not an "index" of the true meaning of Legrand's behavior, at least not in the sense the narrator believes.

But if it is not the feverish desire for gold and for the reinstatement of his "family possessions" (GB 80), then what does motivate Legrand? Perhaps it is, as already suggested, the aim of demonstrating to the narrator what friendship is. But then what does this have to do with the allusions in the tale to the debates over paper and gold in the United States during this time?[39] There are some indications. Friendship in the story, as we have seen, is based on trust: the narrator's lack of trust, his "suspicions touching [Legrand's] sanity" (GB 107), are a breach of the friendship "contracted," as the narrator begins the tale by saying (GB 72), between Legrand and himself. Indeed, it is this lack of trust that is expressed in the narrator's first visit to Legrand: instead of trusting Legrand and accepting his drawing of the bug, the narrator distrusts Legrand and his design, declaring that substantiation is required: "I must wait until I see the beetle itself" (GB 75), demands the narrator. In other words, distrust here amounts to an unwillingness to accept a semblance and an insistence that something more substantial be delivered. In financial terms, this is the insistence on gold, hence the appropriateness of the gold bug in the scene. In fact, as we have seen, Legrand sets about making the gold bug appear in the rest of the story, both in the sense that he himself fabricates the gold-bug fever for the observation of his friend and in the sense that his fabrication makes the gold bug manifest itself in the narrator's mind, which does indeed become "infected" by the fever. But, of course, Legrand makes the gold bug appear quite different from what the narrator believes. For the gold bug appears in all three cases (the actual bug, Legrand's fabrication of the fever, and the narrator's unfriendly contracting of it) as a distraction from the significance of promising and trust, a flight from the necessity and the necessary uncertainty and risk of such contracts. In this sense, Poe's "The Gold Bug" faces us and perhaps, by extension, Americans with the difference between contracting friendship and contracting the infection of suspicion. In this seeming advocacy of paper over gold, Poe could be suggesting that in economic exchange Americans must behave, not as brothers, but as friends.[40] Or is such a thought incredible when it comes to Poe?

Exposure: "The Purloined Letter"

The question of trust in exchange is a prominent, if somewhat over-looked, crux in the fiction of the author of *Tales of Mystery and Imagination*. The issue of trust repeatedly surfaces in Poe's stories on an inscrutable plane associated with paper. Paper would seem to be the metaphor for the various material surfaces on which marks or impressions come to light in Poe's tales: the wall in which appears "as if graven in bas-relief upon the white surface, the figure of a gigantic cat" in "The Black Cat" (567), published in 1843, the same year as "The Gold Bug"; or the face of the hills with engraved figures, the "chasms" with "Ethiopian characters so mysteriously written in their windings" in *The Narrative of Arthur Gordon Pym of Nantucket* (242).[41] Yet paper in Poe is secretive in the sense that Derrida has elaborated in connection with the prose poem "Counterfeit Money" by Poe's French translator, Charles Baudelaire:

Such a secret [the secret meaning of the exchange between the narrator of the poem and his friend who says he has given a beggar counterfeit money] enters literature, it is constituted by the possibility of the literary institution and re-vealed by that institution in all its possibility of secret only to the extent to which it loses all interiority, all thickness, all depth. It is kept absolutely unbreakable, inviolate only to the extent to which it is formed by a non-psychological structure. This structure is not subjective or subjectible, even though it is responsible for the most radical effects of subjectivity or of subjectivation. It is superficial, without substance, infinitely private because public through and through. It is spread on the surface of the page, as obvious as a purloined letter, a post card, a bank note, a check, a "letter of credit"—or "a silver two-franc piece."[42]

And, we might add, a foolscap. The absolutely superficial "structure . . . responsible for the most radical effects of subjectivity or of subjectivation" described by Derrida here resembles as well the nineteenth-century American *trompe l'œil* money paintings like Dubreuil's *Don't Make a Move!* Indeed the allusion Derrida makes to Poe's "The Purloined Letter," published, as we said, just two years after "The Gold Bug," seems to bear this resemblance out and to point in yet another direction. By associating the gun barrel with depth—a distracting illusion of depth—while the paper (the surface) is taken away, Dubreuil's painting reproduces visually Dupin's purloining of the letter while the Minister in that story is distracted by the blank fired in the street, just as the narrator is distracted by the gold bug from the paper in our story. The gold bug in the tale, like the gun barrel in the painting, is a blank, every bit as much as the scene in the Minister's apartment is a hold up. Like Legrand, Dupin, we learn, has the purloining power of fabricating depth while fathoming surfaces.[43] Duplicating the action of the Minister, who pretends to be immersed in deep political matters when he steals the Queen's letter, Dupin is a genius, albeit with the difference that, again like Legrand (and seemingly unlike Kidd), he is a man of principle. But the restoration in the earlier tale was, as we saw, not of wealth or "family possessions," but of friendship and trust among equals (friendship in the Aristotelian sense). In "The Purloined Letter," though, this does not seem to be the case. In the later story we have, not a reinstatement of equality in exchange, but a restoration of an official inequality. While in the former counterfeiting appeared as benevolent sign of friendly exchange (a sobering mystification, as it were), in the latter it surfaces as furious sign of vengeance and a vehicle of personal gain.

The elaborate card game of "The Purloined Letter" really does seem to be all about money and in a way that contrasts with "The Gold Bug."[44] The Queen, who tries to take the King, is deceived or trumped by the Minister—to be understood as the "Jack" perhaps, since the Minister is certainly a knave, or maybe since "knave" derives from the German *Knabe*, and the Minister is, like the suspicious narrator in "The Gold Bug," just a "kid." In any case, the Minister is in turn trumped or duped by Dupin, the "Joker," both in the sense of "a playing card usually printed with a picture of a jester, used in certain games as the highest ranking card or as a wild card" and in the sense, quite simply, of a jester—or, in other words, once again the fool. But if it is the joker Dupin who restores the hierarchy and reinstates the authority of the Queen over the Minister, this is done with a display of power that exposes this very hierarchy as a house of cards. Maybe then, as in the game of whist that is offered as an example of the "analytical" in the first Dupin story, the fool's game *is* in the end about money, which is to say bread—a possibility suggested by the name Dupin (*du pain*).[45] This would account for the "seal formed of bread" (PL 510)—like the seal of the kid in "The Gold Bug"— affixed by Dupin to the counterfeit letter he leaves for the Minister in "The Purloined Letter." And yet perhaps what is being exposed on the final pages of the latter tale—by the friendly narrator—is not just counterfeiting, but in fact a violation of the sort of just fooling in which Legrand engages, the kind which brings about a state of equality and mutual trust that is the true aim of independent democratic states. Then, it seems, in his unjust desire to repay himself with false paper, Dupin would be the real fool.

Thus, while in the earlier detective tale and in "The Gold Bug" distracted reception, the *trompe l'œil* of paperwork, cures the narrators of their inhumane suspicions (about crimes and the diseased intelligences of their friends), in the case of "The Purloined Letter" Dupin's paper-work leaves a decidedly more inhumane impression. "I just copied," reveals Dupin, "into the middle of the blank sheet the words—Un dessein si funeste, / S'il n'est digne d'Atrée, est digne de Thyeste" (PL 511).[46] In place of friendship, then, fraternal vengeance—the paper becomes the medium of a deadly design into which the Minister will already have been drawn by the time he sees Dupin's hand. But let us try not to be distracted with the Minister: Dupin's handling of the paper also draws him into the dead spot of the device.[47] The marks are of no human hand. Here Dupin unfolds. And if this unfolding repeats the exposure to which Dupin's device subjects the Minister, then the tale itself, by doubling Dupin, also becomes in turn exposed, threatened by its formal resemblance to the unfolding of Dupin and his paper device— exposed as a mere machine, a machine for distracting representational illusions, just a game, a trick. Paper is once again the dead spot in the tale: death and finitude *within* the literary medium. For, just as Dupin's deception relies on the distraction of the phony gunshot in the street, the medium of the tale depends upon a diversionary device (here the detective) in order to make its impression. It draws on distraction: on the paperwork that, unbeknownst to the readers, exposes them as much as it does the Minister and Dupin. At this point of distraction, the work of art may be said to sink itself into readers absorbed by a mass medium from which the tale was supposed, through concentration, to distinguish itself.[48]

"The Gold Bug," as we have seen, invites its readers to compare such distraction to the historical experience of paper as money in America, perhaps even to a certain experience of American sovereignty and independence. The allusion to American history deceptively suggests that the medium of the tale is similar to convertible paper money, the trea-sure in the tale being like the precious metal into which the paper money of the literary medium is converted. From this perspective, the aesthetic medium of the tale would distract the reader from its true character which would then be understood to resemble the inconvertible cur-rency (based on nothing but trust) that marked the real historical expe-rience of paper money in America. The American experience of paper as money—the real experience simulated, or the simulated experience realized, by a reading of Poe's tale—would be that of an inconvertible medium drawing on the distraction of convertibility. Declarations of American-ness based on such a medium, or on an experience of it, themselves succumb to referential distraction to the extent that they affirm the self-identity and substantiality of a national subject. This occurs when the medium of Poe's tale is converted into the positivist historical terms of an American experience of paper as an inconvertible or virtual medium.[49] At such a point a certain American reader is frozen in the sights of a referential illusion, fooled just enough for the medium of the tale to leave its distracting impression.

Chapter 2
Off the Map:
Stevenson's Polynesian Fiction

Pirate Fiction

The map in Robert Louis Stevenson's *Treasure Island* (1881) draws on the distracting analogy to paper money in Poe's "The Gold Bug" (Figure 5).[1] Like the "foolscap," the map points to buried treasure, and indeed the treasure resembles the hoard of Poe's tale: it is, we are told, made up of a great "diversity of coinage . . . nearly every money in the world" (TI 186). Based on the monetary analogy we might be led to conclude that the aim in *Treasure Island* would be to convert the paper of the map into the gold of the treasure. Yet this is the distracting illusion that Stevenson takes from Poe. *Treasure Island* is, in this sense, the story of a map and its distractions—the narrative of what happens to Jim Hawkins while he is absorbed in the illusions of the treasure map. This is also the story of the composition of *Treasure Island* that Stevenson tells in the essay written at the end of his life entitled "My First Book" (1894). The depiction of the novel's origins dramatizes as well the absorbing effects of a map—the original map sketched out by Stevenson that was the source of the novel: "I have said it was the most of the plot," he insists, "I might almost say that it was the whole" (MFB 197). Called upon by his "paymaster, the great public," to speak of his treasured work, the famous author—that "familiar and indelible character"—might be expected to indulge in cherished memories of how he turned paper into gold, the "map of an island" into *Treasure Island*. But the tale Stevenson has to tell offers a different account.

It all began, he reports, with some doodling: a map was made and "with the unconsciousness of the predestined" it was "ticketed" "Treasure Island" (MFB 193). Then,

as I pored upon my map of "Treasure Island," the future characters of the book began to appear there visibly among imagined woods; and their brown faces and bright weapons peeped out upon me from unexpected quarters, as they passed to and fro, fighting, and hunting treasure, on these few square inches of a flat projection. (MFB 193)

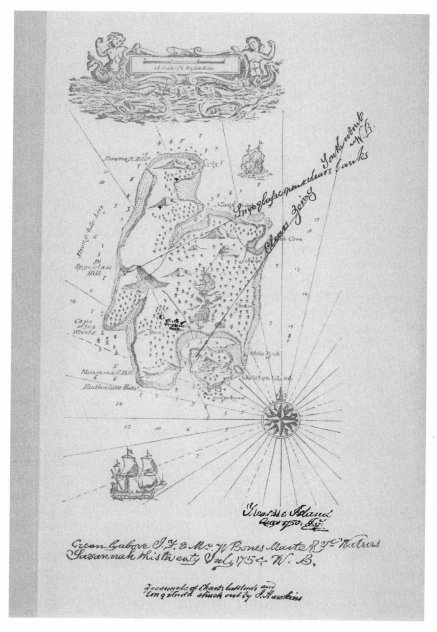

Figure 5. Robert Louis Stevenson's map of Treasure Island. Courtesy of the Beinecke Library, Yale University.

What Stevenson did not know is that, while gazing fixedly at his wonderful map, he was himself being drawn into the story that he had already started putting on paper. For, as he goes on to explain, the fictional treasure map would have the real effect of turning him into a pirate.[2] The map in this scene was supporting an act of unconscious plunder—the misappropriation of literary material that would become his "first book." Awareness of this effect of the map would come only later when, for example, he "chanced to pick up [Washington Irving's] 'Tales of a Traveller' . . . and the book flew up and struck me: Billy Bones, his chest, the company in the parlour, the inner spirit and a good deal of the material detail of my first chapters—all were the property of Washington Irving. But I had no guess of it then as I sat writing by the fireside" (MFB 194). "Plagiarism," Stevenson confesses, "was rarely carried farther" (MFB 194). Other unconscious pilfering came to light later as well: having given the islet next to Treasure Island on the map the name of "Skeleton Island"— again "not knowing what [he] meant"—the author found himself obliged "to justify the name" and "broke into the gallery of Mr. Poe and stole Flint's pointer" (MFB 197). Like a good pirate story, then, the tale of the composition of *Treasure Island* itself begins with the discovery of a treasure map. In this case, the novelist, peering into the map, becomes an unconscious pirate as he receives the foreign materials that will become his own first book.

Then again, it might be more accurate to say that the novel emerges with the disappearance of the treasure map. For, like the sheet of paper in Freud's "Note on the Mystic Writing Pad," the map withdraws in Stevenson's account of *Treasure Island*'s origins. If, beyond the limited graphic receptivity of paper Freud believes he discovers in the mystic writing pad a reflection of his image of the human psyche, beyond the material surface of the map, Stevenson sees in the reciprocating gaze of the "characters" looking back at him the outlines of his first book. Thus, like Freud's sheet of paper, Stevenson's map is both a material support of limited graphic receptivity (a "few square inches" of surface) and a stage on which this finitude is exceeded ("infinite, eloquent suggestion," as it is called at one point [MFB 197]). The map, Stevenson precisely writes, is "a flat projection"—the material support that withdraws from the movement of the literary medium it makes possible. This withdrawal is in fact the main theme of the story of the map narrated in "My First Book." Sent along with the completed novel, we are informed in the essay, the map is lost on the way to the publisher.[3] A copy is made from allusions in the novel, but the literary work proves itself to be a poor map from which to retrace the original. The copy, Stevenson notes, "was never 'Treasure Island' to me" (MFB 197). But of course the original map was never really "Treasure Island" to him in the first place.

This is the whole point of the essay: the map was the device that hid from the author the truly foreign character of what he considered his "Treasure Island," concealing from him that his "first book" involved piracy. With the map Stevenson was drawn into a blind spot where he remained in the dark long enough to become an author without noticing that this also meant becoming a pirate. Moreover, the map managed to hold him in this spot while he produced a pirate novel that takes aim at precisely this blindness. For what is *Treasure Island* about, after all, if not the resemblance, when it comes to the map and the treasure, between the English gentlemen ("Squire Trelawney, Dr. Livesey, and the rest of these gentlemen") who ask Jim "to write down the whole particulars about Treasure Island" and "the gentlemen of fortune" who accompany them on the adventure (TI 3)? Both groups have their codes of honor and social institutions (indeed one could argue that the buccaneers are portrayed in a more positively democratic light) and both crave possession of a treasure that is the property of neither.[4] In fact, the author of *Treasure Island*, grateful that his work "brought (or was the means of bringing) fire and food and wine to a deserving family . . . my own," resembles no character in the novel so much as the pirate Long John Silver who also scrupulously takes but a share of the treasure for the support of his wife and himself (MFB 197; TI 189–90).[5]

In "My First Book" Stevenson seems to want to come clean by revealing how the remarkable paper device of the map blinded him to his piracy during the composition of *Treasure Island*. The map was, he appears to suggest, a source of gifts from the American writers: initially not in the classic sociological sense (of Mauss) but in the purer sense of things that betray no sign that they are being given to the recipient.[6] The twist in this particular story is that these materials appeared as gifts in the classic sense only after their source—the map—had disappeared. As long as it presented itself to the author's gaze, the map provided empirical support for what was not being empirically grasped—it was a blind spot. But after it had disappeared, Stevenson suggests, it became a sign of piracy, indeed a black spot, that "little round of paper, blackened on the one side," which is, as Billy Bones explains to Jim Hawkins, a "summons," a demand for payment (TI 16).[7] From this angle the author might be seen to respond to the summons in "My First Book" by handing over the map or, more precisely, given that the map has disappeared, the story of the original map of Treasure Island that has been lost. In effect this amounts to an admission that the map turned over to the public with the novel in 1883 was a copy, a counterfeit bearing the signature of Captain Flint "forged," as Stevenson notes, by his father.[8] The artfulness of the story of the original map delivered by the novelist to his "paymaster, the great public" in 1894 then would be that it tells of a counterfeiting operation as well—the making of *Treasure Island* from a map. And, indeed, such a tale of counterfeiting fits in well with the stress on forgery throughout Stevenson's fiction. The case of Dr. Jekyll and Mr. Hyde, for example, one in which the latter character gradually acquires the ability to copy the "hand" of the former, itself turns ultimately on the papers placed in the hands of a lawyer whose very name—Utterson—mixes publishing and counterfeiting (not to mention Stevenson).[9]

But the author seems to get carried away by his efforts to implicate his work in the counterfeiting operations represented in his fiction. For the "original" map is itself a gift. Stevenson does not openly acknowledge it—perhaps it is *too* plain—but he takes from Poe the device of the distracting map itself in the novel and in the essay. Since he never recognizes that the device that drew him into his story and made him into a pirate was itself lifted from "The Gold Bug," Stevenson does not consider the possibility that this very device, and not just the "material detail" it conveyed, concealed from him its foreignness. It turns out that even before he started unknowingly to plunder the material for his first novel—before he started to "pore upon [his] map of Treasure Island"—Stevenson was an unconscious pirate. And he remains so, not knowing that it is his "own" map, purely in its potentiality as a receding graphic support and prior to its supporting any "material detail," that makes him into a pirate. The author himself thus continues to be drawn into the apparatus of the disappearing map. Or, conversely, the map continues to draw itself—more precisely, to withdraw itself—secretly into the author's work, in this case into the author's artful attempt to write himself into the work. It is as if, having acknowledged his piracy of the "material details" of his novel, the author artfully calls upon the lost map to reassert his authority over the work. According to this plan, the map, unlike the materials it conveys to him, would be *his* artistic device and as such it would return the work to the author and thus in a sense return the author to himself. The map would limit the piracy, contain it within the outlines drawn by the author himself. The map, in short, would be Stevenson's signature or seal, his device.[10] But this device does not realize the author's intentions, does not provide him with a means of self-recovery, a way of becoming a self-conscious pirate instead of an unconscious parrot—like "Captain Flint," the figure that in fact gets the last word in *Treasure Island*. The map does not return what was taken away while the author's gaze was fixed upon it, namely, a means of gaining mastery and control over what he regards falsely as his aesthetic material.

With the map, then, Stevenson's literary origins are staged as a moment, not of creation in the conventional sense of a spontaneous production, but of distracted receptivity. Even if there is no self-conscious recipient, since the writer has no sense that something is being given, and also no self-consistent thing given, since the map is not given but rather withdraws, Stevenson's encounter with the map occurs as a moment of material exposure. But the material point of contact escapes the phenomenological horizons of self-consciousness (Stevenson), on the one hand, and self-consistent presence (the map), on the other. The withdrawal of the map in Stevenson's essay resembles the action of paper devices in much of his later fiction, in particular the South Sea tale sequences on which he had been working up until his death in Samoa. In this sense Stevenson may be said to succeed in his efforts to write himself into his work even as he gets carried away by them. For it is in getting carried away by the disappearing paper device that the author of "My First Book" most resembles the protagonists of this colonial fiction. The aim of what follows is to explore the implications of this resemblance by tracing the workings of devices similar to Stevenson's map in two of the key tales in his South Sea project. The first, "The Bottle Imp" (1891), was to have been what Stevenson called the "pièce de résistance" in the collection of parables and folktales entitled *Island Nights' Entertainments*.[11] The second, *The Beach of Falésa* (1892), which Stevenson proudly proclaimed to be "the first realistic South Sea story," was planned for a volume that was to have the title of *Beach de Mar*, an unfinished cycle of narratives dealing with the exchanges between the Europeans and the Polynesians.[12] In both stories, as we will see, the paper devices are, like Stevenson's—and Poe's—map, associated with paper money. This association is in itself not surprising given that paper money was every bit as important as maps to the history of European colonialism.[13] More surprising, however, are the implications that begin to emerge when we trace the similarities of these devices to Stevenson's map in his essay on *Treasure Island*. For with the devices the protagonists in these tales are swept into a network like the one into which Stevenson is drawn with his map. Stevenson's South Sea fiction thus invites us to compare the experience of colonialism as a movement to his encounter with the aesthetic medium of what he regards as his own work in "My First Book."

The Financial Imp

Unlike many of his contemporaries from the British Isles, Stevenson's enthusiasm for the New World was connected to his interest in a form of economic or financial exchange that he associated with America.[14] As a young man, Stevenson traveled to California, to San Francisco, on a somewhat risky American adventure—a domestic romance of sorts—that involved leaving behind his more cautious Scottish family (a family of lighthouse engineers) and pursuing the already married woman who

would later become his wife. Amid money troubles and threats of disin-
heritance, Stevenson wrote that what he admired most about America
was a sense of aspiration and adventure, a sense he saw expressed, for
example, in the writing of Whitman and Thoreau.[15] The Scottish writer
was particularly taken by the boldness of Thoreau's economic specula-
tions in the first part of *Walden*—by, as he put it, the "sanity of [Thoreau's]
view of life, and the insight with which he recognized the position of
money."[16] Here is Stevenson on Thoreau:

> Prudence, which bids us all go to the ant for wisdom and hoard against the day
> of sickness, was not a favourite with Thoreau. He preferred that other, whose
> name is so much misappropriated: Faith. When he had secured the necessities
> of the moment, he would not reckon up possible accidents or torment himself
> with trouble for the future. . . . He would trust himself a little to the world. . . .
> [Thoreau] describes contemporary mankind in a phrase: "All the day long on
> the alert, at night we unwillingly say our prayers and commit ourselves to uncer-
> tainties." It is not likely that the public will be much affected by Thoreau, when
> they blink the direct injunctions of the religion they profess; and yet whether we
> will or no, we make the same hazardous ventures; we back our own health and
> the honesty of neighbors for all that we are worth.[17]

Significant here is that Stevenson not only applauds Thoreau's attempt
to underline the economic character of our ordinary language and to
work out a financial philosophy of "hazardous ventures," he imitates it.
While describing the originality of Thoreau's moral accounting, Stevenson himself employs economic language: he speaks of the misappropri-
ating of faith, the securing of necessities, the reckoning up of possible
accidents in the future, trusting to the world, the backing of our own
health and the honesty of our neighbors, and so on. Stevenson mimes,
in other words, that aspect of *Walden* that has been the subject of important work by the American philosopher, Stanley Cavell and others—what
Cavell has described as Thoreau's attempt to call attention in *Walden* to
the "network or medium of economic terms [that] serves . . . as an imitation of the horizon and strength both of our assessments of our position and of our connections with one another."[18]

   But Stevenson's comments on Thoreau are telling from another perspective as well, for they suggest a link between the sort of moral economics evoked in the essay and the idea that was to become the source
of nearly all of his fiction, namely, that of *adventure* (a word that itself,
on the basis of its early signification of fortune, luck, or chance, came
gradually in the early modern period to be associated with economics
or, more specifically, with commerce).[19] If Thoreau's project to think
through life as, in Stevenson's words, a "hazardous venture"—as a risky
economic and ethical enterprise—elicited the young Scottish writer's
admiration, it may also have suggested to him the mingling of ethics

and economics in his own experience of adventure—his voyage to America and eventually to the South Seas (the economics of which became the subject of his late fiction). In any case, Stevenson seems to have begun working out such an idea of adventure in his fiction at this time.[20] In general, Stevenson's critics have ignored such connections. They have mostly been concerned to point out what they regard as contradictions (ultimately of no importance, they imply) between the fiction writer's critical statements and his own literary practice.[21] There have been a few exceptions, but even those readers who have recognized the coherence of Stevenson's reflection on adventure in his criticism and fiction have failed to note its connection to the early admiration of Thoreau's economics. A particularly revealing example of this connection from Stevenson's critical writing at the time is an essay on Victor Hugo, in which Hugo's historical novel *Quatre-Vingt Treize* is praised for the way it represents the French Revolution as a national *adventure*, as the sort of "hazardous venture" on a national scale that Stevenson understands Thoreau to be advocating on an individual level in *Walden*. This praise is especially worth singling out because it runs precisely counter to the dominant Carlylean view of the French Revolution in nineteenth-century England that we noted at the outset, namely, that of a financial farce, a pseudo-revolution based on the chimera of "paper."[22] The comment on Hugo, in this sense, is directly linked to the famous evocation of adventure in the essay "El Dorado," in which Stevenson asserts that the sort of "aspiration" that leads to adventure is "a possession as solid as a landed estate, a fortune which we can never exhaust and which gives us year by year a revenue of pleasurable activity."[23] This emphasis on the peculiar financial character of adventure separates Stevenson from many of his British contemporaries and attracts him to the Americans Thoreau and Whitman. To see how it figures in Stevenson's later South Sea fiction, let us turn first to the late tale, "The Bottle Imp."[24]

"The Bottle Imp" (1891) has been the subject of considerable detective work by the critics. While some have argued that it was borrowed from a local legend Stevenson is supposed to have been told during his first two months in Samoa, others have uncovered a complex series of sources leading back through an early nineteenth-century English melodrama of this title by Richard Brinsley Peake to a German tale, "Das Galgenmännlein" ("The Gallows Imp"), by Lamotte-Fouqué. One critic has even accused Stevenson of piracy. On the other hand, Stevenson himself, in a letter to Arthur Conan Doyle, artfully notes that Samoan visitors, seeing the wealth in his fine house there, have asked, "Where is the bottle?"—requesting him to produce the actual magic bottle of the tale—much as he pretends in "My Last Book" that the readers of *Treasure Island* have demanded that he turn over the original map of the novel.[25] In any case, the exotic story of the magic bottle containing a wish-granting devil must certainly have seemed familiar to a nineteenth-century European and American audience that continued to be fascinated by fantastic tales warning of rags-to-riches fantasies.[26]

As in most stories of this sort and as in many of Stevenson's, "The Bottle Imp" is a tale of caution.[27] In it a young and somewhat naive but adventurous young man, a Hawaiian named Keawe, who comes into possession of a talisman that grants every wish but imposes certain conditions. The narrative draws on a formula exploited by some of the best and most popular writers of the century, including Goethe and Balzac, both of whom Stevenson knew well and admired.[28] This traditional form provides Stevenson with a way of dealing in "The Bottle Imp" with the relationship between aspiration and possession that is the focus of the early critical essays just cited. "A man may pay too dearly for his livelihood," Stevenson says in his essay on Thoreau, "by giving . . . his whole life for it, or bartering for it the whole of his available liberty, and becoming a slave till death."[29] This is exactly what happens in "The Bottle Imp." The young Hawaiian, Keawe, pledges his life for the possession of the magic bottle.

Here is another sense in which "The Bottle Imp" may be described as a tale of caution: not only in that it appears to warn against certain kinds of diabolical pacts, but also because it turns on the deposition of a caution in the sense of a pledge—something given as security in the establishment of a contract or bond (as in caution money).[30] In this case, Keawe offers his life as a caution. He too is in San Francisco, to which he has ventured in order "to have a sight of the great world and foreign cities" (BI 73). And he too is taken with America, in particular with its houses, a point to which we will return. Immersed in "wonder," Keawe comes upon a house that was "smaller than some others, but all finished and beautiful like a toy" (BI 73)—a detail referring us to Stevenson's essay on toys.[31] Looking into the toy house, he sees there a sorrowful old man, who very quickly sells Keawe the magic bottle, significantly, with little of the sense of foreboding often found in scenes of this kind. The simple terms of the contract have been explained by the old man. Upon purchase of the bottle, one pledges one's life against fulfillment of the following conditions: the bottle's owner is granted by the imp "all that he desires—love, fame, money, houses," provided that the bottle be sold at some point by the owner; that it be sold "at a loss"; and that it be sold for "coined money" (BI 74–76).

Let us examine these conditions briefly. After explaining that prolonging one's life is excluded (the imp does not have this power), the old man goes on: "if a man die before he sells [the bottle], he must burn in hell for ever" (BI 75). This condition makes the exploitation of the bottle a matter of time and, as in all speculative investment, of the timing of the sale. As the old man informs Keawe, "all you have to do is to use the power of the imp in moderation, and then sell it to some one else, as I do to you, and finish your life in comfort" (BI 75). In other words, if buying the bottle means acquiring a source of limitless credit, it also involves accepting the obligation of a debt to a future, as yet undetermined, purchaser to whom the bottle must be sold for a loss (the second condition). In this sense, the bottle is related to money—a substance which represents, as Aristotle says, "a guarantee of exchange in the future for something not given."[32] And indeed, according to the *Oxford English Dictionary*, the noun "bottle" itself can mean money ("a collection or a share of money"). The special qualification here, though, is that in this case the token is of owing, rather than of being owed, something in the future: it is a sign of a negative quantity to its holder.[33] Taking the bottle, in other words, means putting oneself in financial debt to another, putting oneself in another's debt—the minute one takes the bottle, one owes someone the difference between the price one paid for the bottle and the necessarily lower price for which one must sell it. The bottle becomes the token of this obligation to pay in the future, an obligation for which one's life is pledged as a caution.

The condition requiring that the bottle be sold for "coined money" might at first seem to place a limit on the size of this debt, by establishing some indivisible monetary unit, and thus to destine someone to be the final purchaser.[34] But, we discover, the debt here seems susceptible to division into infinitely smaller parts. As Keawe's resourceful and rather utilitarian wife, Kokua, tells him later in the story, one United States cent can be divided into about two British farthings, one British farthing into about two French centimes, and so on (BI 625–26).[35] And in this Polynesian story, the possibilities of traveling to other islands in the South Seas with ever-smaller units of currency is, we are led to believe, limitless. In this sense, the debt can hypothetically be resolved into ever smaller amounts in such a way that it remains always possible to pass on the ever-shrinking, but persistent debt (to a new purchaser) and to avoid forfeiture of the caution (the life pledged). The bottle thus betokens an economy that includes a concept, or fiction, of infinitely large and small amounts. A source of potentially infinite credit, it brings with it a debt that is always approaching a fictive absolute zero, as such never to be reached.[36]

The bottle's immediate association in the tale with money and finance is further reinforced by Stevenson's decision to call the demon an "imp." Indeed, Stevenson seems to be borrowing on the particular connotations the word "imp" had acquired in English culture at this time. An imp, the *Oxford English Dictionary* informs us, is a "little device or demon."

Imp, however, the dictionary notes, can also be used as a verb meaning "to engraft feathers in the wing of a bird so as to make good losses or deficiencies, and thus to restore powers of flight—hence, allusively, with reference to 'taking higher flights,' enlarging one's powers." This second meaning is the one that concerns us most because this use of the word "imp" to describe an operation designed to increase powers of flight intersects precisely with Stevenson's financial understanding of "aspiration" and "adventure." For, it is in this sense that the term "to imp" became associated in English with what many saw as the evil of financial credit and in particular paper money. The *locus classicus* is, as we have seen, Pope's *Epistle to Bathurst,* which is devoted to the ethical question of "whether the invention of Money has been more commodious, or pernicious to Mankind."[37] As we saw in the previous chapter, the *Epistle* is one of the best-known examples of early eighteenth-century English satires and polemics that ridiculed the new culture of credit and speculation from the pastoral perspective of landed "retirement," to use Maynard Mack's word.[38] Pope represents the period's widespread belief in the virtue of land and the fraudulence of financial credit—a belief that has been studied extensively by Pocock and others.[39] Let us cite again the lines from Pope in which the figure of imping appears:

Blest paper-credit! last and best supply!
That lends Corruption lighter wings to fly!
Gold *imp'd* by thee, can compass hardest things,
Can pocket States, can fetch or carry Kings. (emphasis added)

The figurative association of credit with flight expressed in Pope's use of the term "imping" would later in the century appear in a substantially modified form in the famous passage from Adam Smith's *Wealth of Nations* on the substitution of paper for gold and silver money, in which Smith argues for the cautious use of paper by comparing it to the wings of Daedalus. ("The commerce and industry of the country," Smith writes, "cannot be altogether so secure, when they are thus, as it were, suspended upon the Daedalian wings of paper money, as when they travel about upon the solid ground of gold and silver.")[40] What Pope and many other eighteenth-century writers considered fraud and artifice is, in Smith's view, a matter of ends and means, in short of finance—what he calls the "judicious operations of banking."

But in spite of the political economic writing of Smith, and after him of Ricardo and others, financial credit, specifically paper, continued to be viewed with deep suspicion, even superstition, well into the nineteenth century in England. Such superstition was regularly projected onto what was seen to lie outside the Empire, whether rival France, upstart America, or, as we will see, the uncivilized South Sea islands. Stevenson, I am suggesting, is different in this regard. Indeed, the difference can already be detected in his admiration for America, which was often viewed as a suspicious financial place for some of the same reasons that elicited Stevenson's praise of Thoreau.[41] Yet Stevenson's appreciation of the positive powers of financial credit as embodied in the image of America in his early writings is far from unqualified. Indeed, in his most important work we also find that admeasure of utilitarianism that accompanied the rise of modern political economy in Britain in the wake of Adam Smith, as a closer look at the workings of the bottle in "The Bottle Imp" will show.

At the beginning of the tale, the "new world"—El Dorado—entices with promises of riches: San Francisco is "a fine town, with a fine harbour, and rich people uncountable; and in particular there is one hill which is covered with palaces . . . 'What fine houses there are!' [Keawe] thought to himself, 'and how happy must these people be who dwell in them, and take no care for the morrow!'"(BI 73). The admiration here is for a scene from which number and calculation are absent: the "rich people" are both "uncountable" and unconcerned with future consequences—they "take no care for the morrow." Equally significant, as we indicated earlier, is the focus in the passage on houses—"palaces," as Keawe sees them—and on ways of dwelling. This scene of domestic promise beyond calculation establishes from the start the key link between the home and the bottle in this particular domestic romance. This is precisely where the bottle comes in. In possession of the bottle, Keawe immediately feels free to express his first desire, namely, "to have a beautiful house and garden on the Kona coast . . . and to live there without care" (BI 78). At this point, however, something happens that upsets the feeling of freedom. For now there are consequences: the death of an uncle whose estate Keawe is to inherit. The fulfillment of aspirations, as it happens, comes at a price—in this case, the bottle, as Keawe himself notes, serves his domestic aspiration by killing his family (BI 78).

This will be the theme for the rest of the tale: the consequences of the bottle's wish-granting power. "The Bottle Imp" becomes a story of trade-offs. The bottle, we are repeatedly shown, is a gift in the classic sense that it brings with it the inescapable system of reciprocal debt that always accompanies economies of gift exchange. As the bottle moves through the story, Keawe is made aware of the price to be paid for using its power in several contexts, material and spiritual. The decisive moment comes, as we might expect, in connection with his wife, Kokua, on whom his domestic aspirations depend. At this point, Keawe has managed to sell the bottle but finds that he has contracted a disease that threatens his marriage to Kokua and forces him to recover the bottle. But when he regains it and wishes his illness away, he finds that he has lost his love for Kokua. Here, in other words, according to the same logic we just saw in the case of his desire for a home, in order to preserve his domestic ties to Kokua, he must destroy them—that, in his words, to bind himself to his wife he must be "bound to the bottle imp for time and for eternity" (BI 90). Not because he will be unable to get rid of the bottle, but, on the contrary, because one *must* get rid of it. The bottle must be passed off—this is its fundamental law. It is Keawe's wife, Kokua (the only woman in the tale) who comes closest to a clear understanding of this law. The bottle, Kokua observes late in the story, involves a peculiar ethical responsibility, which she describes as the obligation "to save oneself by the eternal ruin of another" (BI 97).[42] This is what we might call the law of the pirate, thinking back on "My First Book."

But some question remains about whether, with the bottle, self-preservation requires the destruction of another. After all, in the end, Keawe does save himself and preserve his household without exactly ruining someone else. If he is a pirate, it is of the sort represented by Long John Silver and, by extension, Stevenson, each of whom retires with his wife. Late in the story, a drunken boatswain emerges to relieve Keawe of the bottle. The bottle is, in other words, passed to the drunk— hence another meaning of the word "bottle"—that is, it is passed to the one least likely to respond to its enticements with the "moderation" recommended to Keawe at the beginning of the story by the old man who sells it to him. Here, in keeping with the utilitarian motif we have been tracing, it is made quite clear that it is certainly not Keawe who ruins the drunk but the drunk who ruins himself (indeed Keawe even offers rather insistently to buy the bottle back from the immoderate boatswain). Kokua's perhaps extreme view of the bottle's law must, therefore, be modified: it is not that one ruins others by passing them the bottle, but rather that one might, even unintentionally, provide others with the means by which they will ruin themselves. The ethical difficulty of the bottle is the possibility of putting into the hands of others something with which they will destroy themselves. "Mate, I wonder are you making a fool of me?" (BI 101), the boatswain asks Keawe. This is the moral question—a question of possibility—to which we are ultimately led by the tale's utilitarian stress on the evaluation of consequences.

Keawe's story thus ends appropriately with the departure of the boatswain bottle in hand: "So off [the drunken boatswain] went down the avenue toward town, and there goes the bottle out of the story. But Keawe ran to Kokua light as the wind; and great was their joy that night; and great, since then, has been the peace of all their days in the Bright House" (BI 102). With this departure of the bottle from the story, "The Bottle Imp" itself goes out—not, however, without a final assessment of consequences. In the end, it turns out, Keawe retires to his manor house, the real estate he has derived from "operating judiciously," as Adam Smith would say, with the credit conferred by the bottle. Thus the story of the bottle becomes, like the bottle in the story, the instrument of a particular kind of domestic romance. It affirms that the romance of the home depends upon the utilitarian calculations of means and ends, and in this particular case upon finance (from the Latin *finis* meaning "end"). In other words, the domestic romance of the tale becomes inseparable from the sober calculation of consequences. There is, finally, no escape in this supposedly escapist literature from the evaluation of profit and loss.

But in "The Bottle Imp" domestic romance is not simply wedded to the utilitarian logic of finance. The consequentialist imperative of Stevenson's work extends to the tale itself. Here, though, Stevenson's fiction becomes hard to reconcile with the neat oppositions of utilitarian and anti-utilitarian moral philosophy that dominated debates in nineteenth-century moral philosophy (oppositions which, by the way, the union of the domestic idyll with finance already begins to confuse).[43] For, as with the bottle, responsibility for the tale—the narrative medium through which the domestic romance is achieved—lies with those who would make judicious use of the particular way it joins the imp of finance to the idyll of the home.[44] Responsibility for this tale lies, in other words, with those who choose to read the story to children, recommend it to friends, or assign it to students. And the management of effects or consequences in this context will certainly be no easier than it was for Keawe. Who can tell whether, for instance, the romance with its promise of future happiness through the judicious management of financial means and ends will turn out, in retrospect, to be genuine or counterfeit for those into whose hands it falls? This is the question raised by Stevenson's tale: Who is to say whether the utilitarian domestic romance will become for its readers a magic bottle or, to use the Victorian expression, a "bottle of smoke"—a conventional falsehood, a lie or counterfeit to which one lent credence? ("Withinsides" the bottle, we are told, "something moved like a shadow and a fire" [BI 74].) Perhaps the story of "The Bottle Imp" will also turn out to have been for some such "a bottle of smoke," a literary confidence game, passed along, as Dickens puts it in *Little Dorrit*, "to keep up pretense as a labour and a study . . . in short, to pass the bottle of smoke, according to the rule."[45] The consequences for which we become responsible when we pass along such domestic romances remain relatively unforeseeable. Even when the particular romance happens to urge utilitarian calculation, in the end we pass it along as a sort of gift, in the purer sense of the transmission of something the exact dimensions of which are incalculable, something for which reciprocation will not be possible—something that is not comparable to a financial transaction because it cannot be paid back. For, as we have already suggested, in order for a gift truly to be a gift, we must have in some sense no sure knowledge of what we are giving or being given, or even that something is being given and received.[46]

This brings us back to the map of *Treasure Island*. It is possible that Stevenson was not aware of the connections of the imp with paper money when he composed the tale. Yet later on, he might have chanced to pick up, for example, Pope's letter and then might have realized that this material detail had been lifted from the earlier text dealing with speculative finance in the South Seas. At such a point, Stevenson might have decided to admit the extent of this plagiarism. To do so it would no doubt have been tempting for this adventurous figure of an author to send a message to the public from his outpost in the South Seas and to tell of an original bottle, a magic device that concealed from him his piracy of Pope's imp.[47] In fact, Stevenson seems to engage in such a fancy in his letter cited earlier to Arthur Conan Doyle in which the Samoan visitor's question is reported: "Where is the bottle?" Such a question would be posed from a perspective like the one to which Stevenson addresses his essay on *Treasure Island*. In the case of "The Bottle Imp," the reply might be that, like the map, the bottle was indeed the key to the author's treasure, both in the economic sense of the wealth that is displayed in his house and in the aesthetic sense of the literary riches that circulate in his tale, and that now this wonderful device had vanished.[48] Thus, once again, Stevenson would be drawn as an author into the medium of his tale, not by the proverbial message in the bottle (in this case the figure of the paper money imp lifted from Pope), but by the bottle as such— as the withdrawing material support that makes the sending and receiving of messages possible.[49] Above and beyond the "material detail" it transmits, such a medium—one that refuses to remain within the horizons of a self-conscious subject, on the one hand, and a self-consistent material substance, on the other—bears the possibility of a collective that appears in Stevenson's later fiction to resemble the pidgin culture of Polynesia (meaning "many islands") with its plurality of perspectives and languages. Yet the very possibility of such a medium demands that it not be identified with a geographical location, as we will see in our reading of *The Beach of Falesá*. As we will also see, however, such a medium will not be able to do entirely without the distracting material support we encountered in the map of *Treasure Island* and the foolscap of "The Gold Bug." In this sense, paper money will remain an issue.

South Sea Currencies

A paper is missing from the serial version of *The Beach of Falesá* that appeared in the *Illustrated London News* in 1892. In the novel's first chapter,

"A South-Sea Bridal," there is what seems to be a sham wedding between an English trader (Wiltshire) and a Polynesian woman (Uma). A fellow trader officiates; "the book he made believe to read from," we are informed, "was an odd volume of a novel" (BF 109). Missing from the scene in the first version is a questionable marriage certificate used by the traders to fool, as they suppose, the Polynesian woman into believing that she has become the Englishman's wife. The paper reads:

> This is to certify that *Uma,* daughter of *Faavao,* of Falesá, island of ———, is illegally married to *Mr. John Wiltshire* for one night, and Mr. John Wiltshire is at liberty to send her to hell next morning. (BF 109)

Wiltshire, the narrator of the tale, feels ashamed, considers himself indeed to be a "welsher," the English slang word for swindler that he strangely hears in the Polynesian pronunciation of his name (BF 133). Evidently the English public was expected to share Wiltshire's shame, and this expectation led the publisher, against Stevenson's will, to lift the paper in question from the original serial version of the novel.[50] Angered by the removal of the paper, Stevenson began negotiating—as it happened, with the publisher who had misplaced the original map of Treasure Island—to have it restored to the book edition. Significantly the grounds for this restoration from Stevenson's point of view have less to do with the formal coherence of the novel than with the genuineness of the account. In response to the compromise proposed by the publisher, Stevenson writes: "Well, well, if the dears prefer a week [to one night], why I'll give them ten days, but the real document, from which I have scarcely varied, ran for one night."[51] The "real document" to which Stevenson alludes here is the subject of the portion of his "South Sea Letters" dealing with the Gilbert Islands. These were originally published in the *Auckland Star* during the period when *The Beach of Falesá* was being composed.[52] The prototype of the document lifted from the serial version of *The Beach of Falesá* is cited by Stevenson in the account that appeared in the *Auckland Star.* Speaking of native wives of European traders who were his neighbors in the Gilberts, Stevenson observes:

> All these women were legitimately married. It is true that the certificate of one, when she proudly showed it, proved to run thus, that she was "married for one night," and her gracious partner was at liberty to "send her to hell" the next morning; but she was none the wiser for the dastardly trick. Another, I heard, was married on a work of mine in a pirated edition; it answered the purpose as well as a hall Bible.[53]

The problem with the version of *The Beach of Falesá* published in the *Illustrated London News,* then, is that it places Stevenson is in a position analogous to that of Wiltshire: while the trader defrauds the native

Polynesian, the author defrauds the English reading public. Such jux-taposition, or superposition, of the native and the European contexts is a leading motif of *The Beach of Falesá*.[54] What might seem to be quin-tessentially native practices and beliefs are systematically referred to corresponding European customs.[55] Like Wiltshire, Stevenson's readers become receptive to a communicative medium in which, as we have seen, English slang ("welsher") can be heard in Polynesian pidgin and vice versa.[56] Indeed, as we have already begun to see, this *métissage* char-acterizes the array of outlets through which Stevenson's South Sea writ-ings were published, that is to say, in a plurality of contexts that spans the British Isles, America, the English colonies, and Polynesia. The mixed origins of "The Bottle Imp"—in English popular theater, European *Mär-chen* (a word Stevenson himself applied to the tale)[57] and native South Sea lore—are legible in its original publication in both Samoan in *O le Sulu Samoa* and English in *Black and White* (in the same year, by the way, that the latter journal was publishing portions of the "South Sea Let-ters"). This is, moreover, a feature of the imp figure in the tale itself which is associated both with Polynesian fantasy and with the European economic institution of paper money.[58]

Like the protagonist in *The Beach of Falesá*, Stevenson wants to come clean: The trader, by replacing the counterfeit marriage certificate with one that is genuine; the author, by restoring the genuine counterfeit document. Each of these individual efforts is complicated in a way ex-plored by Stevenson's novel. Wiltshire may not doubt the counterfeit character of the marriage certificate placed in Uma's hands, but the terms he employs to describe her handling of it already begin to raise questions—questions that lead back again to the overlapping of contexts just mentioned. The description is based, once again, on a monetary metaphor: "A nice paper to put in a girl's hand," he observes, "and see her hide it away like gold" (BF 109). For Wiltshire, Uma's attitude toward the paper is a bit of native superstition or fetishism. His characterization of it, however, reveals the European fetishization of gold as the substan-tial embodiment of value. From Wiltshire's perspective she treats it as if it were as good as he believes pure gold to be. The contamination of Wiltshire's portrayal of Uma by his own fetishism is evident again later when he asks her to produce the original marriage certificate so he can make it genuine:

She had it about her person, as usual; I believe she thought it was a pass to heaven, and if she had died without having handy she would go to hell. I couldn't see now where she put it the first time, I couldn't see now where she took it from; it seemed to jump into her hand like that Blavatsky business in the papers. But it's the same way with all island women, and I guess they're taught it when young. (BF 134)

This tactic whereby supposedly native superstition is referred back to European contexts (here the allusion to the mid-nineteenth-century fad for table-turning) is adopted throughout *The Beach of Falesá*.[59] It is evident in Uma's application of the native term "big chief" to Britain's Queen Victoria (BF 146) as well as in Wiltshire's use of the British Romantic trope of the Aeolian harp to describe the deceptive device used by Case to play on what is taken to be the exclusively native superstitious belief in natural animation (BF 151).[60] But the most telling example of this tendency undoubtedly comes in attitudes toward the commodity money of the islands—the copra that is, from the perspective of the European traders, fraudulently adulterated or "imped" by the natives through the addition of water. The fetish in this case is the European ideal or idol of a purifiable substance that embodies value—the gold to which Wiltshire refers in his description of Uma's handling of the (counterfeit) paper certificate. It is this belief in, and ardent want of, an indivisible and pure medium of exchange that has driven Wiltshire's predecessor on the island "clean crazy" about "somebody watering his copra" (BF 102).[61]

The perspective from which pure copra, like pure gold, is genuine is the one from which the paper marriage certificate is a complete fraud. This is precisely the point of view troubled by Wiltshire's tale. The paper certificate handed over to Uma is, like the copra circulating in the islands, an irreducibly mixed medium. Notwithstanding Wiltshire's conscious-ness of a certain fraudulence in the certificate and his later efforts to make it genuine in his eyes, he himself acts on the paper from the begin-ning as if it were binding, feeling "for all the world as though [Uma] were some girl at home in the Old Country, and forgetting myself for the minute, [taking] her hand to walk with" (BF 110). Indeed, far from simply defrauding the native woman, Wiltshire can be seen to imitate what he views as her credulous acceptance of the paper, in the same way that he begins "to speak to her kindly" and to imitate her pidgin English from the very moment of the wedding ceremony (BF 111). The infinitely mixed character of the exchanges and of the media of exchange in *The Beach of Falesá* remains beyond the narrator. While believing that he is engaged in unadulterated fraud, Wiltshire is drawn into a genuinely mixed network of obligation that goes beyond the limits of subjective self-consciousness, on the one hand, and substantial media of exchange, on the other.

According to the logic worked out in *The Beach of Falesá*, the genuine counterfeit marriage certificate that does not appear in the *Illustrated London News* is crucial as evidence of a medium that does not present itself in an unadulterated form. The London publishers try to water down Stevenson's tale. Perhaps they remove the counterfeit document, not simply because it is evidence of fraud and exploitation or of the corruption of an English legal convention, but also because they fail to see that it becomes the basis of a genuine contract in the tale.[62] Some readers, on the other hand, may regard Stevenson's tale as a troubling attempt on his part to water down the counterfeit marriage certificate he had documented in the journalistic account published in the *Auckland Star* with the fictional account of the genuine marriage of the Englishman and the native woman. For such purists the meaning of the document is clear. For other readers, however, the counterfeit paper may indicate the possibility of an empirical moment at which something is missed, such as the one that escaped Stevenson while he was staring at his map of Treasure Island.[63]

The Beach of Falesá depends upon such a missing empirical moment marked out by the dubious document. The paper is in this sense indispensable: it bears a real blind spot where the British subject's interactions with the natives fails to become part of his conscious experience. The moment that is really missing occurs in an encounter with the debased media of a colonial mass culture—the counterfeit marriage certificates issued on the basis of works of fiction, indeed on pirated novels (like Stevenson's *Treasure Island* perhaps), strewn about the sprawling Pacific empire. Stevenson's writings—the journalism and the tales—do not simply describe this mass-cultural commerce: they participate in it. If Stevenson waters down the documents of empire, it is with the aim of exposing and perhaps promoting their potential inconsistency. *The Beach of Falesá* deals with an imperial subject distracted from such inconsistency. Wiltshire is thus a study in imperial distraction: he remains to the end an unreformed and confused purist. Thus, he tears up what he regards as the fraudulent marriage certificate and accepts the authenticity of a marriage ceremony that is utterly unintelligible to him (it is conducted, he reports, "in native" [BF 134]).[64] "Nobody thinks less of half-castes than I do," Wiltshire insists at the close of the narrative, reflecting on his daughters with the sentiment of a concerned father.[65] The trouble, Wiltshire explains, is that he cannot "reconcile [his] mind to their taking up with the Kanakas" (such as he has) and does not "know where [he's] to find the whites" (such as himself) (BF 169). These final remarks demonstrate once again that what proves most irreconcilable and elusive to this British subject is just how mixed up he himself has become in Polynesia. Wiltshire catches his first glimpse of Falesá just as the binnacle light on his ship's compass goes out (BF 101). Such is the vanishing point at which Stevenson's readers encounter the disorienting Polynesia of his South Sea fiction. While reading these tales they are swept, Stevenson seems to hope, into a scattered location that cannot be identified precisely with the Empire as they have become used to seeing it. For this dislocation there are no maps, except those that withdraw.

Chapter 3

Transatlantic Connections: "Paper Language" in Melville

"Paper Language"

Up to a point, Stevenson operates along the lines of what Gilles Deleuze and Félix Guattari call "minor literature." A Scotsman writing in English and living in the South Pacific, Stevenson occupies the position of marginality characteristic of the "minor" writer.[1] His fiction also exhibits each of the three defining traits of minor literature sketched out by Deleuze and Guattari. "Deterritorialized" in its dispersed setting and medium of circulation, politicized in its defiance of the grand narratives of British imperialism, the South Sea fiction is also "revolutionary" in its announcement of an alternative "potential community" or "collective."[2] The parallels might extend farther: the polynesiansim, the cartographism, even a certain Americanness in Stevenson's work correspond to particular motifs identified in Deleuze and Guattari's original outline and elaborated in more detail in later writings, especially by Deleuze.[3] These parallels might appear to converge at the point around which our reading of Stevenson turned, specifically, at the vanishing point marked by his map. From this perspective, the map would have the effect of—would in fact be the very figure of—the decisive "vanishing line" (*ligne de fuite*) traced by minor writers in the major literary tradition, according to Deleuze and Guattari.[4] Such a convergence might indicate a broader correspondence between the "deterritorialization" that gives rise to "minor literature" and the mass mediacy at issue in what we are calling paperwork. After all, Stevenson's encounter is with no ordinary map—it involves a medium that eschews traditional subjective boundaries, the phenomenological horizons of a self-conscious subject (the author himself), on the one hand, and a self-consistent object (a material map), on the other. What is more, as we have seen, Stevenson's map is borrowed from the foolscap of "The Gold Bug": it is less the drawing of a space, than the opening of a network into which the subject itself is drawn. In this sense the map exercises a force similar to that of the newspaper in "The Man of the Crowd," in the Dupin stories and, in a related manner, in the London dailies where Poe encountered Dickens's journalistic sketches.

Like the "vanishing line" of "minor literature," then, paper withdraws in these works at points that break down subjective agency, releasing new, indeed "revolutionary," collective potentiality.[5] In "minor literature," the point of breakdown also has something to do with paper. If paper dramatizes the elusive status of the material support under conditions of mass mediacy, "paper language" characterizes the precarious linguistic state from which "minor literature" derives. In an important late essay, Deleuze finds traces of this "paper language" across the Atlantic in the work of Herman Melville. But by taking up "paper language" in Melville Deleuze hits upon the very element that escapes the dialectical logic of the minor literary program.[6] For paper in Melville surfaces where the national framework that is the necessary starting point for the minor literary program becomes unrecognizable. In spite of the emphasis on virtuality in Deleuze and Guattari's critique of subjectivity and of a certain monolithic concept of national literature, "minor literature" remains the property of a national literary subject—a revolutionary possibility, as they put it, "in the heart of (*au sein de*) what is called a great (or established) literature."[7] By contrast, the medium supported by paper in Melville's writing is a force that exceeds subjective limits, not only on the level of the individual writer, but also when it comes to the national literary movement. This thesis, which has been implied in the interactions and transfers that we have been tracking between Stevenson and Poe, and before that between Poe and Dickens, becomes explicit in Melville's treatment of paper. The broader question of the postnationalist or transatlantic dimensions of Melville's work goes beyond the scope of this study.[8] Our aim will be limited to outlining the trajectory of paper in a few key texts by Melville, a trajectory on which Deleuze touches as he pursues the "paper language" of "minor literature" in a transatlantic context. In his analysis of Melville, and in particular of "Bartleby," Deleuze follows a paper trail receding from the national perspective of the minor literary program and leading to Dickens's *Bleak House.*

"Minor literature" starts with "paper language" (*langage de papier*). The phrase occurs twice in Deleuze and Guattari's portrait of Kafka as "minor" writer.[9] Deleuze and Guattari associate this paper with artificiality or artifice but also with a dryness or poverty of language. The language in question is German, and specifically Prague German for the Jews of Kafka's time.[10] In this "paper" German—Deleuze and Guattari claim— Kafka discovers a foreign quality, like that of a foreign language, inhabiting the very language of the major literature. This heterogeneous element on which the "minor" writer works is, moreover, virtual: it is a force activated in the "paper language" of the major literature.[11] As soon as it is released, however, this force is integrated into the tradition: it is recognized as the actualization of a potentiality "in the heart of the great (or established) literature." In this way, "minor" works convert "paper language," according to an operation overseen by the major, and specifically national, literary tradition. "Minor literature" is thus always the expression of the potentiality—a property—of a major tradition. In this context, as in representational painting, the virtual "vanishing line" traced by the "minor" work serves in the end to establish a certain phenomenological perspective. "Minor literature" is the means through which the major literary tradition posits itself dialectically. In this sense, Deleuze and Guattari's theory ultimately represents a dialectical program for the national literary subject. This is why, unlike the virtual collective of the mass media, the "potential community" of "minor literature" ultimately has consciousness as its horizon, even if the consciousness in question is that of the collective.[12] The "minor" work is, to qualify a term taken from Deleuze and Guattari, a machine for expressing consciousness: the "minor" writer, as they say, "forges the means for another consciousness (*conscience*) and another sensibility."[13]

Yet the "paper language" to which Deleuze and Guattari allude cannot be entirely integrated by such an operation. This is already suggested by the fact that the phrase "paper language" is a citation in the study of "minor literature." No source is identified, but readers of Kafka will find one in a remarkable letter to Max Brod. The passage in question is devoted to the topic of what in German is called *mauscheln*, a verb that might be translated approximately as "to trick" or "to cheat" but also as "to speak with a Yiddish accent." *Wie ein Mauschel reden* means to speak like a Jew or a Jewish merchant (this presumably is where the accent and the cheating come together in the German word). And, it is important to underline, in spite of its associations with the foreign, *Mauscheln* is a German word (not to be found in what the Germans call *ein Fremdwörterbuch*): it derives from the pronunciation of the name "Moses" with a German accent (Duden). *Mauscheln* (we might translate it in this context as "speaking with an accent"), Kafka argues, "must be taken in the broadest sense":

namely as the overt or tacit or even self-pitying appropriation of foreign property not produced by oneself but rather stolen with a (relatively) passing grab, and the foreign property remains, even if not the slightest linguistic error can be identified. . . . Accented speech in itself (*Mauscheln an sich*) is indeed beautiful; it is an organic binding of paper German and gestural language (*eine organische Verbindung von Papierdeutsch und Gebärdensprache*).[14]

The term "gestural language" in this passage calls for analysis and commentary that would lead beyond the limits of the argument we are pursuing. But it is worth noting that a good place to begin such an investigation would be with Benjamin's essay on Kafka, an essay with close connections to his writing on the mass media. Working with the root of the word "gesture" (also the root of the German *Gebärde*), Benjamin's essay explores the singular character of bearing and of bearers—the many messengers and heralds—in Kafka's work.[15] For Benjamin, the singularity of gesture in Kafka lies in that it does not bear consciousness, does not bear the subject in the traditional sense. It would be more accurate to say that in gesture the subject becomes the support for a movement that exceeds subjective limitation. This is what we called the subject of paper in our reading of Derrida in the introduction, a subject that emerges in contrast with the traditional Lockean metaphor of the mind as a sheet of "white paper." If in gesture the subject becomes a support, the support can also at times become the subject of gesture. This is indeed precisely what happens in a passage Benjamin cites from *The Trial*, a scene in fact in which K becomes the bearer or support for paper:

Slowly, with eyes turned cautiously upward, [K] sought to learn what was happening up there, took one of the papers from the desk without looking at it, laid it on his open hand and raised it up gradually to the gentlemen while himself standing up. In doing so he had no definite purpose, but merely acted with the feeling that this was how he would have to conduct himself when he had finished the great petition that was to exonerate him completely. The Assistant-Manager, who was giving his full attention to the conversation, merely glanced fleetingly at the paper, not at all reading over what was there—for what was important to the Chief Clerk was unimportant to him—took it from K.'s hand, said: "Thanks, I already know everything," and calmly laid it back on the table.[16]

K's gesture, his bearing of paper, in this scene is thus characterized by the aimlessness and lack of consciousness typical of gesture in Kafka. He has "no definite purpose," does not look at the paper he rather compulsively bears. We might say that paper is supported by, but does not become the focus, of the gesture. Benjamin introduces K's bearing with the adverb "half unknowingly." Paper in this scene is a support, not for consciousness, but for gesture. Of special relevance for us is the manner in which this bureaucratic paper alludes to Dickens's *Bleak House*, also the source of "paper language" in "Bartleby."[17] "Paper language" in Melville is from the beginning a matter of transatlantic connections.

Bartleby; or the Gesture

The destabilizing force of the transatlantic network implied in Melville's "paper language" escapes the national literary perspective of "minor literature." This becomes clear as Deleuze attempts to extend this perspective in his interpretation of Melville as an American writer. Bartleby's "formula" is taken as a specimen of the "dry," "impoverished" language to which Kafka alludes in his letter. Like the German of the Prague Jews, Bartleby's "formula" is marked by a certain "mannerism," even if it is "grammatically and syntactically correct."[18] It has a foreign element: "at first," Deleuze observes, "the formula seems like the bad translation of a foreign language . . . it carves into the language a sort of foreign language."[19] Bartleby's language is, in other words, "deterritorialized." It is also, secondly, politicized, and thoroughly so in its absolute refusal of choice and position. The formula refuses politics by obliviating will. It is "not a will to nothingness," as Deleuze puts it in one of the most trenchant passages in his essay, "but the growth of a nothingness of the will" (*un néant de volonté*).[20] With this we come to the third and decisive component of the formula, its collective element: the manner in which Bartleby's "paper language" becomes the medium of an "alternative potential community." This third part of Deleuze's triad, of his multiple triads in fact, is crucial for us. This is where the national cast of the minor literary program enters the scene.

The argument on the national level, in short, comes down to the following: the "foreign language in the language" of the English tradition is American (in the sense that French translations are sometimes said to be "from the American"—*traduit de l'américain*). In this framework Bartleby [the character] represents the "vanishing line" where the major English tradition is "minorized" as American literature.[21] Bartleby emerges in the tale as "something strange," an "unknown element" in the tradition of English literature: "Everything began *à l'anglaise* but continues *à l'américaine*, following an irresistible line of flight."[22] This is indeed where, as Deleuze says, "things start to become interesting."[23] For, as Deleuze begins to make this point, paper resurfaces, specifically, in connection with the narrator's description of his efficient management of the two perfectly complementary office clerks (Nippers and Turkey). "The two clerks," Deleuze observes, "are like paper images (*images de papier*), symmetrically inverse, and the narrator fulfills his paternal function so well that we can scarcely believe we are in New York. Everything begins as in an English novel, in London and in Dickens."[24] The clerks are "images of paper," it seems, in that they appear as formalized types. They are presented in a conceptual and literary language that is dry and impoverished—a "paper language," as it were. And here, Deleuze emphasizes, the language is English, or more precisely the language of England and in particular of England's novels. At this point, in other words, we seem to be in a Dickens novel. Not really, though. For, Melville is working on the "paper language" of a Dickens novel in such a way that it is becoming American by "following an irresistible line of flight." This is where Bartleby comes in. But who, with the exception perhaps of the narrator, is more closely associated with paper than Bartleby in the tale? Deleuze's application of the phrase—of the formula—"paper image" to the English treatment of the clerks is dictated by the nationalizing logic of "minor literature." Indeed, paper is linked to the concept of the nation-state represented here by England (elsewhere it is represented by the French or the European, in contrast with the Anglo-Saxon, tradition).[25] It is imperative that the nation-state be represented and that this representation take the form of a paper image. Otherwise, "minor literature" could not convert the "paper language" of the nation-state into a medium of an alternative potential community that is not subject to paternalism or oedipalization, which in this context means not subject to England.[26]

Because it must be representational and convertible—in short, a metaphor—and because it must represent the nation-state, paper must never be associated with American literature for Deleuze. This explains why the phrase "paper image" returns at the end of the essay to mark the failure of the America Revolution as it turns into the "restoration" of the nation-state:

The dangers of a "society without fathers" have often been pointed out, but the only real danger is the return of the father. In this respect, it is difficult to separate the failure of the two revolutions, the American and the Soviet, the pragmatic and the dialectical. Universal emigration was no more successful than universal proletarization. The Civil War already sounded the knell, as would the liquidation of the Soviets later on. The birth of a nation, the restoration of the nation-state—and the monstrous fathers come galloping back in, while the sons without fathers start dying off again. Paper images (*images de papier*)—this is the fate of the American as well as the Proletarian.[27]

What prevents or resists the "paper image" of the nation-state is a certain engagement with the virtual movement of what might be called revolutionary potentiality. In Melville's fiction, Deleuze argues, this is the role played by the figure of the "prophet" (another of Deleuze's third terms). A detailed analysis of Deleuze's characterization of the prophet's engagement with revolutionary potentiality would discover the same vocabulary and logic described earlier in "minor literature." If, as Deleuze argues, the prophet in Melville (and the narrator in "Bartleby") "has seen so much," his vision remains within the phenomenological horizon of a prophetic subject that "recognizes" (*reconnaître*) "vanishing lines" and that "reconciles" (*reconcilier*) oppositions such as the "human" and the "non-human."[28] What remains, in other words, is a dialectical logic of "integration" (the term "integration" almost always appears in connection with the virtual in Deleuze, again as a third and final step in a progression.)[29] In "Bartleby," American literature is seen to posit itself by converting the false "paper language" into a means through which a virtual movement can be integrated without becoming stationary and, as it were, static. As an example of the latter, Deleuze alludes at the end of his essay to the false community of Melville's "Paradise of Bachelors," a group whose counterfeit bond is based on the exploitation of the factory girls portrayed in the companion tale, "The Tartarus of Maids." But if the bachelors represent the failed revolutionary promise of America, how do we explain the fact that they are explicitly presented in the tale as British? Perhaps the best illustration of American failure—of America as a "paper image"—is England. Yet what are we to make of the fact that the maids of the linked tale are workers in an American paper factory? If paper is associated with America in Melville—and every term in this proposition would have to be qualified—the paper in question represents neither the artificial formal medium of the nation-state (a static medium) nor the medium of a genuine integration of a virtual movement as in a work of "minor literature." "Paper language" in Melville is handled differently, as we will see if we look more closely at "Bartleby" and the companion tales to which Deleuze refers at the end of his essay on Melville.

Melville may have gotten some of the material for "Bartleby" from the newspaper ("Bartleby" was itself published serially in *Putnam's Magazine* in 1853). He may, for example, have read the first installment of James A. Maitland's *The Lawyer's Story* in the *New York Tribune* or in the *New York Times* in February of 1853.[30] Or he may have derived the paragraph at the end of the tale about the Dead Letter Office from "sentimental accounts" in various newspapers at this time.[31] Or he may have picked up elements of the tale's basic formula—specifically, the parts of the Bartleby and the narrator—from his reading of the early serial installment of Dickens's *Bleak House* published in 1853 in *Harper's Magazine*, a periodical to which Melville had recently resubscribed. This last possibility suggests that, if Bartleby and the narrator are clearly associated with—and by way of—paper, neither is entirely American. The narrator's practice of Chancery law and Bartleby's law copying hint at links to Dickens's novel (it is thus for good reason that we feel as if we might be in London in Melville's tale). Chancery Court and Nemo, the law copier in *Bleak House*, are of course also profoundly connected to paper. Moreover, in Dickens's novel, paper is a medium of disintegration. There too paper obliviates will. It could be argued that ultimately *Bleak House* brings this disintegrating force under arrest by instituting paternal authority, although the complexity of this operation may point in other directions.[32] Of course, Melville may simply have stopped reading the serial installments of *Bleak House* when the law copier was introduced, and at that point there was no counterforce in sight to bring closure to the "paper language" of Chancery Court, or of Dickens's novel for that matter. Or perhaps Melville did not pay attention sufficiently to the later scenes when John Jarndyce pretends to pull things together. This is, after all, the problem with such novels, as Poe understood; one simply cannot concentrate, they are too long, too distracting. The point is that the British-ness of Melville's story and of its "paper language" extends not just to the clerks, as Deleuze proposes, but also to Bartleby—the "unknown element," the "strange something"—and to the narrator.

In other words, as in "The Man of the Crowd," Melville's "Poeish tale," as one contemporary reviewer called it, seems to stage an interaction between its author and Dickens that is based on paper.[33] Melville gets a certain impression of paper from Dickens—or, not so much from Dickens as from the force of mass mediacy which is supported by paper and into which *Bleak House* is itself drawn. Such mediacy exceeds national limits, as we have seen and as Dickens himself knew very well, somewhat to his chagrin.[34] Melville's "Bartleby" would in this way, like Poe's short story, show how the concentration of the tale ultimately displays the distracting force that in Poe it is supposed to contain. Bartleby's "paper language" marks the spot where the literary medium of Melville's tale is exposed to a mass mediacy that cannot be integrated into a national literary movement conceptualized in terms of a reflexive self-consciousness. This exposure is dramatized in the tale on the level of the individual subject by the narrator's encounter with Bartleby—or, more precisely— with the disintegrating force that Bartleby supports and that the clerks and in turn the narrator himself come involuntarily to support, as they discover when they display the impression the disarticulating formula has made on them. The impression is disarticulating in that it disintegrates grammatically and syntactically—it is not a self-consistent linguistic unit— and in that it disintegrates the self-consistency of its support—in this case, the self-conscious and self-contained subjectivity of supposedly individual subjects. The impression in question, then, extends beyond all self-contained individuality and, accordingly, it precedes the appearance of Bartleby. It is legible in the narrator, even before he introduces himself as a paper-pushing Chancery lawyer, in the dry and artificial legalism—a bit of "paper language"—"Imprimis," a term that itself literally combines initiality and impression.[35] This continues through the physiognomic, Dickensian sketches of the two clerks, types that also recall those employed at the beginning of "The Man of the Crowd." And on it goes, through the "sentimental" passage on dead letters that might very well be the effect of impressions left on Melville by the newspaper. If the narrator is a prophet, it is not because he "sees so much," but rather because he sees so little of what he is supporting when it comes to Bartleby.

Disassembling Collective

The disintegrating force breaking across Melville's tale does not present itself in the form of self-consistent things and characters, but instead traverses and interrupts self-consistency in the manner of Bartleby. What Melville's narrator relates in this sense is the origin of the tale as the withdrawal of self-consistency and specifically of self-consistent supports—in short, the withdrawal of paper. This holds with regard to the collective as well. The withdrawal means that paper is the support neither for a static medium (of the nation-state) nor for a dynamic medium (of the "minor literature"). Paper supports, rather, a medium of a potentiality pure to the point of refusing to actualize, not just the nation-state, but also the nation, a virtuality that cannot be conceptualized as a property of a self-positing nation. This is what happens most explicitly in Melville's companion tales, "The Paradise of Bachelors" and "The Tartarus of Maids." Together, these tales break down the distinction between isomorphic British and American contexts. Moreover, here again paper is the support for the disintegrating force that moves between and through the stories. Such breakdown is part of a broader project in Melville's work that runs from the set of three companion tales of the 1850s and *Pierre, or the Ambiguities* (1852) through *Israel Potter* (1853) and the posthumous *Billy Budd* (1891). Even *Moby Dick* (1851), the work perhaps most often taken to embody American literature, is crossed by the failure of the American reduction of transnational forces.

In "The Tartarus of Maids," a seed merchant narrates his visit to a paper mill in western Massachusetts to buy envelopes to mass market his seeds. In the course of the tale, he associates this visit with the account of a dinner party in a lawyers club in London provided in "The Paradise of Bachelors." Yet in "The Paradise of Bachelors" and "The Tartarus of Maids," the British and American settings are nothing if not scrambled. Not only do the supposedly distinct locations merge so that urban scenes in London reappear in rural Massachusetts, but, on the most general level, the Old World and the New World become reversible.[36] This is underlined, first of all, by the titles of the tales, in which the Old World (England) is referred to a more modern mythological context (Paradise), while the New World (America) is given the older name (Tartarus). This feature is also evident in the literary allusions to eighteenth-century satirical writing (Pope's *Rape of the Lock* comes to mind) in the London story and to Dante in the tale of Massachusetts. Moreover, these confusing patterns emerge as the second tale, "The Tartarus of Maids," takes up in terms of insemination and the bearing of seeds the question of impression and support we have encountered in "Bartleby." There are several obvious parallels here, including the invocation of the traditional

Pauline distinction between spirit and letter, already implied in a sense by the reference to Dante at the outset of the tale, and of course the encounter with a paper machine. Ultimately, as with the narrator of "Bartleby," what the seedsman encounters at the paper mill does not support divine logos. In the seedsman's visit to the paper mill there is no reappearance of the divine logos, but instead the endless reproduction of blank paper issuing from a paper machine:

> Looking at that blank paper continually dropping, dropping, dropping, my mind ran on in wonderings of those strange uses to which those thousand sheets eventually would be put. All sorts of writings would be writ on those now vacant things—sermons, marriage certificates, bills of divorce, registers of births, death-warrants, and so on, without end. Then, recurring back to them as they here lay all blank, I could not but bethink me of that celebrated comparison of John Locke, who, in demonstration of his theory that man had no innate ideas, compared the human mind at birth to a sheet of paper; something destined to be scribbled on, but what sort of characters no soul might tell.[37]

Confronted by the revolutions of the paper machine, Melville's narrator turns over in his mind a revision of Locke's metaphor for the mind that involves seeing it, not only as paper, but as mass-produced paper. In place of the uniqueness and finitude of the self-consistent sheet of paper, he sees instead the massiveness and infinitude of paper "without end." The narrator becomes involved in a mode of production that has nothing in particular to do with subjective consciousness—the machine has nothing in mind for the subject. It is precisely the panic induced by this threatening absence that leads the narrator to seize upon Locke's metaphor and, like his counterpart in "Bartleby," to try to endow the machine with a mind or a soul. The machine, however, refuses the offer and, perhaps most importantly, refuses to reciprocate by giving back or mirroring to the narrator his image—Locke's image—of the mind. This "crisis of reciprocity," as Benjamin would call it, is the whole point of Melville's tale, which narrates the origins, not so much of self-consciousness, as of the medium of the tale itself—the receding origins of the tale's lack of self-consistency and integrity. The shift from self-consistent subjectivity to infinitely divisible medium also operates on the collective level. And here the repression of subjective breakdown dramatized by the narrator's allusion to Locke's metaphor would manifest itself in an effort to repress the related breakdown of the self-contained national entities (England and America).

If the interpenetrating tales are designed precisely to work against such efforts, paper is what might be called the disarticulating material link between them. This is what makes the narrator's allusion to Locke's image of the mind as a sheet of "white paper" so peculiarly telling. For, there is no prophetic vision here, no integrating moment of recognition or reconciliation, just as there is no reappearance of divine logos in the sheets of mechanically reproduced paper that will bear the narrator's seeds, and much more. The narrator of "The Tartarus of Maids" sees in the paper mill anything but a machine for consciousness. Or rather, this is exactly what he does *not* see when he seizes on the traditional Lockean metaphor of the mind as a sheet of "white paper."[38] The metaphorical repression here is similar to the one that occurs when a white sperm whale is taken as a metaphor for a divine will or logos that is in fact at the very point of withdrawal. And this is precisely what happens in the scene in *Moby Dick* in which the whale blubber is cut and falls "fast as the sheets from a rapt orator's desk. Arrayed in decent black; occupying a conspicuous pulpit; intent on bible leaves; what a candidate for an arch-bishoprick, what a lad for a Pope were this mincer."[39] In what is often taken to be the quintessentially American novel, as in the tales we have analyzed, the encounter with paper stages the repressed breakdown of a self-consistent, self-contained subjectivity on the individual as well as on the collective level. In Melville's fiction paper is not the semblance of the nation-state, as Deleuze (and others) argue: it is not the point at which the revolutionary forces of a given collective depart on a virtual "line of flight" giving rise to alternative "collective assemblages," as Deleuze calls them. Paper in Melville is rather precisely at the breaking point where the national collective disassembles.

Chapter 4

The Paper State: Collective Breakdown in Dickens's *Bleak House*

Paper is the material support for psychic and social disintegration in *Bleak House*. For Dickens, as for Melville, the distraction and dispersal of mass mediacy has an overwhelming effect on individual and collective states of stability based on self-containment. In *Bleak House* the metaphor for such a state in the collective sense is the home. In Dickens's sprawling novel the home is scattered with mass-produced paper. Domestic breakdown connects *Bleak House* to an aesthetic tradition that culminates in Lukács's theory of the novel as the genre of "transcendental homelessness." But Dickens's novel does not remain within the framework of this traditional aesthetic perspective. For the scattered state that emerges in *Bleak House* is not that of "transcendental homelessness" either in the individual or in the collective sense of the term. Rather, the homeless motif in this work moves away from the conceptual foundation of a phenomenological theory of the novel as a genre, whether Lukács's classic Hegelian essay or more recent efforts to interpret the novel as an institution of Foucauldian "discipline." Exposed to the dynamism of an especially unsettling mass movement, the home in *Bleak House* leaves this phenomenological space. The handling of mass-produced paper in Dickens's novel dramatizes the decline, not just of the domestic aura, but also of domesticity as a metaphor for a stable sense of place. In *Bleak House* the individual, the collective, and the novelistic medium become involved in a movement that defies the conventional metaphor of the home as a self-contained state. One cannot simply be within, or without, a home in *Bleak House*. The removal of the home from a traditional concept of place in Dickens's work corresponds to the "shattering" of tradition and transmissibility that links modern techniques of mass production to the novel as a literary genre in Benjamin's writings.[1] At issue is a crisis of exchange precipitated by the death of reciprocity. In this chapter we will analyze the role played by paper as a material support in this crisis in *Bleak House*. Dickens might have viewed such a crisis as deriving from the "deranged condition" of England in the "Paper Age."[2] This would account for the flow of paper from Chancery Court. But the novel exposes a mass movement breaking down the self-consistency of Carlyle's paper metaphor. Such a widespread breakdown involves the material support in the broadest possible sense: not just the masses of paper, but also the masses—the individual and collective subjects that become receptive to the process.[3] The following is an attempt to pursue these paper subjects in Dickens's *Bleak House*.

The Hand of Nemo

Paper abounds in *Bleak House*: from the courtroom and law offices to the shops and homes of the novel's protagonists.[4] This is the reader's overwhelming impression of the opening chapters. There are, in order of appearance, the "tens of thousands of Chancery-folio-pages" copied by the copyists (BH 17), the "eighteen hundred sheets" of the lawyers (BH 18), the "heavy charges of papers" hauled off by the clerks (BH 19), the papers copied by a certain "Nemo" and placed before Lady Dedlock by Mr. Tulkinghorn "on a golden talisman of a table" (BH 26), the "bundles of papers" (BH 45) in Kenge and Carboy's law office, "the nest of waste paper" from which Mrs. Jellyby dictates endless philanthropic letters to her daughter Caddy (BH 57), the piles of "waste paper" in Krook's rag and bottle shop (BH 67), and the paper advertising the copying services of Nemo put up in the window of the shop along with a picture of a paper mill (BH 67). In a state where endless copying has become the law subjects are less metaphors, as J. Hillis Miller has suggested, than supports—paper subjects.[5] Moreover, the law of copying in *Bleak House* is not restricted to legal copyists such as Nemo. It applies equally to the young Caddy Jellyby who "can't do anything hardly, except write . . . for Ma" (BH 60) and to the illiterate Krook who demonstrates "a turn for copying from memory . . . though [he] can neither read nor write" (BH 76; Figure 6). Amassing paper and taking on its capacity to bear reproducible marks, Krook ultimately merges with the very substance of the support—the mingling of his ashes with "burnt paper" "is all that represents him" (BH 519).[6] With Krook, mass-produced paper becomes a metaphor for a subject lacking singularity. The death of such a subject is, accordingly, a mere blank: it can bear "all names soever" and is in fact the very stuff of the "tissue-paper" used by the newspapermen of Dickens's day to produce duplicate copy (BH 519, 533).

Nemo is different. In his hand copying is not simply opposed to singularity. Rather, Nemo's hand is singularly posed in the novel. It is the nameless signature—the singular sign of no one—that marks the decline of a subject exposed to mechanical reproduction. The manner noted in this hand diverges from the strictly legal character of the copying while also being identifiable with no one. The singularity in question is,

The Lord Chancellor copies from memory.

Figure 6. Hablot K. Browne, *The Lord Chancellor Copies from Memory.*
Illustration for Charles Dickens, *Bleak House.* Courtesy of the Hay Library,
Brown University.

therefore, not subjective. And yet there is, as Mr. Tulkinghorn observes, a certain heterogeneous element—something "original" and thus "not quite" entirely legal—in this "law hand" (BH 26–27). This is what occurs to Lady Dedlock and produces "her unusual tone" (BH 26). But the occurrence is not described in terms of consciousness: it is a matter neither of intention nor of recognition. If the copyist did not intend to give such an impression—if the impression must be understood to exceed his expectations—Lady Dedlock's apprehension of it also goes beyond the simple recognition of a lost lover's hand. It touches her "like the faintness of death" (BH 27). We might be tempted to interpret the name "Nemo" as expressing the copyist's intention "to escape the involvement in society inevitable if one has any name at all."[7] But this interpretation is inadequate: Nemo describes the disarticulation of the subject as an integrated center of intention. Nemo stands for no one—it is precisely the sort of legalese that obliterates individual will and subjectivity in *Bleak House*. The hand of Nemo is like an omen (Nemo copied backwards), except that it does not point forward to an inevitable outcome but rather enacts an uncertain condition. This is the state suggested by the bearing, the "unusual tone," that comes over Lady Dedlock when, "changing her position, [she] sees the papers on the table" (BH 26).

The adherence to manner and bearing in this scene, then, does more than simply represent the restrictive formalities of class. It dramatizes a condition that no one is in a position fully to recognize.[8] It is not just the "stately" distraction of Leicester Dedlock who is mesmerized by the "legal repetitions and prolixities" that seem to him to be "among the national bulwarks," and not just the "fashionable" distraction of Lady Dedlock who is "bored to death" and who "carelessly and scornfully abstracts her attention" from the legal copying. There is also the distraction of Nemo. What gets into the "hand" of this scrivener as he mindlessly copies Chancery's proceedings? What gets into my Lady's bearing as the "hand" is placed at her "elbow"? And what gets into the manner of the subjects collectively in the novel, or into the manner of the readers collectively of the novel, as they follow the Court's repetitions? The answers to these questions raised by the remarkable hand of Nemo are ultimately beyond the grasp of all concerned, precisely because in each case the bearing in question is less a self-present state than a mass movement. For, the force conveyed by the papers placed before Lady Dedlock early in the novel does not remain within the space circumscribed by the iconic golden table. It does not even stay confined to the face of the papers.[9] The hand of Nemo spreads like a plague.[10] The copied papers are not only scattered throughout the homes, shops, and offices of the novel's opening passages. The copying that reproduces the duplications of Chancery Court is also doubled in the novel by the spread of a contagion.[11] Nemo's hand, taken in two senses, articulates a double mass movement—one involving masses of paper, the other masses of people. To the extent that the multiplication of the contagion is comparable to the spreading of copies (the hand of Nemo), the human subject resembles paper as a material support, or rather as a receding material support. In both cases a proliferating movement is made possible by the withdrawal of a massive support—that of mass-produced paper, on the one hand, and of the urban masses, on the other.[12]

Representations of the urban masses of mid-nineteenth-century London can be found in contemporary works such as Mayhew's classic typological survey *London Labor and the London Poor*.[13] In *Bleak House* there is Jo. Another nobody, the crossing sweep marks the disintegration of the body politic, an unacknowledged and shifting point of social breakdown at which the collective fails to recognize its truly scattered state. Jo moves in the zone of estranging familiarity about which Dickens began to write in his earliest journalistic sketches. From the beginning the specificity of the collective that concerned "Boz" and his readers derived from the singularity of a distracted state that itself repeatedly escapes attention—what is called "habit" in *Sketches by Boz*.[14] Habitually, Boz observes of Newgate Prison, for example, men "pass and repass this gloomy depository of the guilt and misery of London, in one perpetual stream of life and bustle, utterly unmindful of the throng of wretched creatures pent up within it—nay not even knowing, or if they do, not heeding the fact, that as they pass one particular angle of the massive wall with a light laugh or a merry whistle, they stand within one yard of a fellow-creature, bound and helpless, whose hours are numbered, from whom the last feeble ray of hope has fled for ever, and whose miserable career will shortly terminate in a violent and shameful death."[15] Depicted here is a massive repression: the collective's repression of the masses and of its own massiveness.[16] The "throng" presses against the self-consistent and immortal image of the public as "one perpetual stream of life." Yet the wall constructed to contain the pressure is "massive"—the prison wall but also the wall of "habit"—and it displays, rather than shutting out, the vast exposure of the public to the heterogeneity and transience of the dying "throng." The "massive wall" in this sense secretly and intimately associates the collective with its own decline as a self-contained, self-perpetuating community. In *Bleak House* Jo inhabits, or passes away, in such a public passage: "Jo lives—that is to say, Jo has not yet died—in a ruinous place" (BH 256). From the start the crossing sweep recedes, not just in the novel, but also from the novel's shifting perspectives. Even as he is introduced in the third-person narrative Jo seems to remain nearly out of sight—in the midst of London and at the limit of the representational space from which Lady Dedlock, touched by Nemo's hand, is said to have "flitted away." Nemo's hand draws Lady Dedlock away from "the place in Lincolnshire," where she is "at present represented . . . by her portrait," toward the "whereabout of Jo the outlaw" (BH 256). It is place itself, in the various senses probed throughout the novel, that here gives way.[17] If Jo is out of place—kept about by being moved repeatedly elsewhere—this is because fundamentally he is not presentable. The singularity of Jo's condition is thus inconceivably strange to "the place in Lincolnshire" and also to the discursive medium of a novel that can cast only a "distant ray of light upon" his "state."

And yet, Jo's singular and unpresentable condition is precisely what binds the collective in its scattered state. "What connection can there be," the narrator wonders, between Jo's "whereabout" and Lady Dedlock's "place" (BH 256) or between Jo's "state" and the state of the collective that gathers in the unsettling experience of reading *Bleak House*? A partial response comes in one of the most familiar, yet still moving, passages in the novel in which Jo's strange state suddenly turns into that of a reading collective:

It must be a strange state to be like Jo! To shuffle through the streets, unfamiliar with the shapes, and in utter darkness as to the meaning, of those mysterious symbols, so abundant over the shops, and at the corners of streets, and on the doors, and in the windows! To see people read, and to see people write, and to see the postmen deliver letters, and not to have the least idea of all that language. . . . [Jo's] whole material and immaterial life is wonderfully strange; his death, the strangest thing of all. (BH 257–58)

The rhetorical gesture may appear routine, but something remarkable happens in this passage: the strangeness of Jo's condition to the readers is illustrated by a description of the strangeness of the readers' condition to Jo. Strangeness is, in other words, the "connection." The state of being like Jo must be strange, for it obliges readers to see themselves, indeed to read about themselves, as a strange state—to make themselves out at the threshold of reading. At this point reading becomes both condition and limit: a state marked by strange occurrences, like the life and especially the death of Jo. And undoubtedly the strangest thing about Jo's death in *Bleak House* is the sense in which it is collective. Instead of pulling together an integrated community of individuals, this death displays a collective coming apart and dispersing as a mass. From this strange perspective, Jo's death is not individual. It is the death en masse of the collective as a community in the traditional sense. The crossing sweep passes away by becoming immediately one of the many, by disappearing into the crowd.[18] His death is abruptly carried off by a mass movement: "Dead, your Majesty. Dead, my lords and gentlemen. Dead, Right Reverends and Wrong Reverends of every order. Dead, men and women, born with Heavenly compassion in your hearts. And dying thus around us, every day" (BH 734). The death here, like the life, is a matter of "moving on" for all concerned—including the narrator.[19] Jo passes away in the space of such a withdrawal in *Bleak House*. Yet the repetitive movement of Jo's life and death leaves an impression on the collective that fails to recognize itself in the strange vision of the crossing sweep. As with the hand of Nemo, the impression is not a matter of conscious transmission and so not a matter of transmission at all in the conventional sense. What Jo bears is the breakdown of transmissibility that occurs when the collective is struck by the incapacity to hand itself down through the reciprocal exchange of experience. Thus, paradoxically, Jo becomes an "unconscious link" in the novel because he has no experience. He sees everything but knows nothing: "he sums up his mental condition, when asked a question, by replying that he 'don't know noth-ink'" (BH 256). Jo's blank vision transmits like an imperfect recording device.

The manner in which this optic marks, and comes to bind, the collective is suggested by a series of incidents already underway when Jo gives his testimony at the inquest into Nemo's death. Lady Dedlock, who reads the report of what Jo has seen in the "papers," asks him to "shew [her] all of the places there were spoken of in the account [she] read" (BH 261). The tour that follows unfolds mechanically like a series of illustrations and in fact ends with the appearance in the text of Hablot K. Browne's drawing of Jo and Lady Dedlock at the iron gate of the open mass grave where Nemo is also buried ("Cook's Court. Jo stops. A pause. . . . Krook's house. Jo stops again. A longer pause . . ."; BH 261–64). In return for the visit, Lady Dedlock "drops a piece of money in [Jo's] hand, without touching it, and shuddering as their hands approached" (BH 264). This may well be, as Lady Dedlock promises, "more money that [he] ever had in his life," but Jo gets even more than he bargains for in the scene that ensues (BH 261). While retracing the steps of his testimony, the witness keeps picking things up—in this case, taking in, not just the impression of Lady Dedlock's veiled face, but also, it is suggested, the contaminating illness contracted from the mass of decomposing bodies with which the remains of Nemo are merging. This is the deadly combination that Jo will involuntarily bear to the "neighborhood" of Bleak House and to Esther, who is both the mistress of the house and the child of the flawed union (BH 487). From this point on, Jo becomes an unconscious and physically disintegrating support for the unsettling force that finds its way into the hand of Nemo and, as we have seen, into the face of Lady Dedlock when she glances at the copied papers.[20]

Losing One's Place

In that the "ruinous place" from which Jo "moves on" is characterized above all by domestic collapse, the life and death of the crossing sweep binds the collective to a spreading state of homelessness.[21] This is where *Bleak House* intersects with the theory of the novel elaborated by Lukács. With Esther's narrative, Dickens's work seems to come closest to this philosophical perspective on the genre. As it weaves in and out of *Bleak House* the governess's first-person narrative offers an extensive reflection on the individual and collective effects of the disintegrating force to which Nemo and Jo become subject. The autobiographical account interacts with the third-person narrative in a way that shows the novel caught up in a spreading aesthetic condition parallel to the one affecting the subjects individually and collectively in *Bleak House*. By providing the relatively unified perspective of a subject struggling to see itself as part a world of social displacement, Esther's narrative may seem to place the novel on the philosophical terrain that is the basis for Lukács's theory of the novel.[22] But it is precisely this ground that gives way in her account as the subject becomes exposed to the force that we have been tracing by way of Nemo and Jo. By linking the hand of Nemo with a contagious disease, Dickens associates the contemporary social state with the material conditions that were producing epidemics in the London of his day (he had in fact been writing about the latter in *Household Words* during this time).[23] The novelist also, however, associates the proliferation of mass mediacy with the identity crisis that is central to Lukács's Hegelian interpretation of the novel as a genre. Yet, in Dickens's novel, there is no ironic integration of the crisis into experience. More explicitly than in the case of Jo or of Nemo, Esther's bearing of the crisis reveals the point at which the effects of mass production in *Bleak House* become incomprehensible within the traditional phenomenological horizon of individual and collective experience.

This point is illuminated by reading a scene that provides a key to Esther's bearing in the novel—what might be called Esther's "mirror stage." At this point, the heroine is recovering from a life-threatening fever that she and her helper, Charley, have caught from Jo. In other words, the disease had been contracted through what the novel holds up as a positive kind of philanthropy. Thus, the fever reaches Esther in an act involving contact and immediacy—contagious diseases are communicated, even if not consciously—as opposed to what Dickens's third-person narrator ridicules throughout *Bleak House* as "telescopic philanthropy"—that of Mrs. Jellyby, for instance, whose philanthropy operates from a distance, by deliberate and conscious telecommunication (the ceaseless letter-writing on behalf of the African natives of Borrioboola-Gha). Esther survives the fever and is left disfigured. To keep this from her, the looking glass had been removed from the room where she had been quarantined. However, when the patient has gone to recuperate at Mr. Boythorn's house, she finds herself, or so it would seem, in a room with a mirror. There Esther's reflects on what Hegel calls the "self-estranged" subject:

> I had not yet looked in the glass, and had never asked to have my own restored to me. I know this to be a weakness which must be overcome; but I had always said to myself that I would begin afresh, when I got to where I was now. Therefore, I had wanted to be alone, and therefore I said, now alone, in my own room, "Esther, if you are to be happy, if you are to have any right to pray to be true-hearted, you must keep your word, my dear." I was quite resolved to keep it; but I sat down for a little while first, to reflect upon all my blessings. And then I said my prayers, and thought a little more. My hair had not been cut off, though it had been in danger more than once. It was long and thick. I let it down, and shook it out, and went up to the glass upon the dressing-table. There was a little muslin curtain drawn across it. I drew it back; and stood for a moment looking through such a veil of my own hair, that I could see nothing else. Then I put my hair aside, and looked at the reflection in the mirror: encouraged by seeing how placidly it looked at me. I was very much changed—O very, very much. At first, my face was so strange to me, that I think I should have put my hands before it and started back, but for the encouragement I have mentioned. Very soon it became more familiar, and then I knew the extent of the alteration in it better than I had done at first. It was not like what I had expected; but I had expected nothing definite, and I dare say anything definite would have surprised me. I had never been a beauty, and had never thought myself one; but I had been very different from this. It was all gone now. (BH 572)

Part of the similarity to Hegel's portrayal of self-estrangement is evident immediately. Esther recognizes herself as precisely "strange": "my face was so strange," she says.[24] Such reflexivity is characteristic of her discourse throughout *Bleak House*. Beginning with a declaration of inadequate self-knowledge—"I have a great deal of difficulty in beginning to write my portion of these pages, for I know I am not clever" [BH 27])—Esther's narrative ends the novel on an elliptical, reflexive note with the remark that her extended family "can very well do without much beauty in me—even supposing—" (BH 989).[25] Accordingly, Esther begins in the passage by stressing her self-awareness of "weakness" before going on to conduct a dialogue with herself that enables her to face a new self in the mirror (she "started back" at first, she reports, then remembered her own "encouragement"—derived, it seems, from her "placid" reflection in the mirror, from her "reflection" on her "blessings" and also, we assume, from the promise she makes to herself of "beginning afresh"). In the grammatical terms adopted by Hegel, then, Esther makes herself the subject and the predicate of her narrative. Facing the disfigured self-image in its strangeness or "alteration," she becomes dialectically "more familiar" with herself.

But there is something about the disfiguration that does not fall entirely in line with the Hegelian model of consciousness in self-estrangement. It has to do, as Esther simply says, with "nothing definite." There was, she explains, "nothing definite" in the mark she bears, in that "anything definite" would have surprised her and apparently it failed to do so. And yet while she had expected "nothing definite," it was not, as it happened, what she had expected. "Nothing definite," in other words, was and was not expected. This suggests that the singular mark for which Esther's face becomes the support, like the singular hand of Nemo to which it is related, exceeds the horizon of conscious expectation—it is neither fully expected nor unexpected—and thus it resists the subject's effort to internalize it definitively as part of self-conscious experience in the Hegelian sense. The singularity of what Esther bears is introduced in this scene as the veil fails to operate, according to a familiar convention, as a material obstacle to seeing something definite. Not only does the veil itself multiply, starting with the "muslin curtain" and the "veil of [Esther's] own hair," it is also associated with Lady Dedlock, the woman who brought Esther into the world as the child, and so in a certain sense as the bearer, of Nemo.[26] Thus the lifting of the veil leads, not to a revelation of something incorporated into the experience of the subject, but rather to a repetition of what escapes incorporation, of what appears obscurely to Esther as a veil. What appears veiled to Esther and what she unconsciously sees in her disfigured face is a trace of domestic failure—the mark of an illness born to her by Jo unknowingly from Tom-all-Alone's where the crossing sweep had accompanied the veiled Lady Dedlock on a visit to the decomposing corpse of Esther's father.

The role of the contagion in this chain of events indicates another parallel to Hegel. For, self-estranged subjectivity in the *Phenomenology* is also marked by contagion. Hegel calls it "an infection" (*eine Ansteckung*).[27] But the infection is not simply destructive of spirit. And significantly, although it may escape attention on a first reading of Hegel's text, this is already demonstrated by the inventive choice of the word *Ansteckung*, which means, not just infection, but also illumination in the sense of the lighting of a fire.[28] This fire, moreover, provides the means for the infection of self-estranged subjectivity to be converted into a purer flame—the "consuming flame" of self-conscious spirit.[29] By way of self-consciousness, the "dispersed" character of self-estrangement enters into individual and collective experience.[30] Once again, however, things take place differently in *Bleak House*. The key instances of individual and collective reading occur in Dickens's novel at points where this concept of experience breaks

down. As in the *Phenomenology*, in Esther's *Bildungsroman* there is also
the figurative nexus of contagion, self-consciousness, and domestic violation. And, as with self-estranged subjectivity in the *Phenomenology*—for
which, as Hegel says, "it is the power of language as something which per-
forms that which is to be performed"—with Esther too, self-recognition
is fundamentally a question of discovering oneself in language.[31] Yet the
effects of the contagion in *Bleak House* never quite find their place in
Esther's experience. This, more than anything else, is what emerges from
her writing.

The persistent displacement of what Esther must bear is dramatized by
the way Bleak House itself is instituted as a domestic site in the novel. This
becomes clear in the last installments of *Bleak House* as the question of
how the novel will end converges with that of the institution of Bleak
House as a household. As we move toward this point in the novel, various
other matters are resolved (more or less), but, in spite of Esther's agreement to become "the mistress of Bleak House," as Jarndyce's written marriage proposal rather ambiguously asks, this key question persists: will
Esther become Jarndyce's wife and thereby complete the household of
Bleak House? The way in which this question is addressed indicates how
Dickens's novel resists the Hegelian model. John Jarndyce imposes a solution (he "gives" Esther to the young physician, Allan Woodcourt), and he
does so in a scene of legislation differing dramatically from the continuity and immanence that characterizes the conversion of the self-estranged
subject in Hegel's philosophical *Bildungsroman*. Indeed, perhaps most
striking about this scene is the manner in which it insistently calls attention to the abruptness and even violence associated with the instituting of
Bleak House. Clearly there is something *unheimlich* about Bleak House:
Jarndyce builds another house, also named Bleak House, that is, strangely
enough, a replica of the original one (BH 888–89). In this way, according
to a logic suitable to Chancery, Esther does in fact become the "mistress
of Bleak House," although in a different house and with a different husband (namely, Woodcourt). In other words, the final scenes of the novel
suggest that in order for Bleak House to come into being, it must be
moved or doubled—estranged through a process of mechanical reproduction. To take place, Bleak House must, it seems, be displaced.

The unsettling movement of Bleak House demonstrates how the
household in *Bleak House* defies assimilation to a traditional perspective
on place as a materially self-consistent and self-contained state. In this
way, the disintegrating force supported by mass-produced paper in the
novel extends to the concept of place as such in Dickens's novel.[32] The
place one loses in the reading of *Bleak House* is one where experience is
a matter of individual or collective self-consciousness. Bearing this loss
means supporting and transmitting a force of dispersal that exceeds

individual and collective attempts to bind and master its movement. This breakdown of a traditional concept of transmissibility and experience becomes legible in the singular reproduction of Bleak House as a household. Here the logic we have been outlining in Nemo's copying and Jo's repetitive movement reaches the domestic institution in the novel. John Jarndyce may want to see it in terms of a certain concept of paternity. "'Lie lightly, confidently, here, my child,'" he urges Esther, "pressing [her] gently to him. 'I am your guardian and your father now. Rest confidently here'" (BH 964). In this way Jarndyce pretends to institute domestic order by giving Bleak House to Esther and by making of the heroine "a willing gift" to Woodcourt (BH 966). This scheme has the benefit, from his point of view, of allowing the guardian to compensate himself symbolically for the loss of his ward: "there is," as he acknowledges, "a kind of parting in this too" (BH 966). Here, significantly, payment takes the form of the aesthetic pleasure derived from producing the series of predictable events through which the would-be father effects the transfer of Esther and Bleak House—"surprises" that in this case unfold like the execution of a will. "These surprises were my great reward," Jarndyce says, "and I was too miserly to part with a scrap of it" (BH 965).[33] Such are, it seems, the gifts of paternity from the perspective of the retiring bachelor. If John Jarndyce becomes akin to a father in the novel, however, it is not by giving Bleak House to Esther and Esther to Woodcourt but rather by becoming himself engaged in an act of mechanical reproduction that can be traced back to Nemo. Jarndyce copies Bleak House. As long as his action remains within the limits of the play of substitutions that presents itself to him as an exchange of gifts, it remains part of a conscious attempt to master his own decline as a father, that is to say, a face-saving measure.[34] There would be nothing singular in this—all would conform to the laws of reciprocity governing the traditional exchange of gifts, including the conventional rite whereby the father gives the daughter in marriage. What is truly singular, though, once again, is the copying that brings Jarndyce into line with Nemo. For the duplication of Nemo, as the readers will recall, implies the singular decline of the father, the unrepeatable element in the father's copying.[35]

Paternal demise in this sense casts a shadow over the exchanges that mark the institution of Bleak House, leaving it, like Lady Dedlock, touched by "the faintness of death" (BH 27). This shadow hangs over the supposition with which Esther's narrative is left suspended. It is the supposition of a subject, and of a collective, that no longer looks itself in the face. Esther's last words—those of the novel—concern a collective that can very well do without a pretty face, as she says, even supposing that there might be some beauty in the inevitable and singular loss of "old looks" (BH 989). The defacement of Esther enacts the breakdown of a traditional collective that transmits itself in the form of experience contained in images of substantial integrity and retention.[36] It also marks the spot from which a new collective may perhaps start to emerge, one that assumes an experiential deficit as its singular condition of possibility. The loss taken by such a collective is not conscious or affective— it is nothing like the sentimental drama narcissistically staged by John Jarndyce near the end of *Bleak House*.[37] It occurs, rather, at an unexpected and fleeting moment of phenomenal exposure to what is not, and what cannot be, phenomenologically given. Such receptivity is suggested, on a subjective level, by the brief passage that occurs just before Esther encounters Jo, the fading figure that comes to connect London to the suburbs, Tom-all-Alone's to Bleak House, and Nemo and Lady Dedlock to Esther. The collective emerges in this passage from exposure to a "lurid glare [that] overhangs" the invisible urban masses, "the unseen buildings of the city and . . . the faces of its many thousands of wondering inhabitants" (BH 488). Esther goes on in this scene to speak of an unexpected and "undefinable impression" of subjective self-difference that she describes as a Wordsworthian "spot of time."[38] The difference arises from the invisible "wondering" collective that leaves an "impression" without showing its face.[39] This "impression" too involves a loss of face, not just for the collective, but also for the subject that becomes its ephemeral support. This is as true of Esther as it is of Jo. From this angle it is indeed fitting that Jo should see Esther initially as a copy: as a duplicate of another (Lady Dedlock) who was touched by the hand of the copier (Nemo) at the beginning of the novel. Such are the unconscious and fleeting material supports for the unpresentable mass collective in *Bleak House*.

The Mixed Medium of Great Expectations

Dickens's inquiry into the unconscious immediacy of the masses does not come to an end in *Bleak House*. *Great Expectations*, for example, extends the project that was already underway in the earliest journalistic sketches of Boz. Magwitch is perhaps the clearest evidence of this. A trace of Newgate, Magwitch is characterized by the elusive and troubling dimension of the urban everyday of which Boz writes in his sketch on the London prison.[40] *Great Expectations* shows Dickens returning to Newgate and to the matters that concerned him in the journalism that a more traditional literary criticism would have the mature novelist transcend. The novelist's work as a whole is punctuated by visits to Newgate and indeed these repeated returns are prescribed by the 1837 sketch, for, the condition diagnosed there calls for an infinite struggle to overcome the distracting familiarity of everyday scenes involving the masses.[41] "A

Visit to Newgate" expresses the conviction that we are all collectively guilty of overlooking what is close at hand through the mechanical repetitions of everyday life. In Dickens's work this daily oversight discloses something like what Benjamin called "the optical unconscious."[42] G. K. Chesterton provides a concrete link between Dickens and Benjamin on this point, in particular a series of passages from Chesterton's remarkable little study of Dickens that are cited in Benjamin's *Arcades Project*.[43] The excerpts from Chesterton indicate the importance of the street as a locus of common concern to Dickens and Benjamin in their approaches to mass mediacy.[44] These citations also reveal an interest in the unconscious effects of distraction that is shared by the novelist and the cultural critic. Of Dickens's habitual *flânerie*, Chesterton writes in the sections quoted by Benjamin (in French translation):

Whenever he had done drudging, he had no other resource but drifting (*flâner*), and he drifted (*flânat*) over half London. He was a dreamy child, thinking mostly of his own dreary prospects. . . . He did not go in for "observation," a priggish habit; he did not look at Charing Cross to improve his mind or count the lampposts in Holborn to practice his arithmetic. But *unconsciously* he made all these places the scenes of the monstrous drama in his miserable little soul. . . . The undying scenes we can all see if we shut our eyes are not the scenes that we have stared at under the direction of guide-books; *the scenes we see are the scenes at which we did not look at all*—the scenes in which we walked when we were thinking about something else—about a sin, or a love affair, or some childish sorrow. *We can see the background now because we did not see it then.* So Dickens did not stamp these places on his mind; he stamped his mind on these places. (emphasis added)[45]

The mind of Dickens was "stamped," Chesterton artfully suggests, not exactly with these places, but rather on these places, for to be stamped is to be walked on (on these places Dickens stamped), but it is also to receive a shape or impression (on these places Dickens was stamped). As Dickens stamped on these places, then, he was stamped, not by the places but rather by a special kind of stamping that screened the places out of consciousness—by what Chesterton calls "drifting" (*flânerie*). Yet this drifting, it turns out, also bore an unconscious stamp: the places screened out remained in the background, even while not presenting themselves as such. "We can see the background now," Chesterton insists, "because we did not see it then." In other words, the "stamping" produces a state of distracted receptivity resembling the condition of the masses that Benjamin associates with the unconscious optical field opened by photography in his essay on technical reproducibility.[46]

For Dickens, Newgate is just such a screened out place. An indication of how it remains in the background in his work is provided by a journalistic sketch published in 1860 in *All the Year Round*, over twenty years after "A Visit to Newgate" and, as it happened, just five months before

Great Expectations began appearing in that same periodical. In this later sketch entitled "Night Walks," Dickens writes of "a temporary inability to sleep, referable to a distressing impression, [that] caused [him] to walk about the streets all night, for a series of several nights."[47] Thus drifting, Dickens reports, he was drawn back inevitably to Newgate:

My principal object being to get through the night, the pursuit of it brought me into sympathetic relations with people who have no other object every night in the year. . . . In those small hours when there was no movement in the streets, it afforded matter for reflection to take Newgate in the way, and, touching its rough stone, to think of the prisoners in their sleep, and then to glance in at the lodge over the spiked wicket, and see the fire and light of the watching turnkeys, on the white wall. Not an inappropriate time either, to linger by that wicked little Debtors' Door—shutting tighter than any other door one ever saw—which has been Death's Door to many. In the days of the uttering of forged one-pound notes by people tempted up from the country, how many hundreds of wretched creatures of both sexes—many quite innocent—swung out of a pitiless and inconsistent world, with the tower of yonder Christian church of Saint Sepulchre monstrously before their eyes! Is there any haunting of the Bank Parlour, by the remorseful souls of old directors, in the nights of these later days, I wonder, or is it as quiet as this degenerate Aceldama of an Old Bailey?[48]

Mixing once again is the subject of the encounter with Newgate. Dickens goes on in this "night fancy," as it is called, to reflect on the merging of rich and poor, noble and common, day and night, waking and dreaming, sanity and insanity. By way of Newgate's "rough stone" wall, then, he becomes absorbed by the crowding together of what is finely distinguished on a daily basis. As the allusions to debt and money at the end of this passage suggest, the "distressing impression" that gives rise to this night walking is, in a sense, a demand for payment—the night insisting on compensation for what was taken by day, namely, sleep. Drifting arises as a means of making up for the waking deficit of a subject not paying enough attention. Yet the debt in question can never be paid in full, for there is no self-consistent medium of payment. Attention is never entirely free of inattention. Not just a medium of mixing with the masses, then, drifting is also an irreducibly mixed medium—the mixed mass medium of a collective attention deficit. Fraudulent claims to self-consistency can only be made by "a pitiless and inconsistent world" that deceptively tempts its masses up from the country and then executes them for counterfeiting.

Great Expectations outlines the economy of such an inconsistent collective. The medium of exchange in the novel is mixed in the manner analyzed by Chesterton in his comments on Dickens's drifting. *Great Expectations* is the narrative of what happens to Pip while he is concentrating on Estella. What happens, in a sense, is Magwitch. But the name Magwitch is shorthand for a dynamic plurality of forces that eludes a conventional concept of character. Magwitch is less a uniform character than a multitude or a crowd of characters (in this he resembles Balzac's Vautrin). This is what occurs to Pip later in the novel as he sits wondering about the sleeping Magwitch and "loading him with all the crimes in the Calendar" (GE 338). This shifting elusiveness is observed by Pip in his first encounter with Magwitch on the marshes when the convict takes leave of the graveyard, as if moving among a throng of shades: "eluding the hands of the dead people, stretching up cautiously out of their graves, to get a twist upon his ankle and pull him in" (GE 6–7). Magwitch is in this sense the "nameless shadow" that sweeps by Pip at key junctures in the first two volumes of the novel.[49] "What *was* the nameless shadow which again in that one instant had passed?" he wonders after his visit to Newgate with Wemmick (GE 264).[50] Given the dynamism of what he encounters as Magwitch, it is apt that Pip's account is marked from the start by the advent of photography (GE 3)—the technique capable of exploring an infinitely divisible optical field, what Benjamin calls the "optical unconscious."[51] It is also fitting that the series of exchanges into which Pip is drawn with Magwitch turns on the appearance, indeed the apparition, of paper. As many commentators have noted, *Great Expectations* belongs to an entire class of novels from this period that are informed by a transition from a pre-industrial society to speculative capitalism.[52] Dickens's novel may be seen to follow this general pattern as the exchanges between Pip and Magwitch move from barter— the food and drink Pip hands over to Magwitch on the marshes (GE 18)—to money—specifically, the paper money with which the convict seeks to reciprocate (GE 78).[53] Indeed, when Magwitch reappears later in Pip's rooms in London, it is with "a great thick pocket-book, bursting with papers" (GE 332).

But the field of force into which Pip and Magwitch are swept in *Great Expectations* dissolves self-consistent material supports. In this their association reinstates the collective emerging in *Bleak House*. If the distressing impressions to which Pip becomes receptive are the effects of something even more shadowy—even more magical and bewitching—than Magwitch, the same is true of the material medium that passes between, and beyond, the boy and the man. Such a passage surfaces in fact in the scene early in the novel as the "secret-looking man" Pip had met on the marsh (Magwitch, it turns out) reappears in the public house. The man, Pip reports, "looked out [a bright new shilling piece] from a handful of small change, folded it in some crumpled paper, and gave it to me" (GE 78). When told of this gift, Pip's sister asks for a look:

"A bad 'un, I'll be bound," said Mrs. Joe, triumphantly, "or he wouldn't have given it to the boy! Let's look at it."

I took it out of the paper, and it proved to be a good one. "But what's this?" said Mrs. Joe, throwing down the shilling and catching up the paper. "Two One-Pound Notes?" . . .

Then, my sister sealed up [the notes] in a piece of paper, and put them under some dried rose-leaves in an ornamental tea-pot on the top of a press in the state parlour. There they remained, a nightmare to me, many and many a night and day.

I had sadly broken sleep when I got to bed, through thinking of the strange man taking aim at me with his invisible gun, and of the guiltily coarse and common thing it was, to be on secret terms of conspiracy with convicts. (GE 78–79)

Binding in this scene is neither the stellar coin—the "bright" shilling piece—nor the "two One-Pound Notes." Paper is what binds here. Or, more accurately, what unbinds: the singularity of the bond lies in its loosening of certain ties, those of Pip to family and home that have already started to come undone before the paper invades their symbolic center (in the "state parlour" under the "ornamental tea-pot"). From the moment he unbinds the strange man from the metal chains at the beginning of the novel, Pip becomes the unwitting support for this unbinding bond. The support exceeds subjective self-consciousness—it remains, in the background of the novel, as that which Pip always just misses, and what he is bound to miss. And, in a certain sense, as the allusion to the "nameless shadow" indicates, the material support defies identification with any self-consistent substance—including paper. This is the remarkable suggestion of the passage just cited: the bond sealed there is never more potently in force than just before and just after it is identified and recognized as paper money, that is to say, precisely at the moments when it withdraws from metaphorical representation. In this case, it is significant that the withdrawal is from paper money, since Pip is drawn at that instant into a network of "sympathetic relations" for which the money form is certainly inadequate. What takes place between Magwitch and Pip is no simple matter of repayment. It is not even, strictly speaking, an exchange between two self-contained subjects. Pip and Magwitch are brought together on the marshy ground of the graveyard at the infinitely divisible point where life faces death. Yet, as in the case of Esther in *Bleak House*, the encounter is not exactly a facing but rather a defacing of death and life—with the receding zero point or the dead spot of life. This singular face-off emerges at the point where identity is dispersed, where the one splits into a multitude (a movement Benjamin tries to mark with a tag from Latin—a "dead" language—*ad plures ire* [to go over to the many]).[54] This scene and those many scenes it repeats and forecasts in Dickens's work suggest that the encounter with the masses and with the mass media occurs at a point of dispersal. Such are the points to which the readers of *Great Expectations* become collectively receptive while they are concentrating on Pip.

Chapter 5

Pretending to Read:
Hardy's *The Mayor of Casterbridge*

Riveting

The contrast between gold and paper is especially common in the fiction
we have been considering and in literature throughout the nineteenth
century. This distinction is often interpreted as expressing a real crisis
of values in the period akin to the one Benjamin characterizes as the shift
from the traditional work of art to the work of art in an age of the mass
media (the word "aura," it has even been suggested, alludes to the traditional value placed on gold as the substantial presence of value).[1] The
link between a crisis of value of this sort and a critical moment of reading in Benjamin's sense is at the crux of Hardy's *The Mayor of Casterbridge*, "a story of a man of character" (the novel's subtitle). From the
very first page of the book, as this "man of character" appears bearing a
certain "sheet" (a "ballad sheet"), the crisis of value is bound to the
question of paper. Indeed Henchard's gesture in this opening passage—
his bearing of paper—is very much like that of the protagonist of *The
Trial* in the scene cited above in our discussion of "paper language" in
Melville.[2] As in the cases considered in previous chapters, the problem
of value emerges in *The Mayor of Casterbridge* at an intersection between
economics and aesthetics, the former indicated by the role of paper
money in the exchange to which the novel's impressive opening leads.

But the conflict over value—represented in Hardy's novel too in the
traditional nineteenth-century terms of the opposition between gold
and paper—is itself staged in a way that goes beyond the conventional
opposition that informs many of the recent studies of economic issues
in nineteenth-century literature.[3] The theatricality of the first pages of
The Mayor of Casterbridge introduces the conflict surrounding paper that
becomes pivotal in the novel.[4] A good place to begin is at the point where
the tension of the highly dubious wife sale of the novel's opening seems
to breaks[5]:

> "Five guineas," said the auctioneer, "or she'll be withdrawn. Do anybody give
> it? The last time. Yes or no?"

"Yes," said a loud voice from the doorway.

All eyes were turned. Standing in the triangular opening which formed the door of the tent was a sailor, who, unobserved by the rest, had arrived there within the last two or three minutes. A dead silence followed his affirmation.

You say you do?" asked the husband, staring at him.

"I say so," replied the sailor.

"Saying is one thing, and paying is another. Where's the money?"

The sailor hesitated a moment, looked anew at the woman, came in, unfolded five crisp pieces of paper, and threw them down upon the table-cloth. They were Bank-of-England notes for five pounds. Upon the face of this he chinked down the shillings severally—one, two, three, four, five.

The sight of real money in full amount, in answer to a challenge for the same till then deemed slightly hypothetical, had a great effect upon the spectators. Their eyes became riveted upon the faces of the chief actors, and then upon the notes as they lay, weighted by the shillings, on the table. (TMC 77–78)

This passage is striking in many ways, most of which are in fact not immediately obvious to the readers, who at this point, like the spectators, have eyes "riveted upon the faces of the chief actors." The obscure quality of this riveting action is perhaps the main point here, not only in that "rivet" indicates some of what will become the novel's leading motifs—that of wheat (as in "rivet wheat") and of marriage (as in the colloquial expression "being riveted")[6]—but much more in that the riveting also draws attention to the importance of the strange bond between Henchard and the collective, including the collective of readers of the "story of a man of character." "Rivet" (from the French verb *river* meaning "to join, clinch") is an architectural term, as Hardy, himself an architect, well knew. It recalls Ruskin's famous comments on "rivets" in the 1874 "Preface" to *The Stones of Venice*. There Ruskin notes that the first book of this work—what he calls "the groundwork of all [his] subsequent architectural teaching"—"can be of no use to any modern builder, as it absolutely ignores the use of iron, except as a cement, i.e. bars and rivets instead of mortar, for securing stones."[7] It is fitting that Ruskin should assert the value—in opposition to the mere practical utility—of his aesthetic writings by claiming that what has become the dominant modern construction material, iron, is merely a marginal, interstitial question— a matter of mere rivets—in them.[8] In *The Seven Lamps of Architecture* Ruskin expands on the connection between rivets and iron, comparing the latter to the ghost of *Hamlet:* "in recent times," says Ruskin, iron "comes to us in a 'questionable shape.'"[9]

The riveting action of the opening chapter of *The Mayor of Casterbridge* is worth considering in light of the digraphic conflict outlined in the introduction to this study. Hardy was himself interested in stone as an aesthetic medium from several angles—as a restorer of buildings and as the writer of *Jude the Obscure*, the late novel recounting the travails of a stone mason and restorer of churches, who perfects his Latin on stone engravings and who carves in stone his intention to go "thither" and to enter the stone walls of Oxford (the university where Ruskin was in fact a professor of "fine arts" at the time of the novel's setting). The traditional images that link stone to conservation are juxtaposed in *Jude the Obscure* to the forces of modernity represented, for example, by Sue Bridehead, the "unstatuesque" heroine in whom "all was nervous motion." In architectural matters, Sue prefers iron over stone—the "railway station" over the cathedral, which, she informs Jude, "has had its day!"[10] But the relations between Jude and Sue, stone and iron, "gown" and "town," ancient and modern, do not resolve themselves into clear oppositions in *Jude the Obscure*. As the elusive Sue tells Jude, "I am not modern, either . . . I am more ancient than medievalism, if you only knew."[11]

Paper and Parchment: The Heath in *The Return of the Native*

Such resistance to conceptual resolution is also built into the figures of paper in *The Mayor of Casterbridge*—figures of a medium that is both riveting and "questionable" in the novel. But Hardy's reflections on the spectral questionability of paper are by no means limited to "the story of the man of character." Paper is implicated in a crisis of value in the novel that preceded it, *The Return of the Native*. So, before analyzing *The Mayor of Casterbridge*, a closer look at this earlier work is in order. Paper in *The Return of the Native* is associated with the returning Clym Yeobright, just back from the heady world of modern Paris. Clym's face is compared to a "waste tablet," imprinted "as a page" on which appears "the typical countenance of the future."[12] Or, a little later, we are told: "The observer's eye was arrested, not by his face as a picture, but by his face as a page; not by what it was, but by what it recorded."[13] The questionable substantiality of paper is the subject of a scene in which Clym is described facing Egdon Heath, in the sense both of coming face to face with it and also of putting a face—as it turns out, his face of paper—on what Hardy also calls "the face of the heath . . . the great and particular glory of the Egdon waste."[14] Facing the heath:

[Clym's] imagination would people the spot with its ancient inhabitants: forgotten Celtic tribes trod their tracks about him, and he could almost live among them, look in their faces, and see them standing beside the barrows which swelled around, untouched and perfect as at the time of their erection. Those of the dyed barbarians who had chosen the cultivatable tracts were, in comparison with those who had left their marks here, as writers on paper beside writers on parchment. Their records had perished long ago by the plough, while the works of these remained. Yet they all had lived and died unconscious of the different fates awaiting their relics. It reminded him that unforeseen factors operate in the evolution of immortality. (RN 449)

Hardy's strategy of complicating, and even exposing the reversibility, of the relative values assigned to the material supports in question here—paper and parchment—becomes clear when we inquire into the way this passage is linked to the larger scheme of the novel's composition. In Clym's imagination, paper is to parchment as "cultivable tract" is to barrow, and, as is made more explicit elsewhere by the narrator, as "civilization" is to the heath ("civilization was [the heath's] enemy," we are told at the outset [RN 56]). Thus the difference between cultivation and memorialization, ploughed field and stone mound, turning the earth and raising it, is a version of the traditional contrast between paper and stone as material supports. And indeed the parchment-like barrow of *The Return of the Native* itself returns in Hardy's later novel *Tess of the D'Urbervilles* in the more openly stone figure of Stonehenge, which "seemed to be of solid stone, without joint or moulding" (no rivets here, only "the wind, playing upon the edifice . . . like the note of some gigantic one-stringed harp").[15] Clym's way of imagining the relation between heath and field might seem to reaffirm the traditional contrast: of the permanence of the "native" over the evanescence of "civilization," of the "grassy barrows of the happier dead," to invoke Tennyson's "Tithonus," over the "dim fields about the homes/ Of happy men that have the power to die"—in short, of the enduring, memorializing quality of stone over the transient insubstantiality of paper.[16]

That this is not quite the case is suggested by the complicated significance of the barrow in the novel. As we have seen, Clym's "comparison" refers contrasting ways that the earth bears the signs of humanity to different material supports (parchment and paper). And yet, from the beginning of the novel, the barrow becomes significant above all as the platform for a mixed kind of signaling. The more conventional opposition behind Clym's way of facing the heath is already introduced when "Humanity Appears on the Scene, Hand in Hand with Trouble," as the title of the second chapter announces: there is the silent communication on the heath, where "contiguity amounts to a tacit conversation," as contrasted with contact "in cities" (RN 60).[17] But then, in a typically complicating gesture, the two kinds of marking that Clym refers to paper and parchment—the ephemeral cultivation of fields and the enduring erection of barrows—are both represented in the signaling that appears on the barrow. The mixture is presented sequentially in the text: first is Eustacia Vye's signal to her secret lover Damon Wildeve; then comes the signaling of the "heathmen" who build the bonfires, probably as part of "Druidical rites and Saxon ceremonies" (RN 67). The "trouble" with this spectacle, we assume, is the difficulty of assigning what the narrator calls "intelligible meaning" to the dumb show on the barrow. In keeping with what is characterized earlier as the "understatement and reserve" of the heath itself, the action here is gestural: it is a "sky-backed pantomime of silhouettes." That is to say, the figures in Clym's comparison—paper and parchment—are acted out on the barrow in the divergent signaling of Eustacia Vye and the heathmen, but the barrow itself as the earthly basis for the action defies identification with either of these opposed figures. On the contrary, a detailed analysis of this passage will show that the barrow is the very platform on which the dissolution of the opposition between what Clym imagines as paper and parchment is performed. In other words, the barrow bears itself as a stage in the antic display of the qualities with which it refuses to be identified. Let us read more slowly the elaborate "pantomime" performed on the barrow at the beginning of the novel:

> The traveller's eye hovered about these things for a time, and finally settled upon one noteworthy object up there. It was a barrow. The bossy projection of earth above its natural level occupied the loftiest ground of the loneliest height that the heath contained. . . .
>
> As the resting man looked at the barrow he became aware that its summit, hitherto the highest object in the whole prospect round, was surmounted by something higher. It rose from the semi-globular mound like a spike from a helmet. The first instinct of the imaginative stranger might have been to suppose it the person of one of the Celts who built the barrow, so far had all of modern date withdrawn from the scene. . . . There the form stood, motionless as the hill beneath. Above the plain rose the hill, above the hill rose the barrow, and above the barrow rose the figure. Above the figure was nothing that could be mapped elsewhere than on a celestial globe.
>
> Such a perfect, delicate, and necessary finish did the figure give to the dark pile of hills that it seemed to be the only obvious justification of their outline. Without it, there was the dome without the lantern; with it the architectural demands of the mass were satisfied. The scene was strangely homogeneous, in that the vale, the upland, the barrow, and the figure above it amounted only to unity. Looking at this or that member of the group was not observing a complete thing, but a fraction of a thing.
>
> The form was so much like an organic part of the entire motionless structure that to see it move would have impressed the mind as a strange phenomenon. Immobility being the chief characteristic of that whole which the person formed a portion of, the discontinuance of immobility in any quarter suggested confusion.
>
> Yet this is what happened. The figure perceptibly gave up its fixity, shifted a step or two, and turned round. . . . The movement had been sufficient to show more clearly the characteristics of the figure, and that it was a woman's.
>
> The reason of her sudden displacement now appeared. With her dropping out of sight on the right side, a new-comer, bearing a burden, protruded into the sky on the left side, ascended the tumulus, and deposited the burden on the top. A second followed, then a third, a fourth, a fifth, and ultimately the whole barrow was peopled with burdened figures.
>
> The only intelligible meaning in this sky-backed pantomime of silhouettes was that the woman had no relation to the forms who had taken her place, was sedulously avoiding these, and had come thither for another object than theirs. The imagination of the observer clung by reference to that vanished, solitary

figure, as to something more interesting, more important, more likely to have a history worth knowing than these new-comers, and unconsciously regarded them as intruders. But they remained, and established themselves; and the lonely person who hitherto had been queen of the solitude did not at present seem likely to return. (RN 64)

The details of this scene bear analysis. At first Eustacia Vye's signal seems to give the heath its figure by articulating plain, hill, and barrow. At this point the barrow appears to be the "bossy" platform that stands for the appearance of a figure of "unity"—"like an organic part of an entire motionless structure."[18] But then something happens: a "discontinuance of immobility." And yet this disarticulating shift or "displacement" does not simply erase the figure as a sign of the heath. It will be remembered that just prior to the cited passage the reader learned that what looks like "stagnation" in the heath is instead "incredible slowness." Retarded shifting and repositioning is what makes up the heath's "repose"—an ambiguous disposition that "resembled protracted and halting dubiousness." From this perspective (and we have yet to mention that the perspective here is that of the melancholy Diggory Venn who is "musingly surveying the scene"), the vanishing "movement" of the figure, by bringing immobility to a halt, strikes a note that is in keeping with what is called the "condition" of the heath. If the barrow is "noteworthy," then, it is above all in its capacity to bear this note of the heath's "halting dubiousness." This may explain why the "vanished, solitary figure" that appears first on the barrow is said to be "more likely to have a history worth knowing than these new-comers." For, the very fact that the evanescent figure is not "likely to return" signals the paradoxical return of the protracted, incessant reposing of the heath. The return of the heath (a word derived from the pre-Teutonic root for what is not ploughed) is the native re-turn of what has not been turned in the first place. The condition of the heath is like a textual medium in which something emerges for the first time when we read it again. Hence the greater worth of Eustacia's figure appears to stem from a potentiality to bring back suddenly to mind powers of an "incredible slowness" that only seems to have the homogeneity and stagnation of a cold pastoral.

Still, this is precisely how Clym imagines the barrow as a sign of the heath when he compares it to the endurance of parchment and contrasts it near the end of the novel with the perishability of paper. The figures who replace Eustacia Vye on the barrow in this early scene are clearly associated with those "writers on parchment" invoked later. "It is as if," the narrator observes, "these men and boys had suddenly dived into past ages, and fetched therefrom an hour and deed which had before been familiar with the spot" (RN 67). And yet the imagination clings, not to these returning natives, but to the figure that, like the "writers on paper" imagined by Clym later, has the power to die. The imagination is drawn, in other words, to a vanishing signal that transiently marks the return of the incredibly slow process by which the heath itself is incessantly turning. In this sense "the return of the native" signifies both the recurrence and the evolution of the heath—"protracted and halting dubiousness" describes the heath's repeated and discontinuous self-differentiation. In a way that is uncannily recalled by the series of heathscapes given to K by the painter in Kafka's *The Trial*, the heath's images in Hardy's novel are "completely the same" in that they are "not similar."[19] The sequence of the signaling in the passage above is also in keeping with this paradoxical returning of the heath. The order interrupts and inverts the continuity of a conventional historical pattern: the more ancient heathmen come after the more modern woman (Eustacia Vye). Incongruously, the heathmen are "the new-comers." In this context even the allusion to the "history" of the modern figure seems somewhat dubious—does "history" here have the modern meaning of "the past" or the older sense of what we now, and Hardy then, would call "a story"? What happens on the barrow in this scene, then, is the return of original or native "discontinuance," literally a coming apart of "immobility." The slowness of the heath does not proceed in continuous progression but in discontinuous "halting" steps, steps that are themselves in turn charged with a doubleness oscillating irreconcilably between continuity and discontinuity, endurance and transience, or—to use Clym's terms—parchment and paper. It is in light of this "halting dubiousness" of the heath that Eustacia's figure is more worthy of note: not as a figure of paper, even though it resembles the evanescence of paper in Clym's later comparison, nor as a figure of parchment, even while it appears on the site Clym identifies with parchment. Rather, the noteworthiness of Eustacia's figure derives from its manner of leaving on the musing observer an impression of a medium that abruptly begins to oscillate between the figures of paper and parchment introduced later in Clym's comparison. The capacity of the impression to elude resolution makes up the potentiality for "history" that surfaces in the figure of Eustacia on the barrow.

More explicitly, on one level, the barrow with its "pantomime of silhouettes" dramatizes gesturally a quality of the novel as a medium. The dissolving opposition between the figures of paper and parchment enacted on the barrow is also carried out in the turning of the pages of *The Return of the Native*, as the reader "musingly surveys" Hardy's composition. As the reader moves from the later passage in which Clym faces the heath to the earlier one just analyzed, for example, it is as though the ephemeral figure of paper (Eustacia Vye's signal) appeared on the more enduring material support of parchment (Clym's barrow). Or, if these components of the text are reversed and the passages read in order, as though the figure of parchment (Clym's later comparison of the barrow to parchment) appeared on the material support of paper (the earlier site of Eustacia's vanished figure). Of course a precondition for both of these ways of musingly surveying the text is that the reader be already introduced to the template of Clym's simile with its stereotypical figures of paper and parchment, a simile which appears expressly near the end of the novel. Once this precondition is met, once the figures in Clym's comparison have been observed, the reader can return to the scene at the novel's beginning in which Eustacia's signals from the barrow. Now, however, the figures just observed promptly begin to come apart and lose their fixity. No longer opposed, the figures of paper and parchment become instead superposed on one another. Moreover, as the reader continues to turn and return the pages of Hardy's novel, the pattern becomes reversible—the second operation, whereby the figure of parchment appears on paper, turns into the first, whereby the figure of paper appears in a medium that is something other than what Clym imagines it to be, something other than the site of mere vanishing acts. The superposing of the figures of paper and parchment in *The Return of the Native* is thus made possible by a medium that defies assimilation to a stereotypical perspective presented in Clym's simile.

In this context Clym's figure of paper as an ephemeral support does not simply vanish, any more than Eustacia's signal on the barrow does. By losing its referential fixity the figure takes on a potentiality to appear or return in other contexts: as the perishable "cultivable tract," as Eustacia's "vanishing figure," as the reposing heath. Clym's figure does not simply die, then; it becomes susceptible to restatement. Or, in other words, it becomes infinitely understated—again, in keeping with the "reserve and understatement" of the heath on which it can now be superposed. Disarticulated, the figure of paper in Clym's comparison provides the reader with a glimpse of a medium that defies assimilation to the traditional digraphic terms of the metaphor. In the process paper becomes something other than the useful "tract" Clym imagines it to be. On the contrary, as the pages of the novel are turned and returned and the referential function of Clym's metaphor is suspended, the readers become receptive to a medium that refuses the opposition of the simile. At this moment, unlike the figure to which Clym's face is compared, paper is something other than a mere insubstantial support.[20]

Tragic Failure

The possibility of such a moment, and of such a support, returns in the dramatic opening of *The Mayor of Casterbridge*. As with the figure of paper in *The Return of the Native,* the riveting figure that appears in the description of the wife auction draws attention to a joining or securing that is also a coming apart, for the scene bears a social rift as well. But this rift itself may strike the reader as having a traditional, and thus continuous, character, since it recalls one that has long drawn the Aristotelian spectator to tragedy (this is clearly suggested by the theatrical language and trappings of this passage as well as by the overt allusions to Greek tragedy throughout the work). And yet in a sense that is still not clear to the reader at this point, and that perhaps never occurs to Henchard, the very connection that is described with the figure of the rivet here—the connection of the reader to the riveting experience of tragedy made possible by the metaphors of "fate" and "character"—is what is being riven in this scene.

Consider, for example, the passage cited earlier from the beginning of *The Mayor of Casterbridge* and look more closely into the transaction that takes place there. As we have noted, the breakdown in values encountered is presented in terms of paper money. "Five crisp pieces of paper . . . Bank-of-England notes for five pounds" and five shillings are on the table.[21] These "five guineas" are indeed, as we are told, "real money": not in the sense that they refer to "real" gold, as opposed to an artificial paper, currency (the guinea was a gold coin first issued in 1663 and supposedly made of gold from Guinea, while the more modern pound is a note), but in the sense that these particular guineas represent the overlapping currencies really circulating in England at the time of the action (the last guinea was emitted in 1813 and the novel begins around 1830). The difference between a pound and a guinea being a shilling, the guinea in question becomes a mixture of two denominations and a sign that in Henchard's peculiar time the systems of counting, measuring, and dividing are out of joint. At first, this appears to be a straightforward historical disjunction—the guineas seem to historicize the conflict, as ancient gold to modern paper, in the manner of the recent economic literary-historical approaches mentioned earlier. But while this historical scheme can account for many manifestations of the problem Hardy is exploring in the novel, it cannot illuminate the most decisive of these: the one delineated by the riveting action of the passage. That is, the opposition between gold and paper can be seen as an analogy for many others in the novel—the opposition between biological and contractual kinship or, to take the example that has perhaps most interested the critics of the novel, the dichotomy between ancient tragedy and its modern obsolescence—but it cannot shed light on the point at which Henchard's experience becomes most riveting for the reader.[22] For it is precisely a moment when the reader is as much in the dark as "the man of character" about the applicability of such formal and conceptual oppositions that Hardy's novel works to conserve. The drama of reading the novel dissolves the opposition between the prominent media of economic value (paper and gold) or, analogously, the prominent concepts of kinship (contractual or biological).[23]

Part of this drama turns on the meaning of the word "character" in the subtitle. "Character" derives from the Greek verb meaning "to make sharp, cut furrows in, engrave."[24] In this sense "character" literally means writing. But it also translates the Greek noun *ethos,* a key term in Aristotle's theory of tragedy and a cornerstone in Victorian interpretations of the *Poetics.* "Character" in "the story of the man of character" oscillates between writing and *ethos.* In the latter sense, it is linked to fate, as when we are told with respect to the fortunes of Farfrae, Henchard's business associate: "Character is Fate" (TMC 185).[25] Novalis is given in the text as the source of this aphorism, although this tag may have come to Hardy by way of a skeptical citation in George Eliot's *The Mill on the Floss* (where it is called one of the Germans' "more questionable aphorisms").[26] It is also possible that Hardy knew this Heraclitan line from his considerable study of Greek with Horace Moule. S. H. Butcher, Hardy's friend and perhaps the most influential later Victorian Greek scholar, discusses "character" (as Aristotelian *ethos*) in his much reprinted commentary on the *Poetics* and alludes to Heraclitus's phrase in a way that might seem applicable to "the man of character" in Hardy's novel.[27] In tragedy, Butcher comments, "a man's deeds become external to him; his character dogs and pursues him as a thing apart. The fate that overtakes the hero is no alien thing, but his own self recoiling upon him for good or evil. 'Man's character,' as Heraclitus said, 'is his destiny'"(TMC 355).[28] Such a view can certainly be found in *The Mayor of Casterbridge.*

But "character" in the novel draws as well on the etymological roots of the verb that mean "to cut furrows in." In this sense, "character" recalls the ephemeral "cultivable tracts"—the ploughed fields Clym Yeobright compares to paper in *The Return of the Native.* Like the paper in Clym's simile, "character" in the passage describing the "scene" in which Susan and her daughter return to Weydon-Priors, for example, is likewise a figure of transience. "Change" there is "to be observed in the details" (TMC 86). Thus, "character" combines the elements associated with the gold and paper that is the mixed medium of payment in the wife auction. Moreover, "character" in *The Mayor of Casterbridge* brings to mind the "protracted and halting dubiousness" of the heath, in which Clym's opposition between paper and parchment becomes confused. Returning, paradoxically, in the scene when the wife and daughter come back to Weydon-Priors is "discontinuance": the scene betrays "a curious imperfection in Nature's powers of continuity" (TMC 86). Coming back does not mean the coming together of what came apart (the family, for example), but rather the appearance of a discontinuity that was over-looked in the first place and that the reader can in fact see only later. For, what appears is a change, not only in the daughter, but also in the wife: her face has undergone "textural change" (TMC 86). The wife is in fact, we will learn, as much a new woman—in the wake of her mar-riage to the sailor Newson—as her companion is a new daughter. If the scene of her "return" with the daughter has "so much of its previous character," this is in part because the change noticeable in her bears a discontinuous character that appears in the passage opening the novel. Henchard, for his part, overlooks the discontinuous character of the returning scene and reads continuity into it by assuming, for instance, that the daughter and the wife now before him are identical with the previous ones. This assumption lends support to a tragic interpretation of events and contributes to an understanding of the hero's character as an example of *ethos*. It allows Henchard to stay in character, in one sense at least.

But while character may be read as *ethos*, and as determined by fate, the literal sense of the word remains in the background. Indeed, this repressed sense repeatedly resurfaces in the novel, interrupting the read-ing of character as tragic *ethos*. We may be tempted to interpret these interruptions as indications that the true meaning of character in the subtitle to Hardy's novel is writing. Such an interpretation might turn "the story of the man of character" into an allegory of an old-fashioned protagonist moving blindly through a modern "culture of print." From this perspective the novel would be viewed as narrating the historical transition from a traditional world of handshakes and oaths to a mod-ern contractual society, from gold money to paper money, from orality to print, from the tragedy to the novel. But the meaning of character in *The Mayor of Casterbridge* complicates such linear patterns. The inter-ruptions in the reading of "character" as *ethos* dissolve the opposition between ancient tragedy and its modern obsolescence just as the return-ing heath undoes the opposition between parchment and paper in Clym's analogy. What returns in the interruptions in "character" is the discontinuance of tragedy. This discontinuance occurs, moreover, by way of material supports that themselves suspend the opposition between continuity and discontinuity.

One example of such a support, as we have already started to see, is the daughter, Elizabeth-Jane, who faces Henchard some nineteen years after the events with which the narrative begins. She is sent "with a mes-sage to Henchard" by her mother, who has taken note of the mayor's "sudden liking" for Farfrae and who reasons that "if he takes so warmly to people who are not related to him at all, may he not take as warmly to his own kin?" (TMC 127). Of course kinship has itself become a knotty question here. For, as Henchard later learns, there has been a change, not only in the daughter but also in the wife. If, in the words of one critic, "Susan's alliance with the sailor is a marriage disguised as a sale," then she is no longer Henchard's wife.[29] Thus to discover "when and how he will see us—or *me*," as Susan herself puts it, she dispatches Elizabeth-Jane to call on Henchard. The message in this case is very much the medium, and a highly mixed one at that. Even if both the wife and the daughter are a little less than kin to Henchard, Susan calculates that "for her daughter's sake, she should strain a point to rejoin him" (TMC 127), betting, it seems, that Henchard will show more kindness now than he did at the outset, when they were more obviously kin. As it turns out, she is indeed correct to see "promise" in the description of the mayor as having "expressed shame for a past transaction of his life" (TMC 128). For Henchard mis-recognizes Susan and Elizabeth-Jane as the same wife and daughter of the opening scene in the novel. But before handing a note to Elizabeth-Jane—with the very mixture of paper and gold that changed hands in the opening scene—Henchard "arose, came close to her, and glanced in her face," and then:

> The instant that she was gone Henchard's state showed itself more distinctly; having shut the door he sat in his dining-room stiffly erect gazing at the opposite wall as if he read his history there.
> "Begad!" he suddenly exclaimed, jumping up. "I didn't think of that. Perhaps these are impostors—and Susan and the child dead after all!"
> However, a something in Elizabeth-Jane soon assured him that, as regarded her, at least, there could be little doubt. (TMC 138)

Henchard looks closely at Susan's page, as if to search for an authenticating mark, but his inspection is thwarted: he "glanced" in her face.[30] Hence his attempt to read Elizabeth-Jane as the medium of a fatal return fails. Nevertheless, upon her departure a tragic "state showed itself more distinctly" to him—that of Belshazzar in the Book of Daniel. Projected on the wall, it is suggested, is the fateful inscription "*mene, mene, tekel, and parsin*," which, according to the prophet, means: "*mene*, God has numbered the days of your kingdom and brought it to an end; *tekel*, you have been weighed in the balances and found wanting; *peres*, your kingdom is divided and given to the Medes and Persians" (Daniel 5.25–28). This comparison would indicate a fateful recurrence of the wife auction in the figures of number, weight, and division—perhaps even in figures of metal-based coins (the mina and the shekel).[31] But if Henchard is not exactly the father he believes himself to be when faced by Elizabeth-Jane, he is also not an ancient king whose fate is written out for him on the wall. More than anything else, it is the failure of the comparison that shows itself distinctly in this passage as Henchard is left wondering whether anything of the earlier scene is left and whether the woman and the girl might be merely acting the parts of wife and daughter—that "these are impostors," as he says, "and Susan and the child dead after all!" This thought, which interrupts the dramatic possibility of fate and tragic return—and of a certain tragic continuity—is of course abruptly rejected by Henchard. But the very dubiousness of what he considers to be of "little doubt" underscores the scale of the repression necessary to maintain a vision of the tragic continuity.[32]

This is what keeps returning in the novel: the failure of tragedy. The events with which the narrative begins settle into no tragic plot and there is no recognition.[33] Henchard's reading repeatedly reenacts the failure of tragedy, and paper throughout the novel plays a key role in this repetition. As a support for tragic failure, paper becomes the site where human life comes in an elusive sense to rest. Exemplary in this regard are two papers that surface at key points in the novel. The first appears at the death of Susan. Addressed to Henchard, this parting missive promises to elucidate the mysterious significance of all that has happened to him. But while telling of the mixed message conveyed by Elizabeth-Jane in the scene just considered, the note also reinstates the persistent doubts that were not entirely put to rest there. What Henchard bears in his reading of the paper is an overwhelming sense of a life—his life—that is aimless and without pattern.[34] Yet even this is not certain:

> Her husband [Henchard] regarded the paper as if it were a window-pane through which he saw for miles. His lips twitched, and he seemed to compress his frame, as if to bear better. His usual habit was not to consider whether destiny were hard upon him or not—the shape of his ideas in cases of affliction being simply a moody "I am to suffer, I perceive." "This much scourging, then, is it for me?" But now through his passionate head there stormed the thought—the blasting disclosure was what he had deserved.
> His wife's extreme reluctance to have the girl's name altered from Newson to Henchard was now accounted for fully. It furnished another illustration of that honesty in dishonesty which had characterized her in other things.
> He remained unnerved and purposeless for near a couple of hours; till he suddenly said, "Ah—I wonder if it is true!" (TMC 196)

The double-take in this last exclamation interrupts the dramatic illusion of "the paper" as conveying the sense that, as Henchard goes on to say, "the concatenation of events . . . was the scheme of some sinister intelligence bent on punishing him" (TMC 197).[35] Thus, instead of bringing closure to the question of Susan's "honesty in dishonesty," the paper supports a message with a meaning that remains open. It restages the failure of Henchard fully to become a "man of character" in the tragic sense of *ethos*, while also refusing to confirm the absence of design in the events of his life. A similar effect is produced by the "crumpled scrap of paper" left at Henchard's death in which he requests "that no man remember [him]" (TMC 409). Unlike a tombstone, this paper aims to erase the departed from memory. It intends to deprive its readers of the hero's death, to prevent them from taking what the narrator calls "mournful pleasure" in the experience of a life arriving at its end (TMC 410). But the will is not executed in full. The paper on which it is written lingers as a material reminder to forget. The death of the hero is not definitively kept from the readers; it returns in the paradoxical imperative not to forget to forget. The paper is the material that bears forgetting: it agitates the readers to remember that they must forget. It appears to suggest that the readers are collectively in danger of becoming oblivious to what they must remember to keep forgetting. The paper in short solicits a state of attentiveness that is inseparable from—that in fact demands—inattention. Its "directions," the narrator observes on the last pages of the novel, are "a piece of the same stuff that [Henchard's] whole life was made of" (TMC 410). This characterization may help to remind the readers of the state in which the hero is first encountered "reading, or pretending to read, a ballad sheet which he kept before his eyes with some difficulty" (TMC 69). This paper calls for further attention.

The Ballad Sheet

The ballad sheet played an important role in the rise of paper as a material support for the modern mass media. As Martha Vicinus has pointed out, the ballad sheet or broadside ballad "was the most widespread form of written literature from the beginning of printing."[36] The historical origins of the ballad sheet can be traced to the paper "broadsheets" that began to circulate at the time of Churchyard with the establishment of papers mills in England.[37] But what is peculiar about this medium is the way it intensely mixes orality and print. This is implied in the yoking of the words "ballad" and "sheet." "Ballad" derives from the Latin *ballare* meaning "to dance" (also the root of the modern French word *balader*— to walk with no predetermined destination; *flâner* is given by *Robert* as a synonym). Traditionally a ballad is an oral form: "the traditional ballad," notes another scholar, "is a dramatic or humorous story in song, usually impersonal, derived from past folk culture and learnt by ear rather than from literature."[38] The phrase "ballad sheet" itself, then, combines performance and print. The *Oxford English Dictionary* even hints that the specific meaning of "ballad" concerning us here is tied to the emergence of paper broadsheets in the sixteenth century.[39] In any case, we know that the circulation of ballad sheets involved a kind of street theater in which printed bills were hawked and recited by "chaunters" or "patterers"—"the class of street orators" who "indulge in this kind of oral puffery," as Mayhew put it.[40] Vicinus suggests that "the major impetus for buying a broadside among most working people was the chaunter's skillful singing and acting."[41]

Due in part to the development of cheaper paper and printing, the commerce in this particular form of what we might now call "performance art" enjoyed a revival in England beginning in the 1820s—the time set at the opening of *The Mayor of Casterbridge* ("before the nineteenth-century had reached one-third of its span" [TMC 69]).[42] During this period ballad sheets circulated on a mass scale, especially those dealing with "the news" (executions, murders, and wife auctions had long been popular subjects of broadside ballads).[43] These ballad sheets were the precursors of the penny newspapers that began to appear in the 1850s after the repeal of the Newspaper Tax.[44] Meanwhile, Wordsworth and Coleridge, and in their wake Scott, Keats and others, had already exploited the poetic possibilities of the popular ballad, a fitting genre for the program of the *Lyrical Ballads* "to choose incidents and situations from common life, and to relate or describe them . . . in a language really used by men."[45] Hardy was interested in ballads both as a collector and as a post-Romantic poet and novelist.[46] And his peculiar attachment to the ballad brings us back to our main point about paper in *The Mayor of Casterbridge*. Hardy's collecting of ballad sheets may suggest an interest in the frail material support for this mass medium as something other than a simple means of delivering information or entertainment— as the material support for a peculiar state suggested by Henchard's reading in the novel.

Based on the journalistic *fait divers* reported by Hardy in the "Author's Preface," the wife auction at the beginning of the novel is precisely the sort of event about which Henchard might be "reading, or pretending to read" on his ballad sheet (Figure 7).[47] As we have seen, the character of this reading unfolds as a series of scenes in which Henchard encounters puzzling faces and surfaces. Yet, in keeping with the logic we have been tracing in the novel, this reading as such defies representation in *The Mayor of Casterbridge*. So, Henchard is "reading, *or pretending to read*" (my emphasis)—pretending in the sense that he may not actually be reading, that he may be feigning (it is just an act, "pretense"), or that he may only believe or claim to be reading (that he is not really doing it). Or, perhaps the impossibility of saying with certainty what "pretending to read" means here—the impossibility of exhausting in a single stroke the referential possibilities of "pretending to read"—suggests that when one believes or claims oneself to be fully in the act of reading, one is pretending to read.[48] On the other hand, "pretending to read" could mean suspending a certain conscious relation to the things and persons

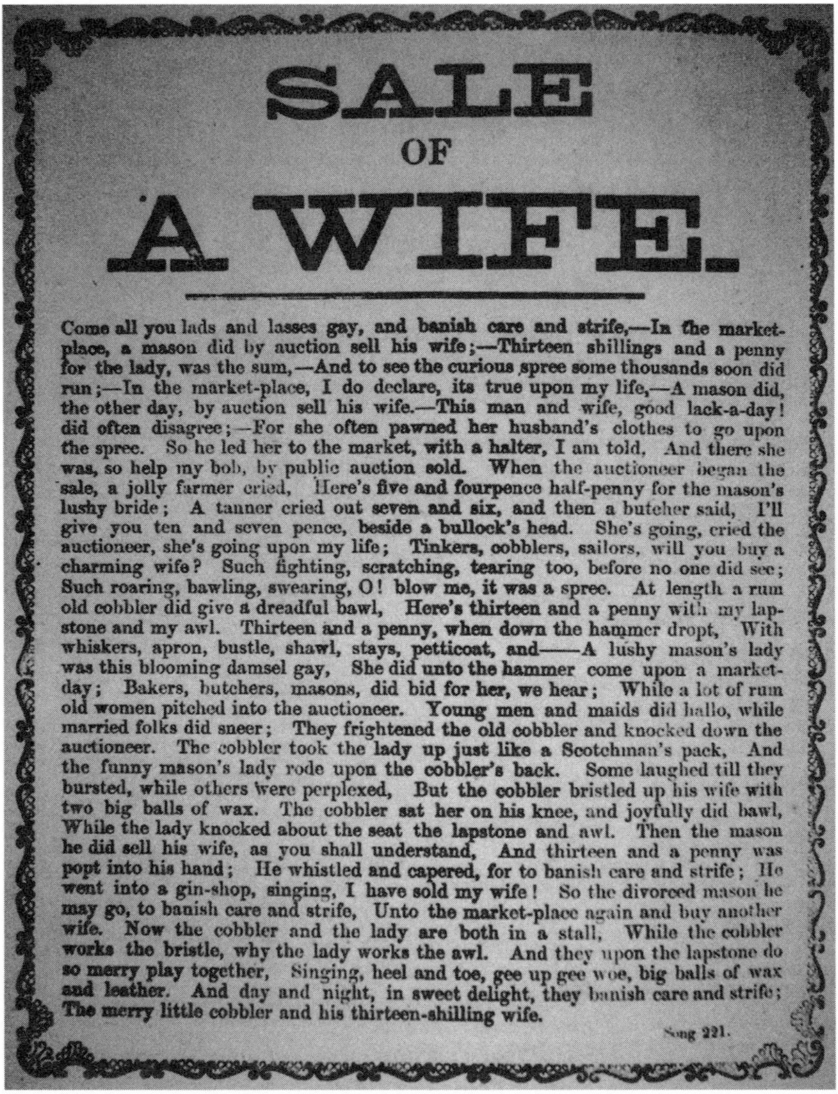

SALE

OF

A WIFE.

Come all you lads and lasses gay, and banish care and strife,—In the market-place, a mason did by auction sell his wife;—Thirteen shillings and a penny for the lady, was the sum,—And to see the curious spree some thousands soon did run;—In the market-place, I do declare, its true upon my life,—A mason did, the other day, by auction sell his wife.—This man and wife, good lack-a-day! did often disagree;—For she often pawned her husband's clothes to go upon the spree. So he led her to the market, with a halter, I am told, And there she was, so help my bob, by public auction sold. When the auctioneer began the sale, a jolly farmer cried, Here's five and fourpence half-penny for the mason's lushy bride; A tanner cried out seven and six, and then a butcher said, I'll give you ten and seven pence, beside a bullock's head. She's going, cried the auctioneer, she's going upon my life; Tinkers, cobblers, sailors, will you buy a charming wife? Such fighting, scratching, tearing too, before no one did see; Such roaring, bawling, swearing, O! blow me, it was a spree. At length a rum old cobbler did give a dreadful bawl, Here's thirteen and a penny with my lap-stone and my awl. Thirteen and a penny, when down the hammer dropt, With whiskers, apron, bustle, shawl, stays, petticoat, and——A lushy mason's lady was this blooming damsel gay, She did unto the hammer come upon a market-day; Bakers, butchers, masons, did bid for her, we hear; While a lot of rum old women pitched into the auctioneer. Young men and maids did hallo, while married folks did sneer; They frightened the old cobbler and knocked down the auctioneer. The cobbler took the lady up just like a Scotchman's pack, And the funny mason's lady rode upon the cobbler's back. Some laughed till they bursted, while others were perplexed, But the cobbler bristled up his wife with two big balls of wax. The cobbler sat her on his knee, and joyfully did bawl, While the lady knocked about the seat the lapstone and awl. Then the mason he did sell his wife, as you shall understand, And thirteen and a penny was popt into his hand; He whistled and capered, for to banish care and strife; He went into a gin-shop, singing, I have sold my wife ! So the divorced mason he may go, to banish care and strife, Unto the market-place again and buy another wife. Now the cobbler and the lady are both in a stall, While the cobbler works the bristle, why the lady works the awl. And they upon the lapstone do so merry play together, Singing, heel and toe, gee up gee woe, big balls of wax and leather. And day and night, in sweet delight, they banish care and strife; The merry little cobbler and his thirteen-shilling wife.

Song 221.

Figure 7. Nineteenth-century ballad sheet "Sale of a Wife." Courtesy of Leslie Shepard.

around one in order to engage in reading.[49] This suspension of the here and now would hold as much for a ballad sheet as for a novel: one must be able to pretend to read, to allow oneself to be drawn in, as we say. In a manner recalled by Henchard's will, then, the ballad sheet bears forgetting. Both papers seek to induce states of inattention: the former, to the death of the man of character in the tragic sense; the latter, to "society." While straining to keep the ballad sheet before his eyes, we read, Henchard's "taciturnity was unbroken, and the woman [Susan] enjoyed no society whatever from his presence" (TMC 70).[50] Yet the homelessness of these characters fails to become part of a collective experience. Henchard's attempt to find the meaning of a wandering life in the less than tragic account of an event not unlike what will soon unfold in the furmity tent is dramatized as a mode of estrangement that suspends social ties. The hero of the novel is from the beginning a distracted reader.

The framing device of the ballad sheet suggests a parallel between Henchard's reading and the reading of Hardy's novel. *The Mayor of Casterbridge* was serialized in the London *Graphic,* an illustrated weekly newspaper that has been described recently as "one of a new breed of newspapers benefiting from advances in the technology of wood engraving to make the news more accessible to a broader market of readers by providing illustrations of prominent events and personalities."[51] In the pages of *The Graphic* the serialized account of "the man of character" broadcasts the decline of tragedy.[52] This decline, however, fails to become a focal point around which the readers of *The Graphic* might come together, since the decline of tragedy as such excludes an experience of tragic finality. This exclusion is the very mode of tragedy's failure in the novel. The singularity of this decline lies in the impossibility that it will ever take place as an accomplished act of individual or collective comprehension. To claim the definitive end of tragedy in this sense remains a pretense. The death of tragedy will be kept from the readers of the novel, above all perhaps, to the extent that they identify it with Henchard's own life and death. Such identifications, like those of the novel's hero, seek to repress the incomprehensible finitude of individual and collective human life by incorporating it into an experience that would on its face represent the overcoming of finitude. Henchard's ballad sheet, especially when we imagine its appearance in *The Graphic,* may suggest the tendency of the mass media to hold out to its readers compensatory images of the kind of defining events that never seem to happen to them. This suggestion is most forceful at the point where Henchard's paper fails to stand for an experience that has come to an end.

Afterword: The Novel Collective

The paperwork that has concerned us in this study cannot be identified with paper in the sense suggested by Carlyle's metaphor of the "Paper Age." Carlyle's phrase relies on the digraphic metaphor put in question by the failure of mass mediacy to present itself substantially. In Dickens's attempts to exploit the distracting effects of novel reading, as in Poe's related efforts to work with aesthetic concentration or "absorption," we have traced the movements of a mass medium marked by the decline of what Benjamin calls the "here and now" of the traditional work of art. By trying to read carefully scenes involving paper and exploring Benjamin's thesis about mass mediacy, we have also been responding to the insistence on reading in his criticism. Mass mediacy, we have been suggesting, takes place in a way that parallels the loss of presence and loss of place in reading. This is what connects the mass media to the novel in Benjamin's work.[1] Reading in this sense is a matter, not of metaphors or concepts, but of the especially dynamic images of which Benjamin writes in his *Arcades Project*: "The image that is read, which is to say, the image in the now of its recognizability—bears to the highest degree the imprint of the perilous critical moment on which all reading is founded."[2] The exceptional forcefulness of this image imperils the when and where of its reception. For the image can be read only at points when and where the traditional sense of a self-consistent when and where is itself shaken. This is what occurs when the collective becomes receptive to mass mediacy: what Benjamin calls "the decline of the aura." The collective that emerges at such moments is a paradoxical one bound together as an irreducible plurality of lonesome readers.[3] While the "now" of the mass media really does take place, then, its occurrence depends upon an intensely scattering empirical moment that cannot be identified with a self-consistent material support. This is what happens in connection with paper in the works we have been reading. In Poe's "The Gold Bug," for instance, what Legrand draws from his pocket withdraws at the start and is "taken" right away: Legrand, seated at a small table "on which were pen and ink, but no paper . . . looked for some in a drawer, but found none . . . and drew from his waistcoat pocket a scrap of what

I took to be very dirty foolscap" (GB 74). Reading at this point—for the narrator and for the readers of the tale—depends upon an empirical moment and thus needs a material support. Yet this support is not self-contained and self-consistent, but rather divided and divisible into alternating terms with which it cannot finally be identified. At the very instant of its appearance in Poe's tale the material support is in this sense immediately scrapped—scratched out by an infinite series of oscillating digraphic figures in the tale: foolscap or paper, on the one hand, parchment or gold, on the other.

The novel collective to which the preceding chapters point cannot be assimilated to a theory of the genre based on the ironic integration of estrangement into experience—what Lukács calls "transcendental homelessness." In Lukács's theory, the "mass" of "lived experiences" (*Erlebnisse*), and with it the "mass" of "isolated individuals," is given "unified articulation" in the transmissible "form" of the "problematic" life.[4] This is the life on which, as Benjamin writes, the isolated readers of the novel seek to warm their hands, that is to say, precisely the kind of experience that is denied to them by their own lives.[5] The novel is, as Benjamin might say, a barbaric genre: the literary mode of a collective that outlives culture understood along the traditional lines of a community based on the reciprocal exchange of experience and of the wisdom gained from it.[6] Thus the novel starts, and indeed repeatedly anew, where experience means nothing.[7] No wisdom or insight can fill in this gap, not even the wisdom of the *docta ignorantia* that Lukács attributes to the irony of the novelist.[8] Self-conscious professions of ignorance, however well advised under normal circumstances, are inadequate to the shock waves produced by the shattering of tradition in which the reading of the novel participates.[9]

The source of the novel collective is the distracted public. Novel readers make up a collective in the sense, not of a self-interested set of individual subjects (a nation or a class, for instance), but rather of scattered yet collectively receptive masses. To elaborate the social and aesthetic implications of this point, much more would have to be said about the strangeness of a collective whose very condition of possibility is a state of scattered receptivity, a collective that exists only when it has yet actually to take shape. As suggested at the end of the previous chapter, such a novel collective would come to exist at elusive points where what we usually think of as social relations are suspended. Our concern has been limited to the ways writers of fiction in the nineteenth century dramatize paper's contribution to the conditions of receptivity from which such an unconscious reading collective might be understood to emerge. The association of paper in this period with a space that shakes public self-consciousness and concentration is suggested by a contemporary painting such as John Orlando Parry's 1835 *London Street Scene* (Figure 8).[10] Parry's illustration shows paper's role in producing a public space marked by what Benjamin calls spatiotemporal "superposition" and "interpenetration," a phenomenon he connects with the "birth of modern feuilletonism."[11] The chapters of this book have pursued an exposition of paper as surfacing repeatedly in nineteenth-century serial fiction at points where the literary text as a self-contained work is itself shaken by the distracting force of a mass mediacy to which it is inextricably linked.

Figure 8. John Orlando Parry, *A London Street Scene, 1835.* Courtesy of the Dunhill Museum, London.

Notes

Introduction: Apparitions of Paper

1. The key source for Carlyle on paper is undoubtedly the chapter entitled "Comsommation du papier" in Louis Sébastien Mercier, *Le nouveau Paris: 1789– 94*, 531–35. For example: "The evil brought about by paper during the different phases of the revolution is such that one could wish that it had never been invented" (532). Mercier also links the massive circulation and consumption of paper with the origins of the Revolution (see 33 and 38, for example). Thanks are due to Philippe Roger for bringing Mercier's comments on paper to my attention. On Carlyle's related remarks on paper in *Sartor Resartus*, see Erickson, 106–8.

2. For the metaphysical signification of support as substance or *substratum*, the entry for the noun "support" in the *Oxford English Dictionary* refers to Locke's *Essay Concerning Human Understanding* (1690). The passage from Locke is worth citing since it indicates the elusive quality of the support as such—apart from the quality or mode it supports:

Hence when we talk or think of any particular sort of corporeal Substances, as Horse, Stone, etc. though the Idea, we have of either of them, be but the Complication, or Collection of those several simple Ideas of sensible qualities, which we use to find united in the thing called Horse or Stone, yet because we cannot conceive, how they should subsist alone, nor one in another, we suppose them existing in, and supported by some common subject; which Support we denote by the name Substance, though it be certain, we have no clear, or distinct Idea of that thing we suppose a Support. (Locke, 297)

For a succinct discussion of the conceptual problem posed by Locke's attempt to provide an empiricist account of substance and support, see Lowe, especially 72–78, and Bennett, 98–108.

3. While media studies generally approach the mass media as beginning in the twentieth century, and in particular with the advent of electronic media, even when they point to the nineteenth-century medium of photography as a precursor, the basic components of the phrase "mass media" can be traced to the first half of the nineteenth century. Under the entry "masses" in the *Oxford English Dictionary* we find the following definition dated to 1837: "the populace, the ordinary people, esp. as viewed in an economic or political context." The dictionary's editors cite Thomas Moore: "One of the few proofs of good Taste

that 'the masses', as they are called, have yet given." As it happens, Moore is alluding here to the reception of Dickens's *The Pickwick Papers* (Moore, 174). On the seminal importance of this, Dickens's first novel in the emergence of a mass literary commerce of the Victorian period, see my *Writing in Parts*, 83–121. Under "medium" in the sense of a "channel of mass communication, as newspapers, radio, television, etc." the editors cite this passage from an 1850 article in the *Princeton Review*: "Our periodicals are now the media of influence. They form and mold the community" ("Cheap Presbyterian Newspaper," 131). It is worth noting that in Carlyle's *French Revolution* the insubstantial character of the medium represented by paper becomes associated with the revolutionary masses. Like paper, which is "made from the *rags* of things that did once exist," the masses in *The French Revolution* are a ghostly medium, a population that has become a mere shadow of its individual "units" (*French Revolution*, 31, 35). Still, like the revolutionary media that called them forth, the masses acquire a met-aphorical character in Carlyle's account, presenting in their very "widespread wretchedness" and "winged raggedness" what is at one point called a "legible hieroglyphic writing" (*French Revolution*, 35–36). Carlyle appears to use the word "hieroglyphic" in the common nineteenth-century sense of a sign of revelation (see Dieckmann, 141–237), but in the context of "The Paper Age" the hiero-glyphic character of what becomes legible in the movement of the masses may also suggest a sign that is more than merely transient (like paper). We will have more to say about the contrast between hieroglyphic writing on stone and cur-sive writing on paper.

4. Canetti makes some suggestive remarks on paper money and crowds (185). On "voided signs" in Carlyle's "Signs of the Times," see Klancher, 71–73. On the similarly inarticulate quality of the masses in Carlyle's *Chartism* (1839), see Plotz, 137–48. The resemblance of the protesting English crowds of the 1830s in *Chartism* to the revolutionary masses of later eighteenth-century France in the *French Revolution*, published just two years earlier, demonstrates how Carlyle's views of the Paper Age refer as much to early Victorian England as to the French Revolution. For an interesting and relevant interpretation of Carlyle's *French Revolution* as a Gothic tale, see Desaulniers, 9–33, 60–104

5. On the logic of metaphor, see Derrida, "White Mythology," *Margins*, 258–71. The traditional sense of the metaphor of substance in question is that of an ontological perspective based on the understanding of substance as spatial extension, a perspective often associated with Descartes. The question of such an alternative concept of substance was at the center of the speculation and debates in the eighteenth century about the status of the mind as a substance and as a support for "impressions," much of it instigated by Locke (see Yolton, *Thinking Matter*, 153–89). The attempt to grasp the elusive substantiality of this support led the English philosopher to the metaphor of the mind as a sheet of "white paper" (Locke, 104). We will be returning to this point.

6. An obvious, but revealing, example would be the explanation of the con-cept of aura and its decline in which Benjamin turns to language and cites a phrase from Karl Kraus: "The closer one looks at a word the more distantly it looks back" (Benjamin, "On Some Motifs in Baudelaire," *Gesammelte Schriften*, 1, 2, 647; *Illuminations*, 200, note 17). The status of the aura in Benjamin's work turns decisively on its "decline." The word "decline" (*Verfall*) does not simply stand for an achieved state, but rather marks a process or a movement under way: it is, in Benjamin's terms, a motif. The word *Verfall* in Benjamin's writing could be illuminated by way of comparison to Heidegger's use of the word in

Being and Time (see sections, 38, 58, 68). For some suggestive remarks on the passage cited from Benjamin, see Weber, *Mass Mediauras*, 106–7.

7. "The whole sphere of authenticity withdraws (*entzieht sich*) from technical—and, of course, not only technical—reproducibility" (Benjamin, *Das Kunstwerk*, 12; "The Work of Art," *Illuminations*, 220). The comments on distraction or dispersal (*Zerstreuung*) come at the end of the essay (see 41; 241). Shaken, in other words, is concentration—here, the sense of an encounter with the literary work as an event that takes places in a unified space and time that can be definitively isolated from other spatiotemporal locations. The word "distracted" echoes the sense of being scattered in the German *zerstreuter* better than "absent-minded," which is how it appears in the English translation. For Benjamin such distraction is considered as a condition of possibility for an alternative kind of collective (a key to Benjamin's work on this topic is in fact the oscillating conflict between distraction and collection—*Zerstreuung* and *Sammlung*). On mass movements in Benjamin, see Weber, *Mass Mediauaras*, 82–87. For a trenchant and illuminating analysis of distraction in Benjamin, see Eiland, especially 57–63. Part of the background here are Kant's remarks on *Zerstreuung* (*distractio*) in the *Anthropology* (see Gasché, 99–101). Benjamin's use of the verb *entziehen* (to withdraw) overlaps with that of Heidegger in his critique of metaphysics. See Derrida, "Le Retrait de la métaphore," 77–93.

8. For a further elaboration on Benjamin's thesis about German Romantic criticism, see Lacoue-Labarthe and Nancy, 387–93; Ferris, 456–61.

9. Assmann, "Stein und Zeit," 92–95.

10. The *assignats* were the first things printed on industrially produced paper; we might even say that the invention of a method of producing paper was an industrial response to the enormous demand for mass-produced paper money. See Hunter, *Papermaking*, 257–64.

11. See Shell, *Art and Money*, 7.

12. Marx, *Kapital*, 51; *Capital*, 83

13. This point raises an objection to almost all of the recent historical studies of money and literature that have taken the emergence of the specific monetary institution of inconvertible or "fiction" currency to mark a fundamental historical break detectable in literary representation, say, during the later decades of the nineteenth century—the influential work of Walter Benn Michaels on American literature and Jean-Joseph Goux on French literature would be leading examples. One could argue that the approach taken by these recent literary-critical works is very much in line with the Carlyle's historical standpoint on the French Revolution.

14. Goux provides a good example of a similar *trompe l'œil* with regard to paper money in recent literary criticism dealing metaphorically with the theme of money. *Coiners of Language*, for instance, takes Gide's novel, *The Counterfeiters*, as representing the historical turning point of the conversion to a society based on inconvertibility: "the particular interest of Gide's novel is that it comes into existence at a turning point, straddling the nostalgic memory of a gold-language or a representative language, and the simultaneously positive and negative prescience that this is no longer tenable, that it no longer corresponds to the actual conditions of the circulation of signs. . . . Poised at the divide between two systems of exchange, the novel expresses the contradiction between a persistent nostalgic attachment to gold currency, and a realistic, or rather theoretical, acceptance of the dizzying novelty of inconvertibility" (Goux, 19–21). By accepting the historical schematism implied in Gide's novel, Goux is compensated

with a straightforward—significantly, his word is "realistic"—historical pattern. Goux is caught in the sights of the referential illusion we will analyze in Poe (see the end of Chapter 1).

15. For an informative discussion of the tradition of criticism that considers the short story in nineteenth-century American literature as a "subset" of the American Romance, see Tallack, 9–21. On the "nationalist" inflections of the distinction between the British novel and the American romance in the nineteenth century and in the criticism that grew up around it, see Thompson and Link, 53–84.

16. The stress on reading works of fiction in the approach taken here to the material support as figured in nineteenth-century literature brings to light a reflection on the instability and inconsistency of the communicative medium overlooked in the traditional account of the rise of "print culture." Johns has recently offered a critical perspective within book history on the traditional view maintained by Eisenstein and Latour that the "print revolution" in Early Modern Europe established a fixed and consistent medium for the production and dissemination of knowledge. Johns's work exposes the stresses and anxieties in the dream of "fixity," as manifested in the discourse of the passions, for example. In this sense, the literary works under consideration here may be understood to draw on the seventeenth- and eighteenth-century discourse on the "physiology of reading" adumbrated by Johns (387–443) as well as on the much older association of paper with ephemerality and fragility that we will outline below. Thanks are due to Jon Klancher for bringing Johns's book to my attention.

17. Kittler, to take an influential example, equates the absence of agency with the instrumentalized action of a non-mechanical machine. This moment of "action" is interpreted by Kittler along the lines of his account of Turing's machine (*Draculas Vermächtnis*, 226–28). Thus Kittler forecloses the possibility of a singular, non-instrumental and involuntary act of reading and substitutes for it the workings of a writing and reading machine resembling a computer without software (*Draculas Vermächtnis*, 236–37). Tholen makes an argument against Kittler's disembodied or de-subjectivized model of human absorption in technologies of inscription that is parallel to the objections raised by critics of Turing himself, such as Rothman, 97–99. In doing so, however, Tholen (like Rothman) reintroduces the horizon of self-contained physicality—of embodiment—and fails to pursue the possibility of a mode of subjective involvement in the machine that does not remain self-consistent. Most recent Anglo-American "new media" theorists have also avoided this possibility by assuming that "materiality" is identical with "embodiment" (see, for example, Hayles, 48–49, 82–83). In spite of introducing considerable complexity into his account of the subjective engagement in technology, Massumi's recent theory of "affect," which extends Deleuze's interpretation of virtuality in Leibniz and Spinoza, also stays within this classic phenomenological context. "Affect" in Massumi's work gives rise to a field in which "self-relation" is "immediate" (Massumi, 13–14). We will return to this limitation of Deleuze's thought. A more thorough account of affect, which is beyond the purview of this study, would have to address the attempts deriving from Kant to reinterpret affect according to the logic of what has been called "doubled affect," that is to say from the perspective of the interaction between transcendental and empirical affect. See Adickes, especially 63–67; Adickes derives his theory of double affect from the commentary on Kant's "Introduction" to the *Critique of Pure Reason* (*Werke*, vol. 3, 45–46; *Critique of Pure Reason*, 30–31) by Vaihinger (vol. 1, 172–74). To compare on affect would be some remarks by

Heidegger in *Being and Time* (see in particular his observations in sections 29 and 69). On the problematic Kantian legacy of affect, see also, more recently, Fenves, 193–200.

18. Within literary studies, there has been much scholarship, especially on the eighteenth and nineteenth centuries, dealing with the "history of writing," as Raymond Williams calls it. In addition to Williams, Michel Foucault has provided the groundwork for much of this scholarship on the role of writing in the emergence of disciplines of knowledge, the professions, and the institution of literature. In such studies, the mass media are usually assumed to be mere outlets and channels through which a quantity of writing is disseminated and circulates. From this perspective literary works are seen to take place within a certain phase of the "history of writing" (examples of this approach, to which I will allude below, include the work of Siskin, Erickson and McGill). By contrast, this book attempts to trace the outlines of an encounter with mass mediacy manifested by the reading of literary works. Our concern is less with the history of the mass media and with literature's role in it, than with the empirical effects of mass mediacy as experienced in the reading of literary works.

19. The interview was first published as "Le papier ou moi, vous savez. . . ," *Pouvoirs du papier, les cahiers de médiologie* in 1997.

20. Derrida, "Le papier ou moi," 239–40. The phrase "temps du papier" occurs later in the interview ("Le Papier ou moi," 270), but the context in which it occurs and even the syntax of the passage make the phrase more ambiguous than Carlyle's lapidary formulation.

21. With respect to the newer electronic media, such as the computer, Tholen explores the suspension of the concept of use and the withdrawal from traditional metaphorical presentation (see especially 51–60). Tholen extends the analysis of metaphor in Derrida's "Le Retrait de la métaphore."

22. Derrida, "Le papier ou moi," 239 (Derrida's emphasis).

23. This is also the sense in which the end of paper's hegemony may be said to have abruptly accelerated at a date coinciding with the subject's (Derrida's) generation, with a lifetime: "The end of this hegemony (its structural, if not quantitative, end, its degeneration, its tendency to retire) have abruptly accelerated during a time that coincides roughly with that of my 'generation': the time of a life" ("Le papier ou moi," 240).

24. Locke, 104.

25. Freud, "Notiz über den 'Wunderblock,'" 3; "A Note Upon the 'Mystic Writing-Pad," 227.

26. Derrida, "Freud et la scène de l'écriture," 336; "Freud and the Scene of Writing," 227.

27. Derrida, "Freud et la scène de l'écriture," 336; "Freud and the Scene of Writing," 288.

28. Freud, "Notiz über den 'Wunderblock," 8; "A Note Upon the 'Mystic Writing-Pad," 232.

29. Freud, "Notiz über den 'Wunderblock,'" 3; "Note Upon the 'Mystic Writing-Pad,'" 227.

30. *Anvertrautes Geld* in German is money placed in trust.

31. Derrida, *Mal d'archive*, 29–39.

32. Fortunately, the interview has been preserved from the hazards of journal publication and has since appeared in the more enduring form of a book: *Papier-machine.*

33. Derrida, "Le papier ou moi," 248, 250–51.

34. Derrida,"Le papier ou moi," 240.

35. Derrida makes this point with respect to language in another in this series of interviews: "It is not certain that man or Dasein would have, by way of language, that appropriate rapport with death of which Heidegger speaks" (*Papier-machine*, 394). Though it will not be possible within the limits of this introduction, more would have to be said about Derrida's allusion to Balzac's *La Peau de chagrin*, a work that not only narrates but also has as its condition of possibility the shrinking material support.

36. In French *le point mort* signifies the condition of an engine or machine when it is not in gear, when it is idling (*Petit Robert*, 2nd ed.). *Le point mort* resembles the condition to which Freud's death-drive tends: "the fundamental tendency of every living being to return to the inorganic state" (Laplanche and Pontalis, 98). See Freud, *Jenseits des Lustprinzips, Gesammelte Werke*, vol. 13, 47; *Beyond the Pleasure Principle, Works*. vol. 18, 44.

37. Papyrus is a laminated sheet of thin strips of the papyrus plant pasted together, while paper is a weave of disintegrated vegetable fibers dried on a screen (Hunter, *Papermaking*, 5, 17–18).

38. Hunter, *Papermaking*, 466.

39. Hunter, *Papermaking*, 213–14.

40. Hou states that "paper money offerings were thus already quite diversified under the Souci (at the beginning of the seventh century), which allows us to think that they had their beginnings at a much earlier period" (Hou, 7). Hunter is more specific, saying that in 106 A.D.—only a year after its invention—"paper [was] used in lieu of metal coins for placing in the tombs of the dead; [this was] the beginning of the use of 'spirit-money,' used to the present day in Chinese ceremonial and religious rites" (*Papermaking*, 466). The introduction of paper money in China came, again according to Hunter, in the second half of the seventh century (Hunter, 203–8, 466). See also Davis, *Certain Old Chinese Notes*, 245–46. Marco Polo's famous account (see Polo, vol. 1, 423–30) put into circulation in Europe a description of paper money in China in the early fourteenth century and especially beginning in the later fifteenth century when this book of travels became one of the first printed books (in German in 1477, and in English in 1579). See Hart, 254–58. In a work that appeared in French in 1735—in the aftermath of the paper money experiments of the Mississippi and the South Sea bubbles—the Jesuit Jean Baptiste Du Halde described the use of paper money in Ancient China in his collation of the reports sent from China over many years by Jesuit missionaries to the order's central office (an English translation of Du Halde's work appeared in 1738; see Davis, *Certain Old Chinese Notes*, 252–53).

41. See Hunter, *Papermaking*, 207–8 and *Chinese Ceremonial Paper*, 40–64.

42. Hou catalogues and translates fragments of the many allusions to paper spirit-money in Chinese literature from the seventh to the eleventh century (see Hou, 5–16).

43. T'ang Lin, *Ming-pao ki*. My translation from the French translation of Hou, 5–6.

44. Hunter, *Chinese Ceremonial Paper*, 40. Hunter's book includes remarkable specimens of ceremonial Chinese paper and also a description of "Chinese paper gods"—paper with printed representations of gods that are believed to "dispel evil spirits" when "displayed in [their] proper place" (65). Hou's book also includes samples of spirit-money as well as a highly interesting analysis of the ritual incineration or "transformation" (*houa*) of the paper money, a process

that allows for the transfer of the paper offerings to a heavenly "treasury" where they can be deposited in the "accounts" that correspond to the birthdate of each existing thing (see Hou, 92–126).

45. "What further discredited [paper] was its Judeo-Arabic origin. The fanaticism that drove the Christian world to destroy everything that smacked of the Moslem civilization proscribed this material from which great advantages were to be derived" (Blum, 34).

46. See also, for example, Hornung: "Hieroglyphic writing in particular was designed to be chiseled into stone or painted on solid walls, that is, on permanent materials, while cursive hieratic writing was meant for papyrus or clay and was used only for keeping temporary records" (20).

47. Jan Assmann, "Stein und Zeit," 92. The term "digraphic" is taken from Assmann, 95.

48. See Diekmann, 1–48.

49. See Assmann, "Stein und Zeit," 95, "Schrift, Tod und Identität. Das Grab als Vorschule der Literatur im alten Ägypten," 64–71, and *Moses der Ägypter. Entzifferung einer Gedächtnisspur*, 166–67; Wienold, 300–8; Fischer, 24–26, 56; and Thiel, 170–205.

50. Blum, 34.

51. See Churchyard, *A Sparke of Friendship and Warme Goodwill* (1588); and Trithemius, *In Praise of Scribes (De Laude Scriptorum)* (1498), especially, 62–63.

52. In a sense the seeds of the conflict had already been planted in ancient Egyptian culture, as Assmann points out (see Assmann, *Stein und Zeit*, 29).

53. The phrase, "in an endless web" (*en continu* in French) is used repeatedly by the historians of paper to describe the paper that was no longer made sheet by sheet in frames. This shift from frame to endless web is recalled by Derrida's comments on, or rather his dream of, an endless "ribbon" or "band" of paper (see "Le papier ou moi," 271–72; on the motif of the frame in Derrida, see *La vérité en peinture*, especially 83–94).

54. For an account of Robert's invention, see André, "Au berceau de la mécanisation papetière" and his exhaustive study, *Machine à papier*, especially 81–86; Hunter, *Papermaking*, 257–64; and Morris, "More Adventures," 9–10. Morris, *Nicolas Louis Robert*, includes facsimiles of five of Robert's ink and watercolor patent drawings and notes: "The drawings are of profound historical significance because without machine-made paper the prodigious nineteenth-century growth of cheap printed materials and the resultant dissemination of knowledge and information would not have taken place. The availability of paper in endless rolls made possible the invention of high-speed rotary printing, which today accounts for the bulk of all printed products, the commonest being books, newspapers, magazines and packaging materials" (9). In his account of the origins of industrial paper production, André points to the dramatic increase in periodical publication, and in particular the invention of the "presse à bon marché" by Emile de Girardin in 1836 as the key to the development of machine-made paper (*Machines à papier*, 259–68). André takes note of the early contract for the assignats in his later article, "Au berceau de la mécanisation papetière." On the impact of the Foudrinier paper machine, for which Robert's machine was the model, on the publication of literature in England in the first half of the nineteenth century, see Erickson, especially 20–48.

55. As we will see, paper was also identified with the illegitimate political authority of the American colonists who had begun printing promissory notes, in defiance of the English throne, in the late seventeenth century. We will return

to the important role played by paper in the conflict between England and the American colonies in Chapter 1. The phrase "financial revolution" alludes to Dickson's influential study of the economic roots on the modern British state in the later seventeenth century. To the list of objects of paper satire in English, in addition to the French and American Revolutions, should also be included Romanticism. See Thomas Love Peacock's *Paper Money Lyrics* (1825): in "A Mood of My Own Mind," for example, Wordsworth's "correspondent breeze" is compared to a speculative bubble.

56. Burke, 224. See also Carlyle, *French Revolution*, 310–11, for example.

57. Murray, 77. Leonard Schlosser's introduction to this recent edition is also informative on this point (13).

58. Murray, 79.

59. Murray, 38.

60. Murray, 38.

61. Some commentators have claimed that the tablets were made of sapphire from the throne of glory. See "Tablets of the Law," *Encyclopedia Judaica*, vol. 15 and Ginzburg, vol. 3, 119, 170.

62. Murray, 39.

63. Assmann, *Moses the Egyptian*. The remarks that follow in this paragraph are greatly indebted to Assmann's erudite and stimulating study (see especially 91–143).

64. Warburton, vol. 2, 54–55.

65. Warburton, vol. 2, 55. See Assmann, *Moses the Egyptian*, 111.

66. Kant, *Kritik der Urteilskraft, Werke*, vol. 8, 365; *Critique of Judgment*, sec. 29.

67. Assmann suggests that Kant would have been familiar with these debates from, among other sources, Friedrich Schiller and Karl Leonhard Reinhold whose *Die Hebräische Mysterien oder die älteste religiöse Freymaurerey* appeared in 1786, a work that became the inspiration for Schiller's ballad "Das verschleierte Bild zu Sais" and his essay "Die Sendung Moses." See Assmann, *Moses the Egyptian*, 115–39. For an interesting discussion of Kant's (other) Egyptian example, the Pyramids, see de Man, "Phenomenality and Materiality in Kant," 129–44 and Davis, "Paul de Man's 'Historical Materialism,'" *Replications*, 232–53.

68. Such a prohibition, as communicated to the Jews by Moses, is also a copy or facsimile and is produced on a support (a stone tablet) made by Moses, since he dropped the original when faced with the spectacle of the Golden Calf.

69. Murray's practical proposal may even be taken to point to what becomes an endlessly complex project in a major strand of nineteenth-century literature and art: that of imagining the infinite potentiality of quotidian materials and practices—in this case an everyday material of communication—to be something more than simply practical and evanescent.

70. The editor of the reprint, Henry Morris, says that the original edition was printed on "unwatermarked wove paper, probably machine-made" (28). The 300 copies of the reprint are on hand-made paper, specifically Hahnemühle Ingres-Büttenpapier.

71. Benjamin, *Arcades Project* Y2,2.

72. Benjamin, *Charles Baudelaire*, 142; *Illuminations*, 187–88.

73. It is noteworthy that the French word *mannequin* signifies both living and lifeless human figures used for the display of clothing fashions, whether on a fashion show runway or in the display case of a boutique.

74. Benjamin, *Charles Baudelaire*, 141; *Illuminations*, 187.

75. See Agamben, *Potentialities*, 177–84.

76. "Just as lithography virtually implied the illustrated newspaper, so did photography foreshadow the sound film," Benjamin, *Das Kunstwerk*, 11; "The Work of Art," *Illuminations*, 219.

77. Meyerson elaborates his thesis about the fundamental importance of *principes de conservation* throughout his remarkable work: from *Identité et réalité* (1908), to *De l'explication dans les sciences* (reissued in 1928 but originally published in 1921); *Du cheminement de la pensée*, 3 vols. (1931); and *Essais* (1936). For relatively succinct, explicit explanations of Meyerson's project see "Préface," *Du cheminement de la pensée*, vol. 1, xi–xiv and "La notion de l'identique," *Essais*, 199–202.

78. Surprisingly, the relevance of this development to aesthetics and in particular to the question of aesthetic value has been almost entirely overlooked. By excessively focusing on the origins of the concept of aesthetic value in eighteenth-century political economy, the current discussion of aesthetic value in literary studies (see Bourdieu, Guillory, Herrnstein-Smith) has tended to universalize the Cartesian conservation principles of classical political economy, in particular those that inform the work of Adam Smith, wherein exchange value is understood as analogous to the conservation of a quantity of substance through a series of exchanges. On Smith and Descartes, see Foley. While this has hardly escaped the attention of historians of the natural and social sciences, the recent literary historians seeking to historicize the concept of aesthetic value have for the most part overlooked the influence of these developments in aesthetic theory after Kant. I have dealt more extensively with the connection between aesthetics, on the one hand, and the natural and social sciences, on the other, in my "The Coming of Paper." On the origins of the natural-scientific concept of energy, see Williams, *The Origins of Field Theory*, 32–63; Elkana, 22–53; and the seminal study by Hesse, 157–225. On the debts of neoclassical economics to theories of energy and the force field, see Mirowski, especially 177–202.

79. Benjamin's concern with such developments in his work on aesthetics is evident, for instance, in the footnote to Meyerson—the first footnote in fact—in his study of the German Baroque *Trauerspiel*. Indeed, the question of conservation principles in natural science and the implications of this question for the philosophy of art or aesthetics were of great concern in the Neo-Kantian philosophical culture of Benjamin's generation of German intellectuals. Important influences here, especially for Benjamin, were Heinrich Rickert (Benjamin's teacher in Freiburg) and Hermann Cohen. On Benjamin's Neo-Kantianism, see Fenves, *Arresting Language*, especially 186–91. I have dealt more extensively with the discourse of virtuality in Benjamin's work and traced the appearance of the word *virtual* in his writing on aesthetics, translation, and history in "Virtual Paris," 206–14.

80. See Schiller, *Die Räuber, Schillers Werke*, vol. 3, 7; an English translation of the passage can be found in Schiller, *Works*, vol. 2, 136. A useful historical survey of the word *Gehalt* can be found in the entry "Gehalt," *Historisches Wörterbuch der Philosophie*, vol. 3, ed. Joachim Ritter (Basel: Schwabe and Co. Verlag, 1974), 139–45. For some remarkable suggestions about Schiller's play itself as developing a critical perspective on this theory of content, see Fenves, 130–34.

81. Georg Lukács, "Hegels Ästhetik," 620.

82. An early example of this can be found in a fragment (probably from the late teens), published posthumously under the title, "On Aesthetics" (*Zur Aesthetik*), in which Benjamin asserts that "the material [of every work of art] . . . is to be thought of as at once inside and outside of the work of art" (later in this passage

Benjamin describes it as being "split" or "sundered" [*gesondert*] (Benjamin, "Zur Aesthetik," *Gesammelte Schriften*, vol. 6, 109–29).

83. These manipulations are variations on themes from Kant's natural philosophy and aesthetics, especially on the link between "divisibility" and "judgment." See, for example, *Versuch, den negativen Größen in die Weltweisheit einzuführen*, *Werke*, vol. 2, 779–81; and *Metaphysische Anfangsgründe der Naturwissenschaft*, *Werke*, vol. 8, 47–62.

84. Benjamin, *Arcades Project*, N7a,1.

85. Samuel Weber has recently referred to this as Benjamin's "-abilities" (*Benjamins-barkeiten*). See his "Benjamin's Style."

86. Benjamin, *Begriff der Kunstkritik*, 25; "Concept of Criticism," *Selected Writings*, vol. 1, 128.

87. Benjamin, *Begriff der Kunstkritik*, 67; "Concept of Criticism," *Selected Writings*, vol. 1, 156.

88. But the kind of dynamic form that interests Benjamin in Romanticism could never completely enter into, much less be grounded in, familiar narratives of progressive shifts, advancement and so on such as one finds even in the most advanced historical accounts of the natural and social sciences. Benjamin was convinced of this long before his late critique of progress in "Theses on the Philosophy of History." His characterization of the Romantic concept of the potentiality of reflection seems to anticipate his later work on history: "the infinity of reflection . . . is not an infinity of continuous advance (*Fortgangs*) but an infinity of connectedness (*Zusammenhanges*)." Called for, according to the Romantics, was not history in the conventional sense but criticism (*Kritik*), that is to say, critical history. Only in critical activity (*Kritik*) does there arise the possibility of "a cognitive moment" (*ein erkennendes Moment*) in which the peculiar dynamism of the aesthetic medium comes to light.

89. On the divergence of Friedrich Schlegel's literary theory from Fichte's theory of subjective self-positing, see the trenchant analysis of Hamacher, *Entferntes Verstehen*, 195–234.

90. "The concept [*Tathandlung*] as a politico-juridical term had acquired the signification 'public, completed act' (as distinct from mere intention) already in the seventeenth century and is encountered in this sense in the eighteenth and nineteenth centuries as well," "Tathandlung," *Historisches Wörterbuch der Philosophie* (the references given here are Friedtlieb, *Prudentia politica christiana* [1614] and Goethe, *Götz von Berlichingen* [1773]).

91. Benjamin's interpretation of Fichte would have to address more fully the critical perspective on dialectical self-positing in the *Wissenschaftslehre*. See, for example, Honneth, especially 28–48. But recent attempts, such as Honneth's, to build upon these critical aspects of Fichte's philosophy, correcting in a sense Benjamin's reductive reading of the *Wissenschaftslehre*, have developed mainly in ways that bear out Benjamin's fundamental differentiation of Romantic (and up to a point his own) aesthetic theory from Fichte's philosophical position. A good example of this is Honneth whose theory of intersubjective "recognition" (*Anerkennung*) based on Fichte maintains a firm distinction between visibility and invisibility, between public and non-public acts, even if it tries to validate the latter and thus to question a certain classic (Habermasian) concept of communication and recognition. That is to say, Honneth does not consider the possibility that gesture could be both visible and invisible, public and non-public—in short, apprehended, and not recognized, in the manner of the unconscious (for examples, see Honneth, 14–15, 36–38). Honneth's critique of

Gadamer's hermeneutic theory of the "horizon of expectation," which parallels Adorno's critique of "authenticity" in Heidegger, remains itself within the phenomenological horizon of consciousness, of "forms of consciousness" (*Bewusstseinsforme*) (70). The analysis of Sartre follows the same pattern. The result in Honneth is a call for the cultivation of a "capacity" for a subjective "opening (*Offnung*) to the many sides of one's own person" (160). For Benjamin, and for us here, the subject is always open and exposed, but not always perceived or apprehended. Tholen makes a similar point in his critique of Luhmann (Tholen, 175–81).

92. Benjamin *Begriff der Kunstkritik*, 24–25; "Concept of Criticism," *Selected Writings*, vol. 1, 128. Such a potential field of infinite action made possible by aesthetic form in Romantic reflection resurfaces in Benjamin's better-known later work on the modern media of technical reproducibility, as we will see.

93. Benjamin, *Begriff der Kunstkritik*, 100; "Concept of Criticism," *Selected Writings*, vol. 1, 177.

94. Benjamin, *Begriff der Kunstkritik*, 78; "Concept of Criticism," *Selected Writings*, vol. 1, 163. And as an act of completion, "The temporal infinity in which this process [of Romantic reflection] takes place," Benjamin says, "is . . . a medial and qualitative infinity. For this reason, progredibility (*Progredibilität*) is not at all what is understood by the modern term 'progress'; it not some merely relative connection of cultural stages to one another. Like the entire life of mankind, it is an infinite process of fulfillment (*Erfüllung*), not a mere becoming" (*Begriff der Kunstkritik*, 86; *Selected Writings*, vol. 1, 168).

95. It is stripped of its infinity, Benjamin also says: *entkleidet,* as if the infinity depended on the appearance or *Schein* of a garment, also a figure for translation in Benjamin *Gesammelte Schriften*, vol. 4, 20–21; *Selected Writings*, vol. 1, 125.

96. Benjamin, *Begriff der Kunstkritik*, 73; "Concept of Criticism," *Selected Writings*, vol. 1, 159–60.

97. Benjamin, *Begriff der Kunstkritik*, 102; "Concept of Criticism," *Selected Writings*, vol. 1, 178.

98. For the clearest assessment to date of this strangeness, see Weber, *Mass Mediauras*, 82–107. Most approaches to the mass media that claim to derive ultimately from Benjamin have followed in the footsteps of Jürgen Habermas's *Strukturwandel der Öffentlichkeit* even while trying to refine or complicate the thesis of the "public sphere." In doing so, they have avoided Benjamin's thesis of a radically dispersed and distracted public. Instead, such approaches have located the problem posed by the mass media in the alienation between the public and private (or the subjective). In spite of different inflections, this is true of most recent work in German and in English. As noted above, Honneth is an example of the former; Warner illustrates the dominant tendency of the latter. Honneth develops an intersubjective theory of "recognition" (*Anerkennung*) along the lines of Luhmann's communication theory (see, for instance, Honneth, 19–20). Warner writes, for instance: "As the subjects of publicity . . . we have a different relation to ourselves, a different affect, from that which we have in other contexts. No matter what the particularities of culture, race, and gender, or class we bring to bear on public discourse, the moment of apprehending something in public is one in which we imagine, if imperfectly, indifference to those particularities, to ourselves. We adopt the attitude of the public subject, marking to ourselves its nonidentity with ourselves" (234). The "nonidentity" here is firmly located and recognized (we "mark it to ourselves") between the private subject and the public subject, both of which remain in themselves self-consistent

entities. The possibility of a public that is not identical with itself, like Benjamin's "distracted public," is excluded from this scene.

99. Benjamin pursues a similarly elusive public in the unrecognizable tragic *Gemeinschaft* of the Baroque *Trauerspiel* and in the "dreaming collective" of nineteenth-century Paris. On the "content" (*Gehalt*) of the tragic hero's achievement for the *Volksgemeinschaft*, which is parallel to the "content" (*Gehalt*) of the idea in history in the passage cited above, see Benjamin, *Ursprung des deutschen Trauerspiels*, 89; *Origin of German Tragic Drama*, 108. For an interpretation of the virtuality of this "content," see Fenves, 239–48. The "dream collective" is throughout the *Arcades Project* (see, for example, K1,1–K1,5).

100. Benjamin, Der Erzähler," *Gesammelte Schriften*, vol. 2, 2, 442; "The Storyteller," *Illuminations*, 86.

101. Irony alludes here to Georg Lukács's *Theory of the Novel*, which Benjamin cites in "The Storyteller." As on the question of "content" (*Gehalt*) in aesthetics in general, the contrast between Benjamin and Lukács on the novel is also illuminating. We will come back to this point in Chapter 4 and in the Afterword.

102. Benjamin, "Über das Programm der kommenden Philosophie," *Gesammelte Schriften*, 2, 1, 159; "On the Program of the Coming Philosophy," *Selected Writings*, vol. 1, 101. See also Benjamin, "Erfahrung und Armut," *Gesammelte Schriften*, vol. 2, 1, 215–16; "Experience and Poverty, *Selected Writings*, vol. 2, 732.

103. The history of paper is indeed indicative of this acceleration. In spite of the fact that the paper-making machine was invented in Revolutionary France, the invention itself was disseminated and had a much more immediate impact in England and in America. See Erickson, 20–48.

104. Benjamin, *Arcades Project*, N2a,3. See also N 3,1 on "legibility."

Chapter 1. Distraction in America: Paper, Money, Poe

1. Poe, "Review of *Twice-Told Tales* by Nathaniel Hawthorne," *Great Short Works of Edgar Allan Poe*, 522.

2. Poe, "The Man of the Crowd," *Tales of Mystery and Imagination*, 108.

3. Descartes, *Metaphysical Meditations*, 2, 13. Cavell detects an echo of Descartes in Poe's prose (see Cavell, "Betting Odd, Getting Even," 18–22).

4. This process parallels the one traced by Brodsky in her trenchant study of the "architectonic line" of Descartes's writing that "translates thought onto an empty surface" (see 7–8, 58–67). On the stabilizing drive at work in this reflexive movement, see Weber, *Mass Mediauras*, 45–51.

5. On the way the mechanical is mapped onto the crowd in British writing about the London crowd that appeared in "mass journals" in the 1830s, see Klancher, 81–97. On the emergence of the distinction between the organic and mechanical in German Romanticism, see Schlanger, for example, 50–51. On machines in Descartes, see Des Chene, 65–102. Apropos of the passage at the beginning of Poe's "The Man of the Crowd" is the following remark by Des Chene: "The machine, then, is open, without secrets, something that can be articulated completely in an ekphrasis" (99–100). Thus the secretiveness and illegibility of the man in the crowd in Poe's tale—the figure who *lässt sich nicht lesen*—refuses the model of the Cartesian machine.

6. Poe's June, 1836 review of Boz's sketches can be found in *Complete Works*, vol. 9, 46–49.

7. I am thinking here especially of the sketches later collected under the

rubric of "Scenes" most of which were originally published in the *Morning Chronicle* and the *Evening Chronicle* from 1834–36. Particularly recalled by the peregrinations of Poe's "man of the crowd" are "The Streets—Morning," "The Streets—Night," "Shops and Their Tenants," "Meditations on Monmouth Street," and "Gin-shops" (Dickens, *Sketches by Boz*, 69–74, 74–80, 80–84, 214–20). Rachman finds similarities between Poe's tale and Dickens's *Sketches by Boz* as well (see especially 71–82). Rachman interprets the "absorption" of Dickens in Poe's text as plagiarism and identifies the old man of the tale with Dickens. On the influence of the journalistic genre of the "street crowd" on Poe's tale, see Elmer, 170–71. On Poe's special interest in the British magazine format as a response to the aesthetic challenges of mass-market journalism, see Allen, 19–39, 101–12, 199–203. In an early review of Dickens (from 1835–36), Poe recommends that American writers imitate British magazine writing (see Poe, *Works*, vol. 16, 73–74). The traces of Dickens's sketches in "The Man of the Crowd" may be taken as an example of what Poe describes in his "Chapter on American Cribbage." Poe writes: "What the poet intensely admires, becomes . . . a portion of his own intellect. It has a secondary origination within his own soul—an origination altogether apart, although springing from its primary origination from without. The poet is thus possessed by another's thought, and cannot be said to take of it, possession" (*Essays and Reviews*, 759). On this point, see McGill, 212–14.

8. I have analyzed this feature of Dickens's writing in *Sketches by Boz* and *The Pickwick Papers* in my *Writing in Parts*, 86–87, 119–21. I will return to this point in Chapter 4. It is revealing that in his appreciations of Dickens's early sketches and *The Pickwick Papers*, Poe concentrated on the tales, "The Black Veil" and "The Madman's MS"; and in his review of *Barnaby Rudge* he was taken, not by the portrayal of the Gordon Riots (which were deemed "an afterthought," having "no necessary connection with the story"), but with the detective-story plot of the novel. On "The Black Veil" see Poe, *Complete Works*, vol. 9, 47–48; on "The Madman's MS" see *Complete Works*, vol. 9, 205; on *Barnaby Rudge*, see Poe, *Complete Works*, vol. 11, 53.

9. The eyes of the man of the crowd suggest the movement of a "vision-machine" (see Virilio, 153): his "eyes rolled wildly . . . in every direction" (113).

10. Benjamin, *Charles Baudelaire*, 144; "On Some Motifs in Baudelaire," *Illuminations*, 189.

11. Another important authority here would be Locke. In "Morella" Poe refers to the passage from the *Essay Concerning Human Understanding* (in Book II, chapter xxvii) in which Locke discusses the distinction between a human uttering gibberish and an animal speaking articulated words and phrases ("Morella," *Poetry, Tales, and Selected Essays*, 235). On Poe's indebtedness to Locke's *Essay* see Sandler.

12. By way of contrast with the "creative" power of "imagination," Coleridge says, "fancy . . . has no other counters to play with but fixities and definites" (Coleridge, *Biographia Literaria* 13).

13. On the passage from Cuvier, see Pollin, "The Ingenious Web Unravelled," 253–54. For an enlightening discussion of Poe's relationship to contemporary natural science and to the emergence of what would become evolutionary theory, see Frank. On the historical connection between photography and modern policing, see Tagg.

14. This interaction is also staged, perhaps a bit too rigidly, by "The Mystery of Marie Rogêt" (1842–43), the sequel to "The Murders in the Rue Morgue." In

the second Dupin story the solving of the crime—in this case one explicitly drawn from a real murder—turns almost exclusively on the collation and comparison of contradictory information in the newspapers. But this time, money—not friendship or benevolence—draws Dupin into the world of the newspaper. Many commentators have interpreted this detail as suggestive of a decisive break between a traditional society of patronage and participation in a classic public sphere and a more modern capitalist culture of the professional who gets paid for his services. If this is the mark of a historical shift, though, it is hard to see what happened between 1841 and 1842. A recent example of this view is Whalen who views the emergence in "The Mystery of Marie Rogêt" of earning money as a motive for Dupin. Whalen also notes the "Dupin makes sense out of a conflicting mass of information and thereby leads the city out of confusion and impending chaos" (229). Whalen does not note that the medium of this "conflicting mass of information" is the newspaper, although he does describe the emergence of the newspaper in the 1830s: "after the Panic of 1837, the cheap dailies and weeklies began to undercut the magazine and book trade" (24). For an assessment of Dupin's work in "The Mystery of Marie Rogêt," see Saltz.

15. In his critical essays, Poe repeatedly stresses the importance of "unity of impression" and "effect." In addition to the passage cited at the beginning of this chapter from the review of Hawthorne's *Twice-Told Tales*, see "The Philosophy of Furniture," in which Poe writes of the "immensely important effect derivable from unity of impression" and of how it is "destroyed" through the interference of "the affairs of the world," and also "The Philosophy of Furniture," where he insists on the need for the "totality of effect or impression" (*Poetry, Tales, and Selected Essays*, 1375, 1430).

16. Shell, *Money, Language, and Thought*, 5–23. As Shell notes, controversy surrounding paper money dominated American political discourse from 1825 through the end of the century.

17. On the financial origins of the modern British state, see Dickson. We will consider a satirical passage from Pope on paper below. Here is a sample from Burke: "All you have got for the present [in France after the Revolution] is a paper circulation, and a stock-jobbing constitution. . . . [The republic of Paris] will make efforts, by becoming the heart of a boundless paper circulation, to draw everything to itself; but in vain" (Burke 142). Instead, Burke prefers to ground exchange on land and believes that "the idea of inheritance furnishes a sure principle of conservation" (Burke 119–20). On Burke see Pocock's "Introduction" to *Reflections on the Revolution in France*, xxi–xxii and xxviii–xxxiii. An interesting eighteenth-century example of the opposing current in England is Charles Johnstone, who presents his 1760 novel *Chrysal; Or the Lives of a Guinea* as having been written by "a schemer, who had wasted his whole fortune in the search after the philosopher's stone, and having his eyes at length opened to this folly, though too late to remedy it, yet was able to divert the grief of his disappointment, by writing these papers, in ridicule of such notions, and from the sale of which he might also expect some relief to his wants" (Johnstone, 11).

18. The United States, Shell observes, is "the first place in the Western world where paper money was widely used" (*Art and Money*, 73).

19. Del Mar's interest in money and the politics of representation may well be part of the reason why economic and financial historians have neglected his work. This may also explain why Del Mar attracted the attention of a poet—Ezra Pound—whose allusions to Del Mar in his 1933 *The ABC of Economics* may also have led to further neglect of his writings on monetary history.

20. Del Mar, *Barbara Villiers*, 40. On John Hull's Boston mint where Massachusetts coined its own Pine Tree shilling, Del Mar says, for instance: "[Hull's mint] defied the Royal prerogative; it was the money of treason; it was coined from piratical plunder; it was dishonest money; it lowered the Royal standard; it inflated the currency; Hull's charge for coinage was exorbitant; etc. Much of this was true; yet except for the first one or two these charges were equally true of the British shilling of that day" (*History of Money in America*, 76–77).

21. The early twentieth-century historian, Andrew McFarland Davis, makes some intriguing suggestions about the parallels between the Colonial American paper money experiments and those of ancient China (Davis, "Certain Old Chinese Notes," vi–vii, 245–86, esp. 284–86). Davis alludes to the influence of William Potter's pamphlets on the colonial experiments.

22. Del Mar, *History of Money in America*, 80. On the contribution of monetary experimentation to the controversy between England and its North American colonies, see Mossman, 102–3; for another perspective, see Jordan, 27–45. The "Mississippi Bubble" refers to the paper money experiment in French Louisiana directed by the Scotsman John Law, who was French minister of finance during the Regency. Law's "system," which originally aimed to foster commerce in the territory, eventually grew into a huge speculative mania or bubble, which burst in 1720. We should note, however, that a difference of opinion similar to the one on the colonial experiments exists on Law and the Bubble. As one nineteenth-century French Saint-Simonian wrote of Law's experiment, "one would not find two writers who are in agreement over the evaluation of this system" ("Considerations sur le système de Law," 6). The Saint-Simonian concludes with a view of Law not unlike that of Breck and Phillips on the Continental Bills: "In spite of all the particular evils produced by the system, we believe that it has had a positive influence on the general progress of society" (18). For Alphonse Thiers, whose monograph on Law appeared at around the same time (a translation was published in the United States around the middle of the nineteenth century), Law was an "unhappy genius" (183). A more recent economist like Schumpeter, however, whose views on money took shape in the face of overwhelming inflation in early twentieth-century Austria, nevertheless considers the Scotsman a leading monetary thinker (Schumpeter, 54); while Galbraith considers Law a fraud and a swindler (*A Short History*, 34–42).

23. Aglietta and Orléan, 146.

24. See Mossman, 29–37, 93–103.

25. Perhaps with the inflated Continental Bills in mind, the new American republic instituted policies betraying a suspicion about paper that would die hard. This fear of paper would not only drive monetary debate and policy in the nineteenth century, it also led to the sense of shame at the nation's paper origins mentioned earlier—the same embarrassment that led the British to project paper onto the revolutions in America and France. Such anxiety was a major factor in the series of financial "panics" that occurred during the first decades of the nineteenth century in the United States (Galbraith, *A Short History*, 44–45; Rothbard, 10–11). Galbraith claims that the word "panic" acquired its financial signification during the crisis of 1819: "the boom collapsed; prices and property values fell drastically; loans were foreclosed; the number of bankruptcies went up. This was the first of the speculative episodes with resulting collapse that were to characterize American economic and financial history for the rest of the century. The word panic as it pertained to money entered the language. Later, in eager search of milder, less alarming terms, reference to crisis, depression,

recession, and now, of course, growth adjustment came successively to denote the economic aftermath" (*A Short History*, 45–46). The suspicion of paper and the belief in specie, the latter intensified in the belief in gold as the substantial manifestation of value itself, together with the difficulties banks had in producing specie on the spot while continuing to extend credit, led to the major panic of 1837, which was occasioned by Andrew Jackson's withdrawal of support from the Second Bank of the United States. The panic over the lack of a central bank precipitated the heated debate between the "paper money men" and the "gold bugs" that brings the longer history of paper money in America into direct contact with Poe's tale that appeared in 1843 in *Dollar* magazine. The actions taken by Andrew Jackson against the Second Bank of the United States—his veto of legislation that would have renewed its charter as the national bank of the country and his withdrawing all government funds from it—have been the subject of much debate among economic and social historians. As one prominent scholar of the period has noted, "the Jacksonian attack on the banks was but a single episode in an extended debate over banking, credit, and currency that lasted throughout the nineteenth century" (Sharp, 6). These actions may have been part of an agrarian revolution, or they may have been driven by a grab for power by a highly acquisitive new entrepreneurial class. In any case, however, the withdrawal of government funds from the Philadelphia giant clearly "discredits [the Jacksonians'] reputation as advocates of credit expansion and laissez-faire" (McFaul, 1).

26. Another example is Mitchell.

27. Bullock quotes Peletiah Webster as stating that the Continental Bill had "polluted the equity of our laws; turned them into engines of oppression and wrong; corrupted the justice of our public administration; destroyed the fortunes of thousands who had the most confidence in it" (Webster, *Political Essays*, 175–76).

28. Breck, for instance, writing in 1843, considered the Continental Bills as a sort of evil. "Vice and immorality," he argued, "were greatly encouraged . . . by that ever-varying currency" (27). "Happily," Breck goes on to say, "such tyranny cannot return: the Constitution of the United States forbidding the enactment of laws making any kind of money legal tender, except gold and silver" (Breck, 27–28). A similar perspective guides Henry Phillips. But while sharing the view that, as Phillips put it some twenty years later at the time of the Civil War and the emission of the Greenbacks, "paper unlike coin was but a conventional sign which could not stand of itself" (2: 16), still Breck does recognize that the Continental Bills were an expression of the sovereignty on the part of the colonies (26). What is more, he acknowledges a certain effectiveness in the artifice of paper money: "But while that artificial currency lasted, it was a happy illusion, which worked the miracle of reality. Without its agency, we should have been subdued, and have crept along, at a colonial pace, as Canada has done. Without it the valley of the Mississippi would have remained a wilderness; the Spaniards would still have been masters of the great outlets of the South; our manufactures would not have been allowed to reach even to the making of a hobnail, and our star-spangled banner would never have been unfurled." (Breck, 39) In general, however, the admiration is subdued and by the time we get to Bullock at the end of the century the colonial paper money experiments have been entirely discredited.

29. Galbraith, *Money*, 45–57

30. For perhaps his clearest and most general discussion of the nature of such

a crisis, see Del Mar's "The Sacred Character of Gold," *History of Monetary Systems*, 66–93.

31. Del Mar, *History of Money in America*, 96. Characteristically, Galbraith observes that the use of paper money in the newly independent colonies was a result of the revolutionary principle of not paying taxes, but he does not go on to consider how this refusal reciprocates the king's refusal of political representation to the colonists (*Money* 45–57).

32. If, as we have seen, the British authorities considered the colonial currencies illegitimate, then it was entirely legitimate in their view to counterfeit the "counterfeit" Continental Bills in order to suppress the "unlawful" uprising. See Del Mar, *The History of Money in America*, 102–3, 113–14; Newman, "The Successful British Counterfeiting," 174–87. It may be that, as one prominent scholar has argued, "historically this appears to be the first use of such tactics. . . . While counterfeiting for personal gain has a record as old as currency itself, counterfeiting as a means of winning a war by undermining the economic stability of the enemy and accelerating the rejection of its currency by its own people was then a novelty" (Newman, "The Successful British Counterfeiting," 174). Newman also notes that Union printers engaged in a similar practice against the Confederacy during the American Civil War. Washington and other Revolutionary leaders were, perhaps justifiably, scandalized (see Newman, 176–79). Benjamin Franklin, a important colonial printer of money himself, would later assess the effects of this two-fold strategy: "This [counterfeiting] operated considerably in depreciating the whole mass, first, by the vast additional quantity, and next by the uncertainty in distinguishing the true from the false" ("The Retort Courteous," 1127). For examples of Franklin's earlier interest in this question, see his "A Modest Enquiry" and "Right, Wrong and Reasonable." And, as it turned out, the British tactic succeeded: despite measures to counter the counterfeiting operation (in 1779, for instance, the Continental Congress ordered an exchange of $40 for $1), by 1781 the entire $200,000,000 issued by the United States of America was worthless (Newman, "The Successful British Counterfeiting," 175).

33. On this tradition in eighteenth-century British writing, see Nicholson's study of what he calls "satires of capital."

34. Thanks are due here to my colleague, Jim Egan, for sharing his knowledge of Cooke's work with me. For some basic information about the rather obscure Cooke see Cohen; on the historical context of Cooke's poem in the debates in the Maryland Assembly at this time over paper money, see Behrens 9–12; for a sample of the early paper money of Maryland, see Newman, *The Early Paper Money of America*, 111.

35. Pope's letter presents the classic argument against the artificial, fraudulent flights of credit and "fortune" from the landed perspective of the "virtue" of property, to use the terms studied by the historian, J. G. A. Pocock. The reference to the queen in the lines just cited, according to the editor F. W. Bateson, refers to the "rumor that Queen Caroline had accepted a large present from Robert Knght, the cashier of the South Sea Company" (Pope, 91, note to line 78). See Pocock, *The Machiavellian Moment*, 457. "We find reason to suppose," notes Pocock elsewhere with reference to Pope, "that the Apocalyptic triumph of nonsense over language at the end of Pope's *Dunciad* had something to do with a society dominated by speculators in paper promises to repay which will never be made good before the end of time; if property is the foundation of personality, unreal property (in which nothing is owned except meaningless words)

makes personalities unreal and their words meaningless" (Pocock, *Virtue, Commerce and History*, 247). Also see the recent study by Nicholson, 8–19, 27–50.

36. Shell, *Art and Money*, 92–94.

37. The similarity between nineteenth-century American *trompe l'œil* paper money art and "The Gold Bug" is suggested by Shell in *Art and Money* (74) and indeed the issue of money (paper versus gold) in Poe's story is the subject of an earlier essay by Shell, "'The Gold Bug': Introduction to 'The Industry of Letters' in America," *Money, Language, and Thought*. My interpretation of the tale here seeks to elaborate some of the implications of Shell's essay, so I would like here to acknowledge my debt, and express my gratitude, to him.

38. Briquet, 199–202; Bofarull y Sans, 24–25.

39. On these allusions, see Shell, "The Gold Bug," *Money, Language, and Thought*, 5–6.

40. On the importance of this question in American history, see McWilliams, 182–83; for some of its philosophical implications see Derrida, *Donner le temps*, 183–217 (*Given Time*, 145–72), and *Politiques de l'amitié*, 330–40.

41. An important parallel to Poe here would be Melville in, for example, "Bartleby the Scrivener," a Wall Street tale in which the usually discrete lawyer-narrator becomes driven to find something deeper in his clerk, Bartleby, to the extent that his subjectivity or, as Melville's narrator puts it, "humanity" comes to depend upon his copyist's having some depth (this is the thrust of his search for Bartleby's "soul," for something "touching on his history" (25). For some suggestive reflections on Bartleby and the image of paper, see Agamben, 39–41, 52–53, 77–84. A similar interest in the maddening inscrutability of surfaces is expressed throughout Melville's 1857 novel *The Confidence-Man: His Masquerades* (see 108–9, for instance). On the latter, see Sussman. We will elaborate on this point in Melville in Chapter 3.

42. Derrida, *Donner le temps*, 215–16; *Given Time*, 170.

43. The police in the tale, of course, made the mistake of losing themselves in depth, in "bulk" and "space": they "divided the surface [of the Minister's house] into compartments" and searched under the "tops" of "tables," "excavated" the legs of furniture, "looked into mirrors, between the boards and the plates," and "probed the beds and bedclothes as well as the curtains and carpets" ("The Purloined Letter," 488). Similarly, in "The Murders in the Rue Morgue" (1841), the police try to discover an underlying motive that would identify the murderer (depth here is motive), while Dupin scans surfaces, reading the depositions in the *Gazette des Tribunaux* and then publishing a counterfeit letter in the newspaper saying that he has found the ourang-outang. Thus in this story, as in "The Purloined Letter" and "The Gold Bug," the key to the enigma is literally in the paper. Even the deceptive nails in the window sashes of the victims' apartment (these *clous* turn out to be important clues here after all) exemplify the *trompe l'œil* of surface: the nailheads only seem to imply extension *into* the window frame: in fact the heads have broken away from their shanks and thus they remain on the surface of the sash when it is opened and closed ("The Murders in the Rue Morgue," 432).

44. On the importance of the origins of playing cards in the history of paper, see Jensen, 88–91. On the use of playing cards as money in colonial Canada, Newman has pointed out: "In Canada in 1685, when the French military payroll was delayed, *monnaie de carte* or *card money* was introduced as a temporary medium of exchange redeemable out of the first coin received from France" (*The Early Paper Money of America*, 7).

45. See the entry "bread," *Oxford English Dictionary*, sense 5: "livelihood, means of subsistence." The dictionary gives the following as an instance from Mariah Edgeworth (1816): "You . . . make your bread by your pen"; and from Byron: "He meant no harm in scribbling . . . 'twas . . . his . . . bread." Much as in English, in French bread is associated with money: as in *gagner son pain* (to earn one's daily bread) (Littré).

46. Barbara Johnson has made some perceptive remarks about the relevance of these lines to Poe's story, and to the dueling interpretations of it by Jacques Lacan and Jacques Derrida (see Johnson, especially 234–36).

47. On the way Dupin is drawn into a symbolic triangle, see Lacan, 51–53. For an analysis of Lacan's exclusion of the textual or literary aspect of the tale and of the presentation of the narrator's implication in the symbolic logic outlined by Lacan, see Derrida, "The Purveyor of Truth," 179–81, 203–6.

48. In this sense Poe's tale combines the two modes of aesthetic receptivity described by Benjamin in his essay on technical reproducibility: "A man who concentrates before a work of art is absorbed by it. He enters into this work of art the way legend tells of the Chinese painter when he viewed his finished painting. In contrast, the distracted masses absorbs the work of art into themselves" (Benjamin, *Das Kunstwerk*, 40; "The Work of Art," *Illuminations*, 239).

49. A good example of such distraction, one that has been influential in recent "economic" literary criticism of American literature, is Benn-Michaels's work on American Naturalism and the gold standard. Even Goux, whose work is more nuanced and who deals with the question of literary historical period rather than that of the nation, exemplifies the historical positivism into which much of this "new economic" criticism falls. In *Coiners of Language*, for instance, Goux takes Gide's novel, *The Counterfeiters*, as representing the historical turning point of the conversion to a society based on inconvertibility: "the particular interest of Gide's novel is that it comes into existence at a turning point, straddling the nostalgic memory of a gold-language or a representative language, and the simultaneously positive and negative prescience that this is no longer tenable, that it no longer corresponds to the actual conditions of the circulation of signs. . . . Poised at the divide between two systems of exchange, the novel expresses the contradiction between a persistent nostalgic attachment to gold currency, and a realistic, or rather theoretical, acceptance of the dizzying novelty of inconvertibility" (Goux, 19–21). By accepting the historical schematism implied in Gide's novel, Goux is compensated with a straightforward—significantly, his word is "realistic"—historical pattern.

Chapter 2. Off the Map: Stevenson's Polynesian Fiction

1. Stevenson was at work on a review of John H. Ingram's edition of Poe's *Works* (1874–75) in the middle of the 1870s. Part of this review appeared in the London journal *Academy* on January 2, 1875 (see Pollin and Greenwood, 317). Pollin and Greenwood point out that "no thorough or even preliminary broad study [on Stevenson and Poe] appears to exist" (322). Watson identifies many details shared by *Treasure Island* and "The Gold Bug," but makes no mention of the map (see Watson, 157–63).

2. Erickson alludes to William Benbowes as a famous literary "pirate" of the 1820's who produced unauthorized editions of Byron and Shelley.

3. The editor for an exhibition of manuscripts and memorabilia at Yale

University's Beinecke Library suggests that one of the models for the pirate Long John Silver was William Ernest Henley, Stevenson's friend who was handling the negotiations with the publisher, Cassell and Company, when the original map was lost (see *R. L. S.*, 26).

4. The best example of this positive light cast on the pirates in *Treasure Island* is perhaps the scene in which the council of buccaneers is convened (TI 158–59). An especially fine illustration of the resemblance between the "gentlemen of fortune" and the gentlemen is the passage in which the latter and the former change places in relation to the stockade after the pirates have been given a counterfeit map by the gentlemen. Jim notes that Dr. Livesay was at that point standing as Silver had been earlier outside the stockade (TI 164).

5. The wording of this phrase from Stevenson's essay is intriguing: "the tale . . . brought (or was the means of bringing) fire and food and wine to a deserving family in which I took an interest. I need scarce say I mean my own" (197). The family in question here was of course from one perspective not "his own" in the sense that it was Fanny Osborne and her son from a previous marriage. In the years prior to the composition of *Treasure Island* Stevenson had gone in pursuit of Mrs. Osborne to the part of California that, some scholars have argued, was the model for Treasure Island (see John Seelye's introduction to the Penguin edition, xxi).

6. This could even go one step farther, in light of the fact that "My First Book" elaborates a theory of receptive literary productivity like the one described by Poe in his "Chapter on American Cribbage," *Essays and Reviews*, 759.

7. The black spot is compared later by Jim Hawkins to money: it was "about the size of a crown piece" (TI 162).

8. 1883 refers to the publication date of the first book edition. The map was not published in the serial edition in *Young Folks Magazine* (October 1, 1881–January 28, 1882).

9. Such counterfeiting is the subject of much of Stevenson's fiction, the most obvious, and most overlooked, example of this being perhaps the lawyer in *Dr. Jekyll and Mr. Hyde* whose very name—Utterson—combines publishing with counterfeiting. According to the *Oxford English Dictionary*, the verb "utter" can mean, "to give currency to (money, coin, notes, etc.); to put into circulation; esp. to pass or circulate (base coin, forged notes, etc.) as legal tender" (sense 2.a.) and also "to issue by way of publication" (sense 2.c.). Critical discussions of Hyde as a figure of the masses and of mass culture would have to be reconsidered in light of the association between Utterson and counterfeiting. See Brantlinger, 173–81; Stewart, 364.

11. Stevenson, *Letters*, vol. 4, 268.

10. "Device" derives from the Latin *dividere*—to divide. Among the rich variety of meanings of "device," including the "something artistically devised or framed; a fancifully conjured design or figure," is "an emblematic figure or design, especially one borne or adopted by a particular person, family, etc., as a heraldic bearing, a cognizance, etc.: usually accompanied by a motto." See "Device," *Oxford English Dictionary*.

12. Stevenson, *Letters*, vol. 4, 100–101, 182.

13. From a certain imperial perspective the formal resemblance between treasure maps and paper money extends to maps of the world in general. Such imperial folly was in fact the subject of a well-known print from the later sixteenth century, the initial period of British imperial expansion in the New World that was accompanied by cartomania. The print, by the Frenchman

Jean de Gourmont, displays an image of the map of the world in a fool's cap. Gourmont's print illustrates nicely the adaptation of the foolscap from Poe's "The Gold Bug" in *Treasure Island*. The characters of Stevenson's South Sea tales often resemble the figure in Gourmont's print. And, as we have seen, in spite of his efforts in "My First Book," Stevenson seems to be drawn into this picture as well when he parrots Poe and unknowingly appropriates the American's foolscap map. But, as in Poe, the foolscap points in another direction in Stevenson as well. For an illuminating discussion of this print, usually called "The Fool's Cap Map," see Helgerson, especially 243–47.

14. For a detailed overview of the theme of exchange in Stevenson's South Sea fiction, see Vanessa Smith, 145–91. The map of Treasure Island, like its flora and fauna and even perhaps its topography, is derived from an American context. Seelye makes this point in his useful introduction to the Penguin edition of *Treasure Island*. Seelye notes the presence of redwood trees and rattlesnakes on Treasure Island and suggests, as others have, that the imaginary island is in California, in fact, and that what Stevenson sketches out unconsciously on the map is based on the "outline of the Monterey Peninsula" (xxii).

15. For Stevenson's comments on the "adventurism" of Whitman, see his "Walt Whitman" in *Virginibus Puerisque*, 195–96.

16. Robert Louis Stevenson, "Henry David Thoreau: His Character and Opinions," *Virginibus Puerisque*, 204.

17. Stevenson, "Henry David Thoreau," *Virginibus Puerisque*, 203.

18. Cavell, *Senses of Walden*, 87–88 and also *This New Yet Unapproachable America*, 115.

19. See the entry "adventure" in the *Oxford English Dictionary*. On the connection between "fortune" and "commerce," see Pocock, *The Machiavellian Moment*, 493.

20. Perhaps Stevenson would have noted a parallel at this point in his career between him and Thoreau. Like Thoreau in *A Week on the Concord and Merrimack River* (1849), Stevenson had published *An Inland Voyage*, an account of a canoe trip, in his case through Belgium and France. *Treasure Island* was appearing in serial in 1882 when the Thoreau essay was published. A recent biographer of Stevenson notes: "One of the most disturbing aspects of *Treasure Island* is its lack of a moral center. Money is the ruling principle and even Dr. Liversey and Squire Trelawny are corrupted by it, leave their bucolic pastures and rush off to the Caribbean with unseemly haste in the hopes of getting rich quick" (McLynn, 199).

21. A recent example of this is McCleary, 193–94.

22. This is, for example, true of Shelley's *Philosophical Review of Reform*, even if it was the considerable merit of Shelley's work to conceive of public debt as a sign, not just of finance alone, but of a social contract involving ethical obligations. On Burke, see J. G. A. Pocock, "Introduction."

23. Stevenson, "El Dorado," *Virginibus Puerisque*, 70–72. A source for Stevenson here may be William Hazlitt's "On the Spirit of Controversy," *Table-Talk: Original Essays on Men and Manners*, 298–99. Hazlitt's importance for Stevenson is suggested by Stevenson, "Books Which Influenced Me," *The Works of Robert Louis Stevenson*, vol. 16, 277.

24. Ultimately, the link between Stevenson's adventure story and Thoreau's economics would be interesting to consider in light of the kinship Stevenson's work has with the romance tradition in nineteenth-century American literature—the family resemblance that would later in fact put him at odds with his American, and later British friend, Henry James.

25. Kirtley claims that Stevenson heard the story in Samoa. Stevenson himself in a prefatory note to his text refers to the English play by Peake first performed in 1828. In 1910 Joseph Beach points to "Das Galgenmännlein" as the source for the English play. On this point, see Vanessa Smith, 181–82. I am also indebted to Vanessa Smith for the letter to Arthur Conan Doyle.

26. See McLynn, 371. On Stevenson as a writer of *Bildungsromane*, see Bozetto.

27. The theme of adventure in Stevenson is balanced by the countervailing prevalence of warnings in his work, even in the theoretical riposte to his friend, Henry James, entitled "A Humble Remonstrance." In this context it is perhaps worth noting that Stevenson's American adventure and his decision to take up the risky career of professional writer were opposed by his security conscious father, Thomas, who wanted his son to enter the traditional family profession of lighthouse engineering (see McCleary, 11–12).

28. On finance in Goethe's *Faust*, see Shell, *Money, Language, and Thought*, 84–130; on this topic in Balzac's *La Peau de chagrin*, see Weber, *Unwrapping Balzac*, 90–116.

29. Stevenson, "Henry David Thoreau," in *Virginibus Puerisque*, 201–2.

30. According to the *Oxford English Dictionary*, "caution" first meant "security, surety" in English and took on the less specific qualitative sense of "taking heed" in the early modern period (the sixteenth and seventeenth centuries).

31. Keawe is in the realm of "imitations" and "substitutes" described by Stevenson in his early essays collected in *Virginibus Puerisque* (1881): he is at what Stevenson calls the "experimental stage" of confidence, "faith," and "hope"—that stage never "altogether quit" which is "not only the beginning but the perennial spring of our faculties." Stevenson, "Child's Play," *Virginibus Puerisque*, 94 and "Virginibus Puerisque," in *Virginibus Puerique*, 11–12.

32. Aristotle, *Nichomachean Ethics*, 5. 5. 14. According to the *Oxford English Dictionary*, the noun "bottle" itself can mean money ("a collection or a share of money").

33. This phrase is taken from Kant's *Versuch, den Begriff der negative Grössen in die Weltweisheit einzuführen in Werken in zehn Bänden*, vol. 2, 775–819. On the question of "negative" debts and "positive" credits in Kant, see Marc Shell, *Money, Language, and Thought*, 133–37. Also of relevance to the significance of the bottle in Stevenson's story is Émile Benveniste's discussion of a particular meaning of the word "debt" as derived for the Latin *debere*: "The sense of *debere* is different, although it is also translated [from Latin] by 'to owe.' One can 'owe' something without having borrowed it: for instance, one 'owes' rent for a house, although this does not involve the return of a sum borrowed. Because of its formation and construction, *debeo* should be interpreted according to the value which pertains to the prefix *de*, to wit: 'taken, withdrawn from'; hence 'to hold [*habere*] something which has been taken from [*de*] somebody" (Benveniste 148–49).

34. This may also reflect contemporary views of coin as the ground for money. Jevons, for example, says "All . . . other commercial property, mortgage deeds, preference shares and bonds, and ordinary shares, resolve themselves into more or less probability of receiving coin at future dates" (Jevons, 249).

35. Stevenson discusses a system of currency conversion that does not reach equilibrium or relative zero in his remarks on the continued use of the monetary unit of the "bit" in the American West. See his remarks on the "long" and the "short" bit in *The Works of Robert Louis Stevenson*, vol. 2, 140–42.

36. In this it brings to mind the passage at the end of "El Dorado" in which

Stevenson alludes to certain "Chimaeras" and the narratives of "aspiration" or "adventure" they instigate. See Stevenson, "El Dorado" in *Virginibus Puerisque* 72

37. Pope "Argument."

38. Also on the *Epistle to Bathurst*, see Wasserman, especially 54.

39. Pope's letter presents the classic argument against the artificial, fraudulent flights of credit and "fortune" from the landed perspective of the "virtue" of property, to use the terms studied by the historian J. G. A. Pocock. The reference to the queen in the lines just cited, according to the editor F. W. Bateson, refers to the "rumor that Queen Caroline had accepted a large present from Robert Knght, the cashier of the South Sea Company," Pope, *Epistle*, 91, note to line 78. See Pocock, *The Machiavellian Moment*, 457. "We find reason to suppose," notes Pocock elsewhere with reference to Pope, "that the Apocalyptic triumph of nonsense over language at the end of Pope's *Dunciad* had something to do with a society dominated by speculators in paper promises to repay which will never be made good before the end of time; if property is the foundation of personality, unreal property (in which nothing is owned except meaningless words) makes personalities unreal and their words meaningless," Pocock, *Virtue, Commerce and History*, 247.

40. Adam Smith, 420. Smith's cautious advocacy of credit in *The Wealth of Nations* is, of course, central to the emergence of modern political economy in Britain, a tradition whose particular way of linking economics and ethics in fact led to utilitarianism. Smith's advocacy of financial paper is thus appropriately based on the qualification that such paper be used as a means to an end, specifically as a way of "rendering a greater part of [the country's] capital active and productive than would otherwise be so." Adam Smith, 420.

41. Think of the American railway ventures of Augustus Melmotte and Hamilton K. Fischer in Trollope's *The Way We Live Now*, a sort of satire of credit; or of the quixotic hero in Dickens's *Martin Chuzzlewit* who blindly seeks his fortune in the fraudulent American company, the Eden Land Corporation.

42. On the basis of this observation, Kokua arranges secretly to purchase the bottle herself from Keawe—to sacrifice or ruin herself, she reasons, to save her husband. An act to which Keawe in turn reciprocates when he discovers his wife's plan: "His wife had given her soul for him," he concludes, "now he must give his for her" (BI 100).

43. I have explored this context more fully in "The Financial Imp" that also deals with "The Bottle Imp."

44. This link between the bottle and the home, between money and domesticity, is suggested in a passage from the influential work of the political economist, W. Stanley Jevons, Stevenson's contemporary. See Jevons, 250.

45. Dickens, *Little Dorrit*, 452.

46. For some suggestive comments on this, see Derrida, *Donner le temps*, 214–15; *Given Time*, 169–70.

47. In Stevenson's late *Ebb-Tide* (1893) bottles, like the map of Treasure Island, conceal a counterfeit—the "fraud," as it called in the novel, perpetrated on the crew (again pirates) who think they are taking a cargo of champagne but who discover it mostly to be water (see *Ebb-Tide*, 225–27). Later on in the novel, the human body is compared by Attwater to a bottle: corpses are called "empty bottles" (243). For a suggestive analysis of how Stevenson's critique of imperialism turns on the interpenetration of empire and colony, see Jolly.

48. Some of the details of the initial description of the bottle associate it with

the treasure map: not only does it provide mastery over the world (world conquerors such as Napoleon and Captain Cook are said to have held the bottle) but it is also the color of it—"white like milk" (BI 74). In addition its glass recalls the window effect of the original treasure map of "Treasure Island."

49. One thinks here of the vessel that is said to have carried another South Sea tale, Poe's "MS Found in a Bottle," away from a narrator as he is drawn magnetically to his death at the pole. The bottle is mentioned only once in the tale—in passing—and there is no additional frame narrative (a narrator who finds the bottle, an editor, etc.). Thus for the readers of the manuscript the bottle has withdrawn. "I may not find an opportunity of transmitting it to the world," Poe's narrator says of his manuscript, "but I will not fail to make the endeavour. At the last moment I will enclose the MS in a bottle, and cast it within the sea" (Poe, "MS Found in a Bottle," *Tales of Mystery and Imagination*, 286).

50. The passage with the text of the paper removed appeared in the *Illustrated London News* issue of July 2, 1892 (on page 11) with a bare-breasted Uma on the facing page.

51. Stevenson, *Letters*, 4, 182.

52. The "South Sea Letters" were serialized in *Black and White* (London), the *Sun* (New York) and in the *Auckland Star*.

53. Stevenson, *In the South Seas*, 200–201.

54. An example of this tactic is to be found in this passage from the "South Sea Letters," in which a trader's wife in church is described with her baby. "It was impossible," Stevenson observes, "not to fancy the baby was a doll, and the church some European playroom" (*In the South Seas*, 200).

55. This tendency to discover parallels between native and European beliefs is also exhibited by the "South Sea Letters." In the letters dealing with the Paumotus Islands, for example, Stevenson writes: "It is plain we have in Europe stories of a similar complexion; and the Polynesian *varua ino* or *aitu o le vao* is clearly the near kinsman of the Transylvanian vampire" (*In the South Seas*, 146).

56. The echoing of Uma's pidgin in Wiltshire's speech begins immediately after the supposedly counterfeit wedding ceremony (see BF 111).

57. Stevenson, *Letters*, vol. 5, 5.

58. Of course another allusion in "The Bottle Imp" might be to tale of Alladin and the magic lamp from another work that is at the intersection of the Occident and the Orient, *The Thousand and One Nights*. Stevenson's interest in this work is most clearly suggested by his publication of *New Arabian Nights* (in 1882) and *More New Arabian Nights* (in 1885), originally entitled *The Dynamiter*.

59. Marx also makes use of the table-turning fad in his characterization of commodity fetishism in *Capital* (*Kapital*, 50; *Capital*, 81).

60. Coleridge's "The Eolian Harp," a possible source here, also questions, rather than asserts, the belief in the animation of nature which may be a matter of "Bubbles that glitter as they rise and break/ On vain Philosophy's aye-babbling spring" (ll. 56–57). See also Shelley's "Ode to the West Wind" which treats the figure of the Aeolian harp with a pun on "lyre" (l. 57).

61. The idol of such purity in the moral realm is the subject of Stevenson's *Dr. Jekyll and Mr. Hyde*. This is what leads to Jekyll's experiment to isolate "pure evil" (85) as an indivisible and pure moral substance, a substance associated with gold in the tale. Jekyll estimates this evil substance to make up one-tenth of his "nature"(compare 32 and 84). The desire is for a nature "more express and single, than [his] imperfect and divided countenance."

62. Wiltshire, for his part, destroys the counterfeit marriage certificate (BF

134), but he does not remove it from his narrative. Uma's reaction to the destruction of the document remains a secret: "Aue!" is her exclamation ("Alas!" is the translation provided).

63. This is what Derrida calls "the phenomenon without phenomenality" in his reading of Baudelaire's "Counterfeit Money" (*Donner le temps*, 189; *Given Time*, 149).

64. "It's a cruel shame I knew no native," Wiltshire remarks earlier in the novel in a scene in which the duplicitous Case serves as his interpreter (BF 122).

65. Edmond interprets Wiltshire's concern for his children as a suggestion about the future of Polynesia that is absent from most European writing about the Pacific. "The mere presence of those mixed race children," Edmond notes, "whose future concerns their father, is striking. For all the sexual commerce across the beach in Pacific romances there are curiously few offspring. Their presence in 'The Beach of Falesea' suggests that the Pacific has a future, albeit a hybrid or creolized one" (176). Stevenson's tale, Edmond concludes, points to "a future in which neither European nor Polynesian will be quite the same" (176).

Chapter 3. Transatlantic Connections: "Paper Language" in Melville

1. "[Minor] literature finds itself positively charged with the role and function of collective, and even revolutionary, enunciation. It is literature that produces an active solidarity in spite of skepticism; and if the writer is in the margins or completely outside his or her fragile community, this situation allows the writer all the more the possibility to express another possible community and to forge the means for another consciousness and another sensibility (*de forger les moyens d'une autre conscience et d'une autre sensibilité*). . . ." (Deleuze and Guattari, *Littérature mineure*, 32; *Minor Literature*, 17).

2. Deleuze and Guattari, *Littérature mineure*, 29–32; *Minor Literature*, 16–18.

3. On the polynesian or "archipelagan" see Deleuze, *Critique et clinique*, 110, and *L'île déserte*, 16–17; on the cartographic, see Deleuze, *Foucault*, 41–51, and *Critique et clinique*, 83–88; on Americanness, see Deleuze, *Dialogues*, 47–53, and *Critique et clinique*, 75–80, 89–114.

4. The phrase *ligne de fuite* has been translated into English as "line of escape," but it can also mean a "vanishing line"—a line leading to the virtual point at which parallel lines appear to converge, for example in a painting designed on the basis of the technique of vanishing point perspective. The term *ligne de fuite* is fundamental to Deleuze's thought and so it can be found throughout his writing. An elaboration on this concept can be found in *Dialogues*, 47–56.

5. "There isn't a subject; there are only collective assemblages of enunciation (*agencements collectifs d'énonciation*), and literature expresses these acts (*agencements*) insofar as they're not imposed from without and insofar as they exist only as diabolical powers to come or revolutionary forces to be constructed" (Deleuze and Guattari, *Littérature mineure*, 33; *Minor Literature*, 18).

6. Deleuze, "Bartleby, or the Formula." Unlike the *lignes de fuite* of which Deleuze and Guattari write, these vanishing points are the traces of a medium—a mass medium—that escapes, not just individual will or intention, but also the collectivized agency that the term "collective assemblages" (*agencements collectifs*) seeks to grasp. For Deleuze and Guattari the question of "revolutionary" popular literature is fundamentally that of "minor literature": "There has been much

discussion of the questions 'What is a marginal literature?' and 'What is a popular literature, a proletarian literature?' The criteria are obviously difficult to establish if one doesn't start with a more objective concept—that of minor literature. Only the possibility of setting up a minor practice or major language from within allows one to define popular literature, marginal literature, and so on. Only in this way can literature really become a collective machine of expression and really be able to treat and develop its contents" (*Littérature mineure*, 33–34; *Minor Literature*, 18–19).

7. Deleuze and Guattari, *Littérature mineure*, 33; *Minor Literature*, 18.

8. For an overview of such perspectives on Melville, see Giles.

9. Deleuze and Guattari, *Littérature mineure*, 30, 34; *Minor Literature*, 16, 19.

10. "Paper language" is described as an "artificial language" (*d'artifice*)" (*Littérature mineure*, 16; *Minor Literature*, 30); as being "arid" (*déséché*) and marked by "impoverishment" (*pauvreté*) (Deleuze and Guattari, *Littérature mineure*, 30 and 34; *Minor Literature*, 16 and 19)

11. Deleuze and Guattari, *Littérature mineure*, 33; *Minor Literature*, 18.

12. Even the term Deleuze and Guattari substitute for the subject suggests integration and order—*agencements collectifs d'énonciation* (collective assemblages of enunciation) (*Littérature mineure*, 33; *Minor Literature*, 18), from the French *agencer*, meaning, "to order," from the Old French root *gent*, meaning "beautiful" (Larousse). Thus, as is evident from some of his earliest writings, virtuality for Deleuze always includes a moment of "integration." See, for example, Deleuze's on what he calls "global intregation" of the virtual in *Différence et répétition*, 272. On how this differs from Benjamin's theory of the virtual, see Weber, "Virtualität der Medien."

13. Deleuze and Guattari, *Littérature mineure*, 32 and 34; *Minor Literature*, 17 and 19.

14. Brod, 358–62 (letter dated June, 1921). This translation is my own. An English translation of it by Richard and Clara Winston can be found in *Franz Kafka: Letters to Friends, Family, and Editors*, 288. On "paper" German, see Wagenbach, 51. Wangenbach cites Kafka's contemporary, the language philosopher Fritz Mauthner: "The Germans in the interior of Bohemia, surrounded by a Czechoslovakian population, speak a paper German . . . it lacks the fullness of a dialect" (Wagenbach, 83; from Fritz Mauthner, *Errinerungen I—Prager Jugendjahre* [Munich, 1918], 51).

15. This preoccupation is announced, in fact, before we even get to Kafka in the way Benjamin approaches his subject in the essay—Pushkin's story of Schuwalkin is the "herald" of Kafka's work, he says. And from this perspective it is more than simply accidental that this heralding involves "*Akten*" and "*Papiere*." For, paper acts primarily as a medium, and as such it also involves, and is involved in, questions of bearing. Thus in the case of the parable from Pushkin, one could say with the utmost rigor that the messenger carries, unbeknownst to him, a token of his status as bearer—as Schuwalkin, the one who unknowingly bears his name, "Schuwalkin."

16. Kafka, 112–13, 131.

17. Kafka's admiration for Dickens and the possibility that *Bleak House* was a source for *The Trial* are the subject of a number of studies (see Tambling, 195–98; Suchoff, 136–37; and Spilke, 242). Deleuze and Guattari analyze *The Trial* as a bureaucracy (*Littérature mineure*, 79–96, 105–7; *Minor Literature*, 43–52, 57–58). Especially significant is that the bureaucratic machine's "virtual movement" as being "already real even though it is not yet in existence" (*le mouvement*

virtuel, qui est déjà réel sans être actuel) (*Littérature mineure*, 107; *Minor Literature*, 58). This corresponds to the dialectical logic we have analyzed above, what Deleuze and Guattari call "the field of immanence" (*Littérature mineure*, 96; *Minor Literature*, 52).

18. Deleuze, *Critique*, 89; *Essays*, 68.

19. Deleuze, *Critique*, 93; *Essays*, 71.

20. Deleuze, *Critique*, 92; *Essays*, 71. This "nothingness of will" (*un néant de volonté*) is what Giorgio Agamben has called "absolute potentiality": "As a scribe who has stopped writing, Bartleby is the extreme figure of the Nothing from which all creation derives; and at the same time, he constitutes the most implacable vindication of this Nothing as pure, absolute potentiality. . . . The formula that he so obstinately repeats destroys all possibility of constructing a relation between being able and willing, between *potentia absoluta* and *potentia ordinata*. It is the formula of potentiality" (Agamben, 253–55). Agamben identifies the "source" of this formula in "a text that was familiar to every cultured man of the nineteenth century: Diogenes Laertius's *Lives of Eminent Philosophers*. We are referring to the expression *ou mallon*, 'no more than,' the technical term with which the Skeptics denoted their most characteristic experience: *epokhe*, suspension" (Agamben, 256). Agamben does not consider the possibility that instead of deliberately deriving the formula from a source, Melville might simply have picked it up, as it were. We will return to this point (to Agamben's elaboration on Deleuze) later in this chapter.

21. Deleuze, *Critique*, 15; *Essays*, 4.

22. Deleuze, *Critique*, 99; *Essays*, 77.

23. Deleuze, *Critique*, 99; *Essays*, 77.

24. Deleuze, *Critique*, 99; *Essays*, 77.

25. See Deleuze, *Critique*, 76, 104–5; *Essays*, 57, 81–82. *Dialogues*, 48.

26. See Deleuze, *Critique*, 113, n. 19; *Essays*, 193, n. 25. The main source of this interpretation of American literature is English: D. H. Lawrence's *Studies in Classic American Literature*, from which all of Deleuze's writing on American letters derives (see especially the chapter entitled "The Spirit of Place" [Lawrence, 7–14].

27. Deleuze, *Critique*, 113; *Essays*, 88.

28. Deleuze, *Critique*, 106–7; *Essays*, 83–84.

29. This could be traced back through *Foucault*, 45, to *Différence et Répétition*, 269–71. This stress on integration is suggested by another example of the paper trail. The figure of the articulated skeleton and the "spinal cord" is linked figuratively to a paper cutout (emphasizing formal integrity): from the study of "minor literature" to the essay on Bartleby: "[Kafka] will abandon sense, render it no more than implicit; he will retain only the skeleton of sense, or a paper cutout (*une silhouette de papier*)" (Deleuze and Guattari, *Littérature mineure*, 37; *Minor Literature*, 21); " . . . Not a skull but the vertebral column, a spinal cord" (Deleuze, "Bartleby," 110–11; 86).

30. See Bergmann.

31. See Monteiro; Parker, "Dead Letters" and "The 'Sequel.'" On all of these possible sources, see the note on "Bartleby" in Melville, *Writings, The Piazza Tales and Other Prose Pieces, 1839–1860*.

32. See my "Losing One's Place," especially 884–85, 887–88.

33. On the remark "Poeish tale," see Melville, *Writings, Piazza Tales*, 576.

34. See Dickens's concerns about the piracy of his novels in America (in *American Notes*), see McGill, 111–40.

35. Melville, "Bartleby the Scrivener," 3.

36. For some examples of where the New World resembles the Old, see 275, 280.

37. Melville, "The Paradise of Bachelors," *Billy Budd and Other Stories*, 284.

38. William Keach's recent exposition of the contradictory discourse of the arbitrary in Locke's linguistic and political theory and his assessment of the impact of this discourse on Shelley and English Romanticism seems to call for further reflection on Melville's relationship to Locke (see especially Keach, 2–6, 26–27).

39. Melville, *Moby Dick*, 325.

Chapter 4. The Paper State: Collective Breakdown in Dickens's Bleak House

1. "By making many reproductions [reproduction technique] substitutes a mass-like (*massenweises*) existence for a unique one. And in permitting the reproduction to engage the receiver in his own particular situation, [reproduction technique] actualizes what is reproduced. These two processes lead to a violent shattering of tradition (*der Tradierten*)—a shattering of the tradition that is the obverse of the contemporary crisis and renewal of humanity. These processes are intimately connected with contemporary mass movements" (Benjamin, *Das Kunstwerk*, 13–14; "The Work of Art," *Illuminations*, 221).

2. "Deranged condition" is Carlyle's famous phrase from the paper on "Model Prisons" in his *Latter-Day Pamphlets*: "The deranged condition of our affairs is a universal topic among men at present; and the heavy miseries pressing, in their rudest shape, on the great dumb inarticulate class, and from this, by a sure law, spreading upwards, in a less palpable but not less certain and perhaps still more fatal shape on all classes to the very highest, are admitted everywhere to be great, increasing and now almost unendurable" (*Latter-Day Pamphlets*, 48). For the standard view of Carlyle's influence on Dickens, see Butt and Tillotson, 177–80. More recent, and more nuanced, interpretations of the relationship have been offered by Arac, 114–38 and Tambling, "Carlyle in Prison," 311–33.

3. Benjamin suggests this receptive character of the masses when he calls them a "matrix": "The mass is a matrix from which all traditional behavior toward works of art issues today in a new form" (*Das Kunstwerk*, 39; "The Work of Art," *Illuminations*, 239). The word "matrix" here appears in the Latin form. On the technical signification of matrix in typography, see the entry "matrix" in the *Oxford English Dictionary*.

4. The abundance of paper in *Bleak House* is reminiscent of Carlyle's "Paper Age" in *The French Revolution* and also remarks on paper in *Sartor Resartus*. Passages from the latter on Monmouth Street in London (see *Sartor Resartus*, 243) are recalled by Krook's rag and bottle shop. But Dickens's early sketch on Monmouth Street, one roughly contemporary with Carlyle's, is decidedly different, as we will see later in this chapter. For an interpretation of paper in *Our Mutual Friend* on the basis of a distinction between public and private spaces see Altick, especially 252–53. Maxwell describes the great quantities of paper in Bleak House as a representation of the outbreak of bureaucracy in mid-Victorian London (see especially 171).

5. Miller's "deconstructive" interpretation of *Bleak House*, which was originally published in 1971 (as the introduction to the Penguin edition) and which influenced a generation of critics, begins with the abundance of documents in Dickens's novel (see 84–85). On the metaphorical quality of characters in Dickens, Miller observes: "The characters to which [Dickens] gives such

emblematic names are linguistic fictions. They exist only in language" (189; see also 195).

6. For an illuminating interpretation of Krook's shop as a site of recycling in Dickens, see Ginsburg, 143–45.

7. J. Hillis Miller, 190.

8. The condition is of *Zerstreuung* in the double sense, outlined above, of distraction and dispersal suggested by Benjamin. This distracted condition is to be distinguished from what Carlyle famously called the "deranged condition" (Carlyle, *Latter-Day Pamphlets*, 48). Butt and Tillotson rather too quickly identify Dickens's perspective with that of the author of *The French Revolution* (177–79). "Derangement," as described by Carlyle, is a condition simply to be overcome, a matter of arrangement (of "putting one's house in order"), whereas "distraction" is the irreducibly dynamic condition of a social movement that repeatedly unsettles arrangements, of domestic displacements, in Dickens's fiction.

9. The force that we have been metonymically calling the hand of Nemo seems to jump across the phenomenological boundary of the "papers" as a self-consistent material support and to be transferred to the face of Lady Dedlock. It is as if the human face becomes the copy of the face of the "papers." Dickens is interested in precisely such transfers—including what happens when the reader watches Mr. Tulkinghorn trying to read the elusive meaning of Lady Dedlock's face as she moves to read the papers on the table. In such occurences Dickens may be understood to explore the human subject as a support for the singular reproduction of Nemo, as we will see later especially in the scene involving Esther's face.

10. The association of "hand" with contagion is suggested at the beginning of the novel by the description of the "groping and floundering condition which this High Court of Chancery, most pestilent of hoary sinners, holds, this day, in the sight of heaven and earth" (BH 12).

11. It is noteworthy that the contagion in question is not clearly identified. Is it smallpox, typhus, or erysipelas? See West, 30–34.

12. The sense in which the masses become a support with the industrialization of culture is made explicit in Benjamin's essay on technical reproducibility when he compares the masses' capacity to bear impressions with the typographical device of matrix (*Das Kunstwerk*, 39; "The Work of Art," *Illuminations*, 239).

13. There are in fact more than twenty entries in Mayhew's work devoted to the varieties of crossing sweeps. See Mayhew, vol. 2, 465–507. For some astute observations and distinctions on the figure of the crowd in nineteenth-century British "mass journals" of the 1830s, see Klancher, 76–97.

14. This is the distracted state of what is called "habit" in *Sketches by Boz*. See, for example, the beginning of "A Visit to Newgate": "'The force of habit' is a trite phrase in every body's mouth; and it is not a little remarkable that those who use it most as applied to others, unconsciously afford in their own persons. Singular examples of the power which habit and custom exercise over the minds of men, and of the little reflection they are apt to bestow on subjects with which every day's experience has rendered them familiar" (234). On this passage, see my *Writing in Parts*, 89–91.

15. Dickens, *Sketches by Boz*, 234

16. The word "throng" in this passage implies pressure, in the sense that a crowd is said to press. "Throng" is etymologically related to the German word *Drang*, the root of Fruedian "repression"—*Verdrängung*. The French translation of *Verdängung*—*refoulement*—evokes the crowd (*la foule*) more explicitly.

17. The senses of place are especially crucial to the initial portrayal of Lady Dedlock, one of the "representatives of her little world" (BH 21). See especially Chapter Two (BH 17–23), which closes with Mr. Tulkinghorn asking "permission to place" the papers copied by Nemo on the golden table.

18. Aesthetic receptivity is likened by Benjamin to death in the sense of the Latin phrase "to go over to the many" (*ad plures ire*). See Benjamin, "On Some Motifs in Baudelaire," *Gesammelte Schriften*, 1, 2, 638–39; *Illuminations*, 198, note 13, and also *Arcades Project* N7a,4: "The receptivity of great, much-admired works of art is an *ad plures ire*." Also see the note to the English translation of the *Arcades Project*, 990, note 22.

19. The blindness to Jo's death is emphasized by the first sentence of the next chapter that immediately follows the passage just cited (and is part of the same serial installment): "The place in Lincolnshire has shut its many eyes again" (BH 678).

20. As a material support, Jo displays the spread, mentioned earlier, of the force in question beyond the self-consistent substance paper. Nowhere is he linked explicitly with paper. This is also the case with Esther, as we will see.

21. "[Tom-all-alone's] is a black, dilapidated street, avoided by all decent people; where the crazy houses were seized upon, when their decay was far advanced. . . . Now, these tumbling tenements contain, by night, a swarm of misery. As, on the ruined human wretch, vermin parasites appear, so, these ruined shelters have bred a crowd of foul existence that crawls in and out of gaps in walls and boards. . . . Twice, lately, there has been a crash and a cloud of dust, like the springing of a mine, in Tom-all-alone's; and, each time, a house has fallen" (BH 256–57).

22. Esther is in Lukács's sense the empirical subject that at the same time recognizes the unreconcilably strange and inimical relation between the inner and outer world—a subject that is limited both to the world and to interiority (*weltbefangenes und in der Innerlichkeit beschränktes Subjekt*). Esther is, in other words, an ironic subject as described by Lukács: lacking the "cold and abstract superiority" of the satirist, her irony derives from the fact that she is forced to apply to herself what she sees of the world. By treating herself as a "free object of free irony," as Lukács says, Esther becomes a "purely receptive subject" (*rein aufnehmendes Subjekt*) (Lukács, *Theorie des Romans*, 68; *Theory of the Novel*, 75). But Lukács's irony ultimately converts the exile from meaning into the transmissible form of an experience—a conscious experience—of negativity.

23. See, for example, Dickens, "Healthy by Act of Parliament," 460–63 and "Address from an Undertaker to the Trade," 302–3.

24. The relevant passage in Hegel is: "Or, self-consciousness is only *something*, it only has *reality*, insofar as it estranges itself" (*Phänomenologie*, 363–64; *Phenomenology*, 297).

25. Significantly, at the beginning of the narrative Esther is not mirrored: as proof, presumably of her lack of cleverness, Esther tells of her youthful professions of ignorance to her doll who, as she now recalls, looked back "not so much at me, I think, as at nothing" (BH 24).

26. In confronting a veil before her reflection (in veiling herself), Esther encounters a figure closely associated with her mother whose identity is still unknown to the heroine at this point in the novel. It is Lady Dedlock who wears a veil while visiting the half-buried corpse of her former lover, Captain Hawdon ("Nemo"), in the company of Jo. Lady Dedlock is veiled in several respects in the novel. Her expression, for instance, is described as veiled—she conceals her

thoughts behind a shroud-like veil suggested by her name (Ded-lock). But this veiled expression is the sign of another veiling in the novel—namely, the false shroud figuratively placed over the baby she conceived with Captain Hawdon (Esther). Lady Dedlock had been deceived, by her sister, into believing that the baby had died at birth. When Esther sees the veil of her own hair in this passage, then, it is in fact an aspect of herself—specifically, her self-estranged relation to her mother, Lady Dedlock—that is veiled and that appears as a veil.

27. The infection comes to light at the moment in the *Phenomenology* when the merely conventional quality of the individual as a legal person (that emerged in Roman society) can no longer contain a force of spiritual self-estrangement and irony (that rises with the dissemination of the Enlightenment). The tension produced by this conflict generates the process of *Bildung*—the highly dynamic mimetic activity of self-estranged spirit as it assumes and discards conventional forms (the famous example is Diderot's *Rameau's Nephew*). Such mimetic self-estrangement, Hegel insists, is essentially linguistic in character ("This estrangement though occurs alone in language, which appears here in its essential meaning" [Hegel, *Phänomenologie*, 376; *Phenomenology*, 308]). Here is the passage in which Hegel calls this linguistic self-estrangement "an infection":

> The "I" is *this* "I"—but likewise *universal*; its appearance is at once immediately the manifestation and the disappearance of *this* "I" and thereby its remaining in its universality. The "I" that utters itself is *heard* or *perceived*; it is an infection (*Ansteckung*) in which it goes over immediately into unity with those for whom it is there and is universal self-consciousness. That it is *perceived* or *heard* means that its *existence* itself immediately fades away; this its otherness is taken back into itself; and this is its very existence: as self-conscious *Now*, as being there not to be there and as being there through this disappearance. This disappearance is thus itself its remaining; it is its own self-knowing and its self-knowing as that which has gone over into another self that has been perceived and is universal. (Hegel, *Phänomenologie*, 376; *Phenomenology*, 308–9)

28. "Infection" in the German language derives from an analogy between the transmission of contagious illness from household to household in a community and the similar spread of fire. Infection and fire are in this sense metaphorically joined in the word as modes of domestic violation. *Trübners Deutsches Worterbuch*, vol. 1, for instance, gives the following explanation: "The leaping over of smoke and flames from the burning house to the endangered neighbor yields in our language in the sixteenth century its particular image for infectious diseases." *Trübners* further notes the frequency of this usage among the German *Klassiker,* who "loved figurative formulations," citing among others, Wieland and Schiller. I have dealt with this scene more extensively in my "Losing One's Place."

29. Hegel, *Phänomenologie*, 366–67; *Phenomenology*, 300. On this purgative or cathartic force of *Geist* in Hegel, see Szondi, 323–24; and also Derrida, *Glas*, 14–31 and 262–63. The process of conversion depends, as these few comments already begin to suggest, upon a reading that adheres to the Hegelian doctrine of "the speculative sentence" (*spekulative Satz*): the doctrine dictating that "the dispersal of content" be "bound" and converted into the substance of spirit (Hegel, *Phänomenologie*, 57–62; *Phenomenology*, 36–41). Miller translates *Satz* as "proposition" rather than "sentence." The word "dispersal" translates the German "*Zerstreutheit*" (Hegel, *Phänomenologie*, 58; *Phenomenology*, 37). The binding action of the subject here is parallel to that of the state on the collective level—the political ordering of dispersed economic conditions. See the passage at the end of the *Phenomenology* (529–30) on the emergence of collective self-consciousness

out of cult society. A more extensive consideration of this point would lead to Hegel's *Philosophy of Right* (1821) and hence beyond the scope of this project. Let me be clear, however, that I am not suggesting that Hegel's concept of the state is simply "reactionary" or "totalitarian," a well-worn thesis popularized in the twentieth century by Popper in *The Open Society and Its Enemies* (1945). The critique of this reductive misreading of Hegel starts from Eric Weil, *Hegel et l'État* (1950) and Herbert Marcuse, *Reason and Revolution* (1955). For a trenchant account of the conflict over Hegel's concept of the state and a subtle exposition of the *Philosophy of Right* on this question, see Ritter, especially 7–17, 40–72, 81–84, n. 4. Particularly relevant to the connection between the logic of the *Phenomenology* that I have outlined above and Hegel's concept of the question as a highly dynamic, indeed "revolutionary," institution of social order is Ritter, 63–72. Hegel's theory of the state, Ritter concludes, has "the methodological task of rendering the historical substance of modern society valid" (69).

30. Then, Hegel explains, "no longer the predicate of a subject, content is rather substance, the essence and the concept of what is being said" (Hegel, *Phänomenologie*, 58; *Phenomenology*, 37). As reading turns into a state of self-consciousness, the speculative sentence bears the substance that allows the dispersed character of self-estrangement to enter into individual and collective experience. On the political conversion of economic dispersal, see Avineri, 147–54 and Kelly, 110–52. On substance and experience in Hegel, see, for example, Hegel, *Phänomenologie*, 38 and 58; *Phenomenology*, 21 and 37. On reading and sublation in Hegel, see Hamacher, *Pleroma*, 5–17. For some illuminating remarks on the role of reading in the arrival of the second or "knowing subject" in the position of the first or logico-grammatical subject, see Warminski, 168–69. Through speculative reading, we might say, the individual and the collective become, not merely worldly supports for spirit, but rather "spiritual substance" in the world. And the world, in turn, becomes a substantial place that can as such be integrated into experience by way of self-consciousness.

31. Hegel, *Phäomenologie*, 376; *Phenomenology*, 308.

32. Recent historically oriented approaches to domesticity in *Bleak House*, inspired mainly by Michel Foucault, that have sought to surpass the "Idealist" Hegelian logic of Lukács's account of "transcendental homelessness" have tended to overlook this shattering of place in the novel's dramatization of domestic displacement. In an influential and representative interpretation of *Bleak House*, D. A. Miller, for example, interprets homelessness in *Bleak House* and in the nineteenth-century novel generally as belonging to the disciplinary logic of "total surveillance" and, in effect, as a warning "that one hold one's place" in a home, which, he says, maintains itself "by becoming its own house of correction" (D. A. Miller, *The Novel and the Police*, 103). The source of Miller's interpretation of discipline in the novel is what Foucault calls "total surveillance." The model for "total surveillance" is of course Bentham's Panopticon, a prison design that envisions a circular prison in which fully visible inmates would think themselves under constant surveillance by unseen guards in a central watchtower. See Foucault, *Surveiller et punir*, 201–2; *Discipline and Punish*, 200–201. It is interesting, from our point of view, that Foucault describes the operation of the Panopticon on the "masses." The Panopticon converts the "masses" (*la foule, masse compacte*) (of prisoners) from a "collective effect" (*effet collectif*) into "a collection of separated individualities" (*une collection d'individualités séparées*) (Foucault, *Surveiller et punir*, 203; *Discipline and Punish*, 201). The perspective on domesticity derived by Miller from Foucault's account assumes that the domestic setting in question

is, as such, fixed and constant, and that the displacements of the subject are from one pre-existent and self-consistent place to another—from room to room, so to speak, within the great house of disciplinary power. Yet in fact, as we have seen, this is precisely *not* what happens in *Bleak House*. Fundamental to the domestic institution in Dickens's novel is that it *moves*—it is displaced and brings about a decidedly new place and a new sense of place. This important fact makes it hard to see *Bleak House* as advising that one "hold one's place." In fact, the dead end of holding one's place is made explicit in the counter-example of Lady Dedlock, who attempts unsuccessfully to avoid losing her "fashionable" place at Chesney Wold by concealing the potentially disturbing evidence of Captain Hawdon's irrepressible return; just as, in a parallel way, the Dedlock household, true to its name, seeks in vain to maintain itself as an institution by excluding altogether the sort of tremors this shocking evidence would set off. Even Richard Carstone seems to perish in the novel less by losing his place in the sophistry and deferrals of the Chancery suit than in trying to establish a firm position in its shifting discursive sand. Indeed, the emphatically written, mechanically reproduced character of the evidence in this particular case seems to raise another possibility, namely, that the institution of the home in the novel is analogous to the reading of the novel's own installments. Reading, moreover, precludes that one hold one's place since this activity requires one to keep moving: one holds one's place only when one stops reading. In this sense *Bleak House* suggests that the subject, the home, and the novel are all involved in a movement that resembles reading—an exercise in which holding a place means abruptly and repeatedly losing one.

33. Jarndyce seems to find a similar, if clearly less benevolent, kind of reward in his knowing interview with Mr. Guppy (see BH 896–97).

34. On the importance of saving face in gift exchange, see Mauss, *Sociologie*, 206; *The Gift*, 39.

35. On this point, see Derrida, *Donner la mort*, 64.

36. This is the kind of beauty supposed by Benjamin in his novel theory: "a new beauty," as he says, "in what is vanishing" (Benjamin, "The Storyteller," *Gesammelte Schriften*, 2, 2, 442; *Illuminations*, 87). The theory of the novel elaborated by Benjamin from the early notes on "Reading Novels" to "The Storyteller" responds to the call in "On the Program of the Coming Philosophy" for attention to the "dignity (*Dignität*) of experience that is ephemeral" (*Gesammelte Schriften*, vol. 2, 1, 158; *Selected Writings*, vol. 1, 100–101). D. A. Miller reduces Esther's supposition simply to signify her desire to have her beauty back: "one easily supplies what Esther keeps from saying ('even supposing I have my beauty back')" (*The Novel and the Police*, 101). Yet the gist of the passage, and of the series of incidents leading up to Esther's defacement, points toward the possibility that there may be beauty in losing beauty—the possibility explored by Benjamin's theory of the novel. Robbins argues that there is a connection between Esther's philanthropy and her loss of face, proposing that this "self-effacement" is part of an ethos of professionalism in the novel ("Telescopic Philanthropy," 153). But the process of willful self-effacement Robbins draws out of *Bleak House* depends upon a mode of subjective agency missing from the key scenes of "philanthropy" in the novel. It is this "need" of conscious subjective agency expressed by Robbins's essay that leads him to issue the demand for the very kind of "instruction" and practical wisdom—"skill or craft"—that the reader of Dickens's novel must do without (see "Telescopic Philanthropy," 157–58).

37. This moment of exposure also differs, as we have suggested, from the

fulfillment and self-fulfillment presented by the ironic consciousness of Lukács's novelist ("the conscious and emerging wisdom of the writer") (Lukács, *Théorie des romans*, 79; *Theory of the Novel*, 84).

38. "There are in our existence spots of time, / That with distinct pre-eminence retain/ A renovating virtue . . . (Wordsworth, *The Prelude*, XII, 208–210). On Dickens's admiration for Wordsworth, see Slater, 41–42.

39. The "wondering inhabitants" of London described in this passage resemble in this sense the "dreaming collective" of Benjamin's *Arcades Project* (see, for example, K1,1–K1a,2).

40. Magwitch is also of course affiliated with the popular criminal biographies of the *Newgate Calendar*. "I would sit and look at him," Pip reports, "wondering what he had done, and loading him with all the crimes in the Calendar" (GE 338).

41. See *Barnaby Rudge* (Chapters 64–65); *Oliver Twist* (Chapter 52); and *Great Expectations* (GE 260–62). On Newgate in Dickens, see Collins, *Dickens and Crime*, 27–41.

42. Benjamin, *Das Kunstwerk*, 36; "The Work of Art," *Illuminations*, 237.

43. Chesterton's essay was originally published in 1906. Benjamin cites a 1927 French translation by Achille Laurent and L. Martin-Dupont.

44. See, for example, Dickens, "The Streets—Morning," "The Streets—Night," and Shops and Their Tenants" (*Sketches by Boz*, 69–74, 74–80, 80–84) and Benjamin, *Arcades Project*, A11,3; J3,2; M11, 1; M11,2; M11,3; M11a, 1.

45. Benjamin, *Arcades Project*, M11,2–M11,3; Chesterton, 45–46.

46. It is perhaps not merely happenstance, by the way, that Benjamin takes as an example of such an infinitely divisible field the interval of a footstep: "Even if one has a general knowledge of the way people walk, one knows nothing of a person's posture during the fractional second of a stride" (*Das Kunstwerk*, 36; "The Work of Art," *Illuminations*, 237).

47. Dickens, "Night Walks," *Selected Journalism*, 73.

48. Dickens, "Night Walks," *Selected Journalism*, 73–75.

49. The passing of this shadow repeats an earlier scene in which, as in the passage just cited, the shadow appears to "tinge" the image of Estella. As Pip "followed her white hand, again the same dim suggestion that I could not possibly grasp, crossed me. My involuntary start occasioned her to lay her hand upon my arm. Instantly the ghost passed once more, and was gone" (GE 238).

50. During this visit to Newgate with Wemmick, Pip meets a counterfeiter (a "Coiner") about to be executed reminiscent of the utterers to which Dickens alludes in "Night Walks" (GE 262). This again links Magwitch to Newgate: the convict was initiated into the criminal arts by Compeyson whose "business was the swindling, handwriting forging, stolen-bank note passing and such-like" (GE 348).

51. On the connection between photography and Dickens's realism, in particular his depiction of urban space in *Bleak House*, see Armstrong, 135–43. Armstrong makes some very suggestive remarks on this connection in her discussion of Hablot K. Brown's illustrations for *Bleak House* and relates this to the way Esther's encounter with Jo and with the masses generally is an exposure to the differential space of photography (see 148–59).

52. This view is expressed by criticism from House, 159–60, to Walsh, 73–98.

53. In this sense, Pip's narrative reiterates the pattern of Magwitch's account of how he went from being a man who does nothing but "eat and drink" to becoming the "pardner" of Compeyson (GE 348).

54. See note 18.

Chapter 5. Pretending to Read: Hardy's The Mayor of Casterbridge

1. On this suggestion about "aura," see Shell, *The Economy of Literature*, 85–86. Much current discussion of aesthetic value has been concerned to approach it as a sociological question. This effort is summed up by John Guillory's proposal "to translate the (false) philosophical problem of 'aesthetic value' into the sociological problem of 'cultural capital' (Guillory, 327). The falsity of the philosophical problem, Guillory argues, lies in a relationship (a false one) between aesthetic and economic value—the identification of "use-value" with aesthetic value. Called for, in Guillory's view, is a "translation" of aesthetic use-value into the language of "cultural capital." But the relationship of aesthetics to economics that surfaces in our readings suggests another possibility, namely, that aesthetic value manifests itself in the suspension of the ongoing translation of the aesthetic medium into the figurative and thematic economy (the "cultural capital") of value metaphors. It is precisely in the suspension of, or in the withdrawal from, the metaphorical economy of such translation that the aesthetic medium may be conserved. The identification of aesthetic value with use-value, which Guillory (following Pierre Bourdieu) attributes to Kant, is no doubt a false philosophical problem. The sociological translation envisioned by Guillory and others neglects the genuine philosophical problem broached by Kant and reinterpreted by Benjamin's approach to aesthetic media. For the conservation Kant explores in his aesthetics is not that of "use-value" or "incommensurability," as is often claimed (See Guillory, 317), but of a "power of judgment" (*Urteilskraft*)—of a potentiality to judge singularly, in a manner that is universal and at the same time not reducible to the application of concepts or forms. This neglect can in large part be traced to a reliance on the reductive account of Kant's aesthetics offered by Bourdieu, mainly in his book, *Distinction*. Opting to regard aesthetics as a matter of sociologically pre-determined categories of "consumption" and "taste," however, involves ignoring Kant's most enduring contribution to the modern discourse of value, namely a theory of conservation based on divisibility rather than self-consistency. For all of the obvious differences between the two, economic thought leading up to Neoclassical economics in the later nineteenth century and aesthetic theory in the aftermath of Romanticism are fundamentally, if indirectly, elaborations of a stress on potentiality in Kant's natural and aesthetic philosophy. In the chapter "The Discourse of Value: From Adam Smith to Barbara Herrnstein Smith" Guillory devotes only one footnote to the Neoclassical theory of exchange that for nearly all economic historians, including those who disagree with it, offered a very different theory of value from the one handed down by Adam Smith (380, note 27). On the importance of the Kantian treatment of potential in nineteenth-century natural philosophy and then economics, see Georgescu-Roeggen; Mirowski; Hesse. Recent criticism stressing the link between aesthetic value and economic value has neglected this theoretical thrust of Neoclassical economics in a way that is parallel to its neglect of divisibility and potentiality in aesthetics—by assuming immediately a sociological perspective. Guillory, for example, dismisses Neoclassicism as irrelevant on the basis of the (utilitarian) argument by Robert Heilbroner that "few economists actually use utility analysis as a serious means of resolving the value problematic" (Guillory, 380, note 27; Guillory's citation is from Robert Heilbroner, *Behind the Veil of Economics: Essays in the Worldly*).

2. On this passage, see Chapter 3. I have dealt with this scene more extensively, but by no means exhaustively, in my "Coming of Paper." From another

perspective, Irving Howe has described evocatively the gestural aspect of Hardy's fiction and of the opening scene in *The Mayor of Casterbridge* (see Howe, 20–21, 84–92).

3. For paradigmatic statements of this view, see Goux, 19–21, Michaels and Vernon, 7–8.

4. Benjamin, "Franz Kafka," *Gesammelte Schriften*, vol. 2, 2, 418; "Franz Kafka," *Illuminations*, 120.

5. Evidently, the source for the wife sale was an account Hardy read in the *Brighton Gazette* for May 25, 1826 (see Winfield, 226). Such events were often the subject, however, of ballad sheets like the one Henchard is "reading, or pretending to read."

6. The two meanings of "rivet" are given by the *Oxford English Dictionary*, see the third substantive and second verbal significations, respectively.

7. Ruskin, *The Works of John Ruskin*, vol. 9, 14. On Hardy's borrowing from *The Stones of Venice* in *The Dynasts*, see Swann, 187–88.

8. It should be noted, however, that as is often the case with Ruskin, and as we saw above, this statement from the "Preface" to *The Stones of Venice* is not without nuances: the interstitial rivets are, after all, what "secures stones" and Ruskin does devote some interesting remarks to them later in this volume (see 87 and 95) as well as in *The Seven Lamps of Architecture, Works*, vol. 8, 66.

9. Ruskin, *The Seven Lamps of Architecture, Works*, vol. 8, 66. Ruskin bemoans the rise of iron in English construction, a development that, he says, "has changed our merry England into the Man in the Iron Mask" (66). "True architecture," he goes on, "does not admit iron as a constructive material, and . . . such works as the cast-iron central spire of the Rouen Cathedral, or the iron roofs and pillars of our railway stations, and of some of our churches, are not architecture at all (67). It is precisely this phantasmal questionability of iron, "the magic of cast iron," that Benjamin seeks to unfold in his late *Arcades Project*. It was the sight of enormous constructions in iron, a merely "functional and transitory" material, like paper, that led Parisian observers to wonder fearfully at an iron tower made of "two and a half million rivets"—the Eiffel Tower (see *Arcades Project*, F 1,1, F 1,7, F 2,9 , F 3a,4, F 4a, 2). On the conflicting conservation principles in the aesthetic theories of Ruskin, Proust and Benjamin, see my "The Coming of Paper."

10. Hardy, *Jude the Obscure*, 107. Of Sue Bridehead we are told: "There was nothing statuesque in her; all was nervous motion" (*Jude the Obscure*, 73). Jude's inscription of "thither" on the stone is described on 61; for examples of other inscriptions in the novel see 30, 254, 308.

11. Hardy, *Jude the Obscure*, 107.

12. Hardy, *The Return of the Native*, 194, 225. On "waste tablet," see the comments in Chapter 1 on the figure of "waste paper" in Ebeneezer's Cooke's "Sotweed Redivivus."

13. Hardy, *The Return of the Native*, 225.

14. Hardy, *The Return of the Native*, 53. The motif of the face in this novel and in *The Mayor of Casterbridge* may be connected to Hardy's reading of Walt Whitman's "Crossing Brooklyn Ferry," which is explicitly cited in *Tess of the D'Urbervilles* (213). Partly drawing on the traditional image of the page as a face, Whitman's poem, like Hardy's *The Mayor of Casterbridge*, also deals with paper as a medium of aesthetic exchange.

15. Hardy, *Tess of the D'Urbervilles: A Pure Woman*, 483.

16. Alfred Lord Tennyson, "Tithonus," lines 69–71.

17. The title of the second chapter of *The Return of the Native* is "Humanity

Appears on the Scene, Hand in Hand with Trouble." The first chapter is called "A Face on Which Time Makes But Little Impression."

18. The word "bossy" connotes both stone and paper, according to the *Oxford English Dictionary.*

19. "[The third picture or image (*Bild*)] was, however, not similar [*nicht ähnlich*], it was much more completely the same heathscape [*die völlig gleiche Heidelandschaft*]," Kafka, *Der Prozess,* 140; *The Trial,* 163 (translation modified). The paintings or images of the heathscape are linked to the image of paper in *The Trial,* which I have explicated in my "The Coming of Paper."

20. It should be noted that an effect similar to the one we have been tracing can be discerned in paper as a metaphor for Clym's face. Although we glossed over it earlier, Clym's countenance is called, as we saw, not a "waste paper," as it might have been, but a "waste tablet." Thus, instead of being unambiguously joined to the figure of paper in Clym's simile, "waste"—in this case the evanescent marking of commercial transactions on a sheet before they are carried over into the more permanent, but again somewhat dubiously named, "journal"—is paired with "tablet," a term that more commonly denotes "a small, flat, and comparatively thin piece of stone, metal, wood, ivory, or other hard material" (*Oxford English Dictionary*). This complication is supported by the fact that Clym's paper physiognomy is said to contain the "substance" of the heath: "He walked along towards home without attending to paths. If anyone knew the heath well it was Clym. He was permeated with its scenes, with its substance, and with its odours. He might be said to be its product" (RN 231).

21. The precise division between quantity of gold and paper was underscored in Hardy's revision for the Wessex edition of 1912. Earlier versions had one five-pound bank note with five coins.

22. A useful sample of the criticism dealing with the question of tragedy in the novel is provided by Wolfreys in his collection of essays on *The Mayor of Casterbridge: Contemporary Critical Essays,* 203–4. Recent examples of critics interested in the contrast between tragedy and novel in this context are Moses, 29–66 and Musselwhite, 50–88.

23. On the complicated modernity of *The Mayor of Casterbridge,* see Meisel, 22–36.

24. "Character," *Oxford English Dictionary.*

25. Examples of critics who see Hardy as trying to adapt tragedy to the modern world of his novels are Moses, who argues that he fails to do so (see 31–32 and 55–60), Chapman, who claims that with Hardy "tragedy becomes psychological rather than social" (152). King offers a slightly different version of the latter thesis (see 103, for instance). Lothe notes the importance of the word "character" in the title of *The Mayor of Casterbridge* as an allusion to Aristotle's theory of tragic *ethos* (119–20), but, like the other critics mentioned, neglects the other signification of the word and thus also the conflict that is, as I am arguing, fundamental to the novel.

26. See Martin Seymour-Smith's note 188 in the Penguin edition (428).

27. Hardy reports that a visit with Butcher brought his old Greek tutor, Moule, to mind. See Hardy, *The Life,* 369.

28. S. H. Butcher, *Aristotle's Theory of Poetry and Fine Art, with a Critical Text and Translation of The Poetics* (first edition published in 1895), 355.

29. Epstein, 51.

30. It is worth noting how the name "Elizabeth-Jane" confuses metallic and promissory money. "Elizabeth" derives from the Hebrew "Elisheba," which means

"to whom God is the oath" (*Webster's New Universal Unabridged Dictionary*, 2nd ed.); at the same time, an "Elizabeth" is a "coin of Queen Elizabeth" (*Oxford English Dictionary*). "Jane," on the other hand, is also the name of "a small silver coin of Genoa introduced into England towards the end of the 14th century" (*Oxford English Dictionary*). "Susan" means lily (*Oxford English Dictionary*). The name may allude to lilies as the "sceptres of queens" and represent the power of women (see Ruskin, "Of Queens' Gardens"); or it may recall the "lilies of the field" in Matthew's teaching about the need for faith that follows on his delaration that "You cannot serve God and mammon" (see Matthew 6.24–33).

31. These Hebrew words may be verbs meaning "to number," "to weigh," and "to divide." But the first two are also units of monetary currency: the mina and the shekel (one mina is equal to sixty shekels). See the gloss on these lines in *The New Oxford Annotated English Bible, with the Apocrypha, Expanded Edition*, 1076. See also in the same edition "Measures and Weights in the Bible," 1547.

32. The digraphism that informs the naturalization at issue in this passage is marked in a sense by the exclamation "Begad!"—a "gad" being either a metal bar used for measuring land or a stylus. Thus Henchard's ongoing translation of the "confused picture" returning here comes to a halt with an outburst that also restates, in a congealed form, the conventional digraphic opposition. It should be emphasized that what Henchard overlooks when he turns away from the possibility introduced by the exclamation "Begad!" cannot simply be called writing, say, in the thematic sense that he fails to see that his relationship to Elizabeth-Jane is contractual—a matter of writing, as it were, as opposed to blood. Contractual kinship is hardly presented in the novel as the unambiguously "correct" interpretation that eludes Henchard: it is not clear, for example, that the second Elizabeth-Jane, or for that matter her mother, are contractually bound to Henchard. On the contrary, the novel works to maintain this very ambiguity. In his interview with Elizabeth-Jane Henchard does not overlook the fact that he is bound to her by the modern, civilized institutions of writing—metaphorically speaking, that he is her kin on paper—but rather the very aspect of the medium naturalized by the alternating figures of kinship that mediate, in this case, Elizabeth-Jane's face as a sign of debt: the "something" about which "there could be little doubt."

33. The events at Weydon Fair are indeed at one point called a "tragical crisis" (TMC 91).

34. Henchard's attempts to make linear sense of his experience starts just after the chaos of the novel's opening day. In order to "get out of" the day's "confused picture," Henchard decisively shapes the scattered impressions that made up the experience into a linear pattern: "we walked here, and had the furmity, . . . and sold her." On the basis of this ordering of events, Henchard orients himself: "Yes, that's what happened," he insists, "and here I am." But the confusion of the picture keeps returning in the novel to scramble this outline, refusing Henchard a settled perspective from which to view the event as a fixed, unified object. In Kantian terms he is subject to the conceptual "perplexity" or "embarrassment" that constitutes aesthetic judgment: he is able to make the occurrence into a "perceptual" but not a "conceptual" unity. And, though we may not know it, at the moment we first read this passage from the beginning of the second chapter of the novel, we are in a situation not entirely unlike that of Henchard. We too are kept from getting completely out of the "confused picture" that, as we discover, is diffused across the rest of the novel. To the extent that the "confused" character of the "picture" keeps us in it—more precisely,

keeps us returning to it, for how can one be truly "in" such a confused picture—we remain riveted to the scene in a manner somewhat resembling that of Henchard.

35. Henchard's double-take here is of course a repetition of the scene involving Elizabeth-Jane's face and the wall of his house. In it the protagonist learns what the readers might well have suspected: as Susan artfully puts it in the letter, "Elizabeth-Jane is not your Elizabeth-Jane" (TMC 196). The clearest indication comes in an earlier passage, yet another repetition, in which as Henchard notes an "altered" color in Elizabeth-Jane's hair, the readers are told ominously that an "uneasy expression came out on [Susan's] face, to which the future held the key" (TMC 159). At this point the reader may know what Henchard does not. In that case we would have what is sometimes called dramatic irony, a discrepancy between the knowledge of the protagonist and the spectator of traditional tragedy. The readers, like the spectators of tragedy, under these circumstances know the truth of a moment to which, from the perspective of the protagonist, the future holds the key. But this tragic scenario depends upon the readers' pretense to knowledge about the true nature of Henchard's relation to Elizabeth-Jane, which is precisely what the novel seeks to withhold. The readers in this sense repeat Henchard's reenactment of tragic failure. There is no clear-cut sense of dramatic irony.

36. Vicinus, 7. Reproductions of early nineteenth-century ballad sheets can be found in the following: *Broadside Ballads of the 18th and Early 19th Centuries* (selected by J. Stevens Cox), Shepard, *John Pitts*, 99–121, and Shepard, *The Broadside Ballad*, 144–52.

37. See "Broadside," *Oxford English Dictionary*, sense 3.

38. Shepard, *The Broadside Ballad*, 33.

39. "Ballad," *Oxford English Dictionary*, sense 3. See also Shepard, *The Broadside Ballad*, 51–52.

40. Mayhew, vol. 1, 227. See also Shepard, *John Pitts*, 62–63.

41. Vicinus, 12.

42. On this revival, see Shepard, *John Pitts*, 33–80.

43. "So the broadside ballad was born, in a period of social upheaval [the sixteenth century] with religion and politics as its main preoccupations, with the ecclesiastical edict and the royal proclamation as its immediate ancestors. Soon the range of subject-matter rapidly expanded to include marvellous signs and wonders, monstrous births, merry love songs, and all the gossip of the day. The popularity of the new street ballads coincided with the steady decline of the traditional and professional minstrel, and by the period of Elizabeth I, minstrels had become legally ranked with rogues, vagabonds, and beggars. The printed balladsheet must have contributed largely to the downfall of ancient traditional balladry in favour of new popular street songs. Who would pay a minstrel to sing long old-fashioned ballads of far-off times when you could buy a smart up-to-date broadside for one penny?" (Shepard, *The Broadside Ballad*, 51). Shepard's plates illustrate well the continuity of subject from the early broadside ballads through the street ballad sheets of the first half of the nineteenth century to today's sensationalist tabloids.

44. Shepard observes about ballad sheets as proto-newspapers: "the broadside ballad-sheets on crimes and topical events paved the way for the cheap newspapers. In 1855 the Newspaper Tax was removed, and six years later the paper duty. In the late 1850s penny; and halfpenny newspapers began to appear" (*John Pitts*, 83). Mayhew provides sales figures from 1837 to 1849, reporting that two

and a half million copies of some broadside ballads were printed in 1849, specifically those dealing with the murderers, J. B. Rush and Mr. and Mrs. Manning (Mayhew, 308).

45. William Wordsworth, "Preface to Lyrical Ballads," 410–11. It would be worth approaching Baudelaire's poetry within the context of this revival in "street literature." Indeed the poem explicated by Derrida, to which we referred above— "La fausse monnaie" ["The Counterfeit Coin"]—recalls a street ballad entitled "Counterfeit Halfpence," in which the ballad is compared to money. This ballad is cited in "Introduction" to *Later English Broadsides and Ballads*, 2.

46. On Hardy's collection of ballads, see Jackson-Houlston, 141–47. Jackson-Houlston reprints Hardy's collection of "Country Songs of 1820s Onwards" (182–93). Though Jackson-Houlston finds in it too much "generalization" (141) about ballads, Thom Gunn (19–46) convincingly shows how indebted—formally, stylistically, and thematically—Hardy's poetry is to the ballad.

47. The ballad sheet, entitled "Sale of a Wife," that appears as Figure 7 is from John Ashton's 1888 *Modern Street Ballads*. In this ballad, as in *The Mayor of Casterbridge*, the buyer is a sailor and the "public" considers the auction a "joke" (Ashton, 1 and 3; *The Mayor*, 78). In another ballad dealing with a wife auction, "Smithfield Wife," a sweep pays one pound, five shillings (a reproduction of the original can be found in *Broadside Ballads of the 18th and Early 19th Centuries*, n.p.).

48. Here is an overview of the senses given by the *Oxford English Dictionary* for the verb form of "pretend": "I. 1. trans. to stretch, extend, or hold (something) before, in front of, or over a person or thing (e.g. as a covering or defense) Obs. . . . 2. To bring or put forward, set forth, hold out, offer for action, consideration, or acceptance . . . 3. a. *refl.* To put oneself forward in some character; to profess or claim . . . b. Without reflexive pronoun, in same sense as a; gradually passing into one closely akin to 7: To put forth an assertion or statement . . . about oneself; now usually implying mere pretension with out foundation: to feign *to be* or *do* something (A leading modern sense) . . . 4. *trans.* To give oneself out as having (something); to profess to have, make professor of, profess (a quality, etc.). Now always in a bad sense: To profess falsely, to feign (some quality) . . . 8. To intend, purpose, design, plan. *Obs.* . . . 9. To aspire to; to take upon one, to undertake; to venture, presume; to attempt, endeavour, try. . . ."

49. Perhaps, then, Henchard "pretends to read" the ballad sheet also in the obsolete sense given as the first meaning in the *Oxford English Dictionary*: "to stretch, extend, or hold (something) before, in front of, or over a person or thing (e.g. as a covering or defence)." Perhaps, in other words, what Henchard "kept before his eyes with some difficulty" (TMC 69) is a material support that cannot be held up as a stable support for reading. Pretending would be obsolescent in this sense as well. The outmoded sense of the word describes a practice in decline—Henchard pretends to act as though he were not precluded from holding before his eyes the true character of what occurs to him. The ballad sheet that appears on the opening pages of *The Mayor of Casterbridge* is also obsolete, but it does not simply pass away after passing before the eyes of the readers of Hardy's novel. There is evidence that Hardy considered the ballad form obsolete. See Hardy, *The Life*, 20 and also Jackson-Houlston, 144.

50. The distinctions in this scene parallel closely those sketched by Benjamin I "The Storyteller": "What was really peculiar, however, in this couple's progress, and would have attracted the attention of any casual observer otherwise disposed to overlook them, was the perfect silence they preserved. They walked side by side in such a way as to suggest afar off the low, confidential chat of people

full of reciprocity; but on closer view it could be discerned that the man was reading, or pretending to read, a ballad sheet which he kept before his eyes with some difficulty by the hand that was passed through the basket strap" (TMC 69). The difference between communication on the heath and in the cultivated world of cities is represented here as a contrast between the "low, confidential chat of people full of reciprocity" and the reading of a ballad sheet. Paper is contrasted with oral communication, the mute solitude of the modern reader with the open reciprocity of a more traditional orality—perhaps even, it is tempting to say, the novel with storytelling, to invoke the terms of Benjamin's "The Storyteller" (Benjamin, "Der Erzähler," *Gesammelte Schriften*, vol. 2, 2, 442; "The Storyteller," *Illuminations*, 87). As we have seen, the historical background of the ballad sheet encourages this association of paper with the novel, in particular with *The Mayor of Casterbridge*. But it also begins to dissolve the opposition between paper and orality as modes of communication.

51. Wright, *Hardy and His Readers*, 146. In America, *The Mayor of Casterbridge* was simultaneously serialized in *Harper's Weekly*.

52. Wright provides an instructive description of Hardy's interest in contemporary debates about character in novels and in tragedy, arguing that in *The Mayor of Casterbridge* what "had begun as a straightforward melodrama, full of 'graphic' incidents, seems to have developed in the course of writing, partly as a result of Hardy's reading of high-brow debates about the novel, into a fully fledged tragedy" (160). Yet much of the material found in Wright's chapter on the novel points to an interpretation of *The Mayor of Casterbridge* as a work in which tragedy dissolves into melodrama.

Afterword: The Novel Collective

1. See Benjamin, "Der Erzähler," *Gesammelte Schriften*, vol. 2, 2, 442–43; "The Storyteller," *Illuminations*, 87.

2. Benjamin, *The Arcades Project*, 463 (N3,1).

3. This "solitude" (*Einsamkeit*) of the reader is the determining condition of the novel for Benjamin ("Der Erzähler," *Gesammelte Schriften*, vol. 2, 2, 443; "The Storyteller," *Illuminations*, 87. On this "solitude" and on the "perplexity" (*Ratlosigkeit*) of the novel reader, see Weber, "Reading—'To the Very End of the World,'" 822–23.

4. Biographical form provides the "bad infinity" of the novel with "boundaries." This infinity is presented in Lukács's text as a "mass" (*Masse*) of individual lived experiences (*Erlebnisse*) and as a "mass" of isolated living individuals (*isolierte Menschen*) (Lukacs, *Theorie des Romans*, 76; *Theory of the Novel*, 81).

5. The contrast between Benjamin's novel theory and that of Lukács is paralleled by their respective approaches to tragedy. Here again there is divergence in spite of the fact that Benjamin cites Lukács to support his own position (see Benjamin, *Ursprung des deutschen Trauerspiels*, 82, 112; *Origin of German Tragic Drama*, 102, 131 and compare to Lukács, "The Metaphysik der Tragödie," *Die Seele und die Formen*, 248–49, 237–38; "The Metaphysics of Tragedy," *Soul and Form*, 173, 165).

6. The link between the novel and barbarism is made by the overlap between Benjamin's essay "Experience and Poverty" that was published in 1933 and "The Storyteller" that appeared in 1936. The latter essay drew on fragments and drafts going back to 1928, among these a piece entitled "Novel Reading" (*Roman lesen*)

that Benjamin described as a "new theory of the novel" in a letter to Scholem (see *Briefe*, 482). On this point, see Tiedemann's notes in Benjamin, *Gesammelte Schriften*, vol. 2, 3, 1276–77. The most explicit connection between the essays on barbarism and the novel is the thesis on the poverty of experience which appears, almost verbatim, in both: see "Erfahrung und Armut," *Gesammelte Schriften*, vol. 2, 1, 214; "Experience and Poverty," *Selected Writings*, vol. 2, 731–32; "Der Erzähler," *Gesammelte Schriften*, vol. 2, 2, 439; "The Storyteller," *Illuminations*, 84.

7. This is what Benjamin calls the "zero point" (*Nullpunkt*) of experience in an early essay. See Benjamin, "Über das Programm der kommenden Philosophie," *Gesammelte Schriften*, vol. 2, 1, 159; "On the Program of the Coming Philosophy," *Selected Writings*, vol. 1, 101.

8. With respect to the "dialectical reflection" of the novelist, Lukács writes of the "empty space (*leerer Raum*) of the distance between [idea and reality] that would have to be filled by the author's consciousness and wisdom" (*der bewußten und hervortretenden Weisheit des Dichters augefüllt werden müßte*) (Lukács, *Theorie des Romans*, 79; *Theory of the Novel*, 84). This same logic leads to the passage later in this section of the essay in which Lukács alludes to Nicholas of Cusa's teachings on *docta ignorantia*—"the certainty . . . that through not-desiring-to-know and not-being-able-to-know [the writer] has truly encountered, glimpsed and grasped (*erblickt und ergriffen*), the ultimate, true substance, the present, non-existent God" (Lukács, *Theorie des Romans*, 88; *Theory of the Novel*, 90). On Nicholas of Cusa's concept of *docta ignorantia*, see Winkler, 32–54; Flasch, 97–120; and Blumenberg, 34–108 (especially 105–8). Benjamin's theory of the novel is in keeping with Lukács on the issue of the gap between life and meaning, as suggested by the citation *The Theory of the Novel* in "The Storyteller." But Benjamin's novel theory extends his critique of the Kantian concept of experience, from early essays such as "On the Program of the Coming Philosophy" through "Experience and Poverty." The reinterpretation of experience on the basis of linguistic mediacy leads Benjamin to propose an approach to the novel that is not bound to the phenomenological theory of consciousness and intentionality that ultimately oversees Lukács's interpretation of the genre, in spite of the theory of irony. Thus Benjamin considers mystified the conventional perspective from which novel reading is seen to involve "empathy" (*Einfühlung*), and pursues parallels with practices that do not fall under the purview of consciousness, such as eating (see Benjamin's "Reading Novels," *Selected Writings*, vol. 2, 728–29; *Gesammelte Schriften*, vol. 4, 1, 436 and his fragments on novel reading and eating, *Gesammelte Schriften*, vol. 4, 2, 1014). It is in this sense that Melville may be understood to link eating and copying in "Bartleby." On Benjamin's application of the term language to a sphere "beyond the regions circumscribed by human intentionality," see Fenves, *Arresting Language*, 200–5. On the potentially disrupting influence of irony in Lukács's theory of the novel and on the manner in which it is reigned in by a more traditional phenomenological view of intentionality and temporality, see de Man, "Lukács's *Theory of the Novel*," *Blindness and Insight*, 56–59.

9. Without "meaning" (*Sinn*), Lukács says, the "reality" (*Wirklichkeit*) of the novelist "would disintegrate into the nothingness of inessentiality (*ins Nichts der Wesenlosigkeit zerfallen würde*) (Lukács, *Theorie des Romans*, 84; *Theory of the Novel*, 88). Such disintegration, which is unbearable from the perspective of Lukács's novelistic subject, is the senseless bearing suggested by Benjamin's remarks on novel reading.

10. For some illuminating comments on Parry's painting, see Curtis, 63–67.

11. Benjamin, *Arcades Project*, S2,1. See also, for example, *Arcades Project*, M1a,3,

M2,4. The transportation to the streets of London of Vesuvius—in particular the deadliness of an eruption that aesthetically freezes everyday social life—corresponds to what Benjamin describes in a quotation from Hugo von Hofmannsthal as the power to "transport ourselves into even the purest of all regions— into death" (*Arcades Project*, S2,2). This comment points to a parallel between the everyday conditions of modernity and a certain aesthetic tendency the novel shares with the mass media.

Selected Bibliography

Adickes, Eric. *Kants Lehre von der doppelten Affektion unseres Ich als Schlussel zu seiner Erkenntnistheorie.* Tübingen: Mohr, 1929.

Agamben, Giorgio. *Bartleby ou la création.* Trans. Carole Walter. Saulxures: Circé, 1995.

Aglietta, Michel and André Orléan. *La violence de la monnaie.* Paris: Presses Universitaires de France, 1982.

Altick, Richard. "Education, Print, and Paper in *Our Mutual Friend.*" In *Nineteenth-Century Literary Perspectives,* ed. Claude de L. Ryals, 237–54. Durham, N.C.: Duke University Press, 1974.

André, Louis. *Machine à papier: innovations et transformations de l'industrie papetière en France 1798–1860.* Paris: Editions de l'EHESS, 1996.

———. "Au berceau de la mécanistion papetière: la papetrie d'Essonnes des Didot à Robert." In *Les trois révolution du livre,* ed. Alain Mercier, 277–82. Paris: Imprimerie Nationale, 2002.

Arac, Jonathan. *Commissioned Spirits: The Shaping of Social Motion in Dickens, Carlyle, Melville, and Hawthorne.* New Brunswick, N.J.: Rutgers University Press, 1979.

Aristotle. *De Anima.* Trans. R. D. Hicks. Cambridge: Cambridge University Press, 1907.

Armstrong, Nancy. *Fiction in the Age of Photography: The Legacy of British Realism.* Cambridge, Mass.: Harvard University Press, 1999.

Arnold, Matthew. *Poetry and Criticism.* Boston: Houghton Mifflin, 1961.

Ashton, John. *Modern Street Ballads.* London: Chatto and Windus Piccadilly, 1888.

Assmann, Jan. *Moses der Ägypter: Entzifferung einer Gedächtnisspur.* Munich: Carl Hanser, 1998.

———. *Moses the Egyptian: The Memory of Egypt in Western Monotheism.* Cambridge, Mass.: Harvard University Press, 1997.

———. "Schrift, Tod und Identität: Das Grab als Vorschule der Literatur im alten Ägypten." *Schrift und Gedächtnis,* 64–71. Munich: Fink, 1983.

———. "Stein und Zeit: Das 'monumentale' Gedächtnis der altägyptischen Kultur." In *Kultur und Gedächtnis,* ed. Jan Assmann and Tonio Hölscher, 87–114. Frankfurt am Main: Suhrkamp, 1988.

———. *Stein und Zeit: Mensch und Gesellschaft im alten Ägypten.* Munich: Wilhelm Fink, 1991.

Avineri, Shlomo. *Hegel's Theory of the Modern State.* London: Cambridge University Press, 1972.

Bacon, Francis. *The Advancement of Learning. The Works of Francis Bacon*, vol. 3. Stuttgart: Friedrich Frommann, 1963.

Behrens, Kathryn L. *Paper Money in Maryland: 1727–1789.* Baltimore: Johns Hopkins University Press, 1923.

Benjamin, Walter. *The Arcades Project.* Trans. Howard Eiland and Kevin McLaughlin. Cambridge, Mass.: Harvard University Press, 1999.

———. *Der Begriff der Kunstkritik in der deutschen Romantik.* Frankfurt am Main: Surhkamp, 1973.

———. *The Correspondence of Walter Benjamin.* Trans. Manfred R. Jacobson and Evelyn M. Jacobson. Chicago: University of Chicago Press, 1994.

———. *Gesammelte Schriften.* 7 vols. Frankfurt am Main: Suhrkamp, 1972–89.

———. *Illuminations: Essays and Reflections.* Trans. Harry Zohn. New York: Schocken, 1978.

———. *Das Kunstwerk im Zeitalter seiner technischen Reproduzierbarkeit.* Suhrkamp: Frankfurt am Main, 1966.

———. *The Origin of German Tragic Drama.* Trans. John Osborne. London: Verso, 1985.

———. *Das Passagen-Werk.* 2 vols. Frankfurt am Main: Suhrkamp, 1982.

———. *Selected Writings.* 4 vols. Cambridge, Mass.: Harvard University Press, 1996–2003.

———. *Ursprung des deutschen Trauerspiels.* Frankfurt am Main: Suhrkamp, 1974.

Benjamin, Walter and Gerschom Scholem. *Briefwechsel 1933–1940.* Frankfurt am Main: Suhrkamp, 1980.

Bennett, Jonathan. "Locke's Philosophy of Mind." In *Cambridge Companion to Locke*, ed. Vere Chappell, 89–114. Cambridge: Cambridge University Press, 1994.

Bensmaia, Réda. "The Kafka Effect." In *Kafka: Toward a Minor Literature*, ed. Gilles Deleuze and Félix Guattari, trans. Terry Cochran, ix–xxi. Minneapolis: University of Minnesota Press, 1986.

Bentham, Jeremy. *Deontology, A Table of the Springs of Action, and The Article on Utilitarianism.* Ed. Amnon Goldworth. Oxford: Oxford University Press, 1983.

Benveniste, Émile. *Indo-European Language and Society.* Trans. Elizabeth Palmer. Miami: University of Miami Press, 1973.

Bergmann, Johannes Dietrich. "'Bartleby' and *The Lawyer's Story*." *American Literature* 47 (November 1975): 432–36.

Biasi, Pierre-Marc de. *Le papier: une aventure au quotidien.* Paris: Gallimard, 1999.

Birkerts, Sven. *The Gutenberg Elegies.* Boston: Faber and Faber, 1994.

Bloom, Murray Teigh. *Money of the Their Own: The Great Counterfeiters.* New York: Charles Scribner's Sons, 1957.

Blum, André. *On the Origin of Paper.* Trans. Harry Miller Lydenberg. New York: R.R. Bowker, 1934.

Blumenberg, Hans. *Aspekte der Epochen schwelle: Cusaner und Nolaner.* Erweiterte und überarbeitete Neuausgabe von "Legitimität der Neuzeit," vierter Teil. Frankfurt am Main: Suhrkamp, 1976.

Bofarull y Sans, Don Francisco de. *Animals in Watermarks.* Hilversum, Holland: Paper Publications Society, 1959.

Bouchary, Jean. *Les faux-monnayeurs sous la révolution française.* Paris: Marcel Rivière et Cie, 1946.

Bourdieu, Pierre. *La distinction: critique sociale du jugement.* Paris: Minuit, 1979.

Brantlinger, Patrick. *The Reading Lesson: The Threat of Mass Literacy in Nineteenth-Century British Fiction.* Bloomington: Indiana University Press, 1998.

Breck, Samuel. *Historical Sketch of Continental Paper Money*. Philadelphia: John C. Clark, 1843.

Briquet, C. M. *Les filigranes: dictionnaire historique des marques du papier.* Vol. 4. Facsimile of the 1907 edition. Amsterdam: Paper Publications Society, 1968.

Brod, Max and Franz Kafka, *Eine Freundschaft: Briefwechsel.* Frankfurt am Main: Fischer, 1989.

Brodsky Lacour, Claudia. *Lines of Thought: Discourse, Architectonics, and the Origin of Modern Philosophy*. Durham, N.C.: Duke University Press, 1996.

Brunschvicg, Léon. *Les étapes de la philosophie mathématique*. Paris: Félix Alcan, 1912.

Buci-Glucksman, Christine. *La folie du voir: une esthétique du virtuel*. Paris: Galilée, 2002.

Bullock, Charles J. *Essays on the Monetary History of the United States*. London: Macmillan, 1900.

Bulwer-Lytton, Edward. *England and the English*. New York: George Routledge and Sons, 1874.

Burke, Edmund. *Reflections on the Revolution in France*. New York: Penguin, 1986.

Butcher, S. H. *Aristotle's Theory of Poetry and Fine Art, with a Critical Text and Translation of The Poetics*. 4th ed. London: Macmillan, 1932.

Butt, John and Kathleen Tillotson. *Dickens at Work*. London: Methuen, 1957.

Canetti, Elias. *Crowds and Power*. Trans. Carol Stewart. New York: Seabury Press, 1978.

Cantor, G. N. and M. J. S. Hodge. "Introduction: Major Themes in the Development of Ether Theories from the Ancients to 1900." In *Conceptions of the Ether: Studies in the History of Ether Theories, 1740–1900*, ed. G. N. Cantor and M. J. S. Hodge, 1–60. Cambridge: Cambridge University Press, 1981.

Cantor, Geoffrey, David Gooding, and Frank A. J. L. James. *Michael Faraday*. Atlantic Highlands, N.J.: Humanities Press, 1996.

Carlyle, Thomas. *Latter-Day Pamphlets*. London: Chapman and Hall, 1898.

———. *On Heroes, Hero-Worship and the Herioc in History*. Berkeley: University of California Press, 1993.

———. *Sartor Resartus: The Life and Opinions of Herr Teufelsdröckh*. New York: Odyssey Press, 1937.

———. *The French Revolution: A History*. Oxford: Oxford University Press, 1989.

Cavell, Stanley. "Betting Odd, Getting Even." In *The American Face of Edgar Allan Poe*, ed. Shawn Rosenheim and Stephen Rachman, 3–36. Baltimore: Johns Hopkins University Press, 1995.

———. *Disowning Knowledge in Six Plays of Shakespeare*. New York: Cambridge University Press, 1987.

———. *The Senses of Walden*. New York: Viking, 1972.

Chapman, Raymond. "'The Worthy Encompassed by the Inevitable': Hardy and a New Perception of Tragedy." In *Reading Thomas Hardy*, ed. Charles P. C. Pettit, 138–55. New York: St. Martin's Press, 1998.

Chartier, Roger. "Du livre au lire." In *Pratiques de la lecture*, ed. Roger Chartier, 62–88. Marseille: Rivages, 1985.

"Cheap Presbyterian Newspaper." *Princeton Review* 22, 1 (January 1850): 122–43.

Chesterton, G. K. *Charles Dickens*. New York: Schocken, 1965.

Churchyard, Thomas. *A Sparke of Friendship and Warme Goodwill*. London, 1588.

Cohen, Edward H. *Ebeneezer Cooke: The Sot-Weed Canon*. Athens: University of Georgia Press, 1975.

Coleman, C. *The British Paper Industry, 1495–1860: A Study in Industrial Growth*. Oxford: Clarendon, 1958.

Conley, Tom. *The Self-Made Map: Cartographic Writing in Early Modern France.*
Minneapolis: University of Minnesota Press, 1996.

Cox, J. Stevens. *Broadside Ballads of the 18th and Early 19th Centuries.* Guernsey:
Toucan Press, 1976.

Curtis, Gerard. *Visual Words: Art and the Material Book in Victorian England.* Aldershot, Hants: Ashgate, 2002.

Danahay, Martin A. "Matter Out of Place: The Politics of Pollution in Ruskin
and Turner." *Clio* 21, 1 (Fall 1991): 61–78.

Davis, Andrew McFarland. *Certain Old Chinese Notes or Chinese Paper Money.* Boston:
George Emery Littlefield, 1915.

———. *Currency and Banking in the Province of Massachusetts Bay.* New York: Macmillan, 1900.

Davis, Whitney. *Replications: Archaeology, Art History, Psychoanalysis.* University Park:
Pennsylvania State University Press, 1996.

Deleuze, Gilles. *Critique et clinique.* Paris: Minuit, 1993.

———. *Essays Critical and Clinical.* Trans. Daniel W. Smith and Michael A. Greco.
Minneapolis: University of Minnesota Press, 1997.

———. *Foucault.* Paris: Minuit, 1986.

———. *L'île déserte et autres texts: textes et entretiens, 1953–1974.* Paris: Minuit, 2002.

———. *Le pli: Leibniz et le baroque.* Paris: Minuit, 1988.

Deleuze, Gilles and Félix Guattari. *Kafka: pour une littérature mineure.* Paris: Minuit,
1975.

———. *Kafka: Toward a Minor Literature.* Trans. Dana Polan. Minneapolis: University of Minnesota Press, 1986.

Deleuze, Gilles and Claire Parnet. *Dialogues.* 2nd ed. Paris: Flammarion, 1996.

Del Mar, Alexander. *Barbara Villiers: Or A History of Monetary Crimes.* New York:
Cambridge Encyclopedia Company, 1899.

———. *History of Monetary Systems.* Chicago: Charles H. Kerr, 1896.

———. *The History of Money in America: From the Earliest Times to the Establishment
of the Constitution.* New York: Cambridge Encyclopedia Company, 1899.

De Man, Paul. *Blindness and Insight: Essays in the Rhetoric of Contemporary Criticism.*
2nd ed. Minneapolis: University of Minnesota Press, 1983.

———. "Phenomenality and Materiality in Kant." In *Hermeneutics: Questions and
Prospects,* ed. Gary Shapiro and Alan Sica, 121–44. Amherst: University of
Massachusetts Press, 1984.

———. *The Resistance to Theory.* Minneapolis: University of Minnesota Press, 1986.

Derrida, Jacques. *De l'esprit: Heidegger et la question.* Paris: Galilée, 1987.

———. *Donner la mort.* Paris: Galilée, 1999.

———. *Donner le temps: 1. La fausse monnaie.* Paris: Galilée, 1991.

———. "Freud and the Scene of Writing." In *Writing and Difference,* 196–231.
Trans. Alan Bass. Chicago: University of Chicago Press, 1978.

———. "Freud et la scène de l'écriture." In *L'écriture et la différence.* 293–340.
Paris: Seuil, 1967.

———. *Given Time: I. Counterfeit Money.* Trans. Peggy Kamuf. Chicago: University
of Chicago Press, 1992.

———. *Glas.* Paris: Galilée, 1974.

———. *Mal d'archive: une impression freudienne.* Paris: Galilée, 1995.

———. *Margins of Philosophy.* Trans. Alan Bass. Chicago: University of Chicago
Press, 1982.

———. "Le papier ou moi." In *Papier-machine: le ruban de machine à écrire et autres
réponses.* 239–72. Paris: Galilée, 2001.

———. *Passions.* Paris: Galilée, 1993.

————. *Politiques de l'amitié, suivi de L'oreille de Heidegger.* Paris: Galilée, 1994.

————. "The Purveyor of Truth." Trans. Alan Bass. In *The Purloined Poe: Lacan, Derrida and Reading,* ed. John P. Muller and William J. Richardson, 173–212. Baltimore: Johns Hopkins University Press, 1988.

————. "Le retrait de la métaphore." In *Psyché: inventions de l'autre,* 63–93. Paris: Galilée, 1998.

Desaulniers, Mary. *Carlyle and the Economics of Terror: A Study of Revisionary Gothicism in "The French Revolution".* Montreal: McGill-Queen's University Press, 1995.

Descartes, René. *Discourse on Method and the Meditations.* Trans. John Veitch. Buffalo, N.Y.: Prometheus Books, 1989.

Des Chene, Dennis. *Spirits and Clocks: Machine and Organism in Descartes.* Ithaca, N.Y.: Cornell University Press, 2001.

Dickens, Charles, "Address from an Undertaker to the Trade." *Household Words* 1, 13 (June 22, 1850): 301–4.

————. *Bleak House.* New York: Penguin, 1996.

————. *Dombey and Son.* New York: Penguin, 1985.

————. *Great Expectations.* New York: Penguin, 1996.

————. "Healthy by Act of Parliament." *Household Words* 1, 20 (August 10, 1850): 460–63.

————. *Little Dorrit.* New York: Penguin, 1985.

————. *Selected Journalism 1850–1870.* New York: Penguin, 1997.

Dickson, P. G. M. *The Financial Revolution in England: A Study in the Development of Public Credit, 1688–1756.* New York: St. Martin's Press, 1967.

Dieckmann, Liselotte. *Hieroglyphics: The History of the a Literary Symbol.* St. Louis: Washington University Press, 1970.

Donagan. Alan. "Sidgwick and Whewellian Intuitionism: Some Enigmas." *Essays on Henry Sidgwick,* ed. Bart Schultz, 123–42. Cambridge: Cambridge University Press, 1992.

Du Halde, Jean-Baptiste. *Déscription géographique, historique, chronologique, politique, et physique de l'Empire de la Chine et de la Tartarie chinoise,* vol. 1. Paris: Lemercier, 1735.

Eagleton, Terry. *Criticism and Ideology.* London: Verso, 1976.

Edmond, Rod. *Representing the South Pacific: Colonial Discourse from Cook to Gauguin.* New York: Cambridge University Press, 1997.

Eigner, Edwin M. *Robert Louis Stevenson and Romantic Tradition.* Princeton, N.J.: Princeton University Press, 1966.

Eiland, Howard. "Reception in Distraction." *boundary 2* 30, 1 (Spring 2003): 51–66.

Einzig, Paul. *Primitive Money: In its Ethnological, Historical and Ecnomic Aspects.* 2nd ed. Oxford: Pergamon Press, 1966.

Eisenstein, Elizabeth L. *The Printing Press as an Agent of Change: Communications and Cultural Transformations in Early-Modern Europe.* 2 vols. Cambridge: Cambridge University Press, 1979.

Eliot, Geroge. *The Mill on the Floss.* New York: Penguin, 1985.

Elkana, Yehuda. *The Discovery of the Conservation of Energy.* Cambridge, Mass.: Harvard University Press, 1974.

Elmer, Jonathan. *Reading at the Social Limit: Affect, Mass Culture, and Edgar Allan Poe.* Stanford, Calif.: Stanford University Press, 1995.

Epstein, Leonora. "Sale and Sacrament: The Wife Auction in *The Mayor of Casterbridge.*" *English Language Notes* 24, 4 (June, 1987): 50–56.

Erickson, Lee. *The Economy of Literary Form: English Literature and the Industrialization of Publishing, 1800–1850.* Baltimore: Johns Hopkins University Press, 1996.

Febvre, Lucien and Henri-Jean Martin. *L'apparition du livre.* Paris: Albin Michel, 1958.

Fenves, Peter. *Arresting Language: From Leibniz to Benjamin.* Stanford, Calif.: Stanford University Press, 2001.

Ferris, David. "'Truth is the death of intention': Benjamin's Esoteric History of Romanticism." *Studies in Romanticism* 31, 4 (Winter 1992): 455–80.

Fischer, Henry George. *L'écriture et l'art de l'Égypte ancienne: quatre leçons sur la paléographie et l'épigraphie pharaoniques.* Paris: Presses Universitaires de France, 1986.

Flasch, Kurt. *Nikolaus von Kues: Geschichte einer Entwicklung.* Frankfurt am Main: Vittorio Klostermann, 1998.

Foley, Vernard. *The Social Physics of Adam Smith.* West Lafayette, Ind.: Purdue University Press, 1976.

Foucault, Michel. *Discipline and Punish: The Birth of the Prison.* Trans. Alan Sheridan. New York: Vintage, 1979.

———. *Surveiller et punir: naissance de la prison.* Paris: Gallimard, 1975.

Frank, Lawrence. "'The Murders in the Rue Morgue': Edgar Allan Poe's Evolutionary Reverie." *Nineteenth-Century Literature* 50, 2 (September 1995): 168–88.

Franklin, Benjamin. "The Retort Courteous." *Writings,* 1122–30. New York: Literary Classics of the United States, 1987.

———. "A Modest Enquiry into the Nature and Necessity of a Paper Currency." *Writings,* 34–42. New York: Literary Classics of the United States, 1987.

———. "Right, Wrong and Reasonable." *Writings,* 595–600. New York: Literary Classics of the United States, 1987.

Freud, Sigmund. "A Note Upon the 'Mystic Writing-Pad.'" *The Standard Edition of the Complete Psychological Works of Sigmund Freud,* vol. 19, 227–32. Trans. James Strachey. London: Hogarth Press, 1961.

———. "Notiz über den 'Wunderblock.'" *Gesammelte Werke,* vol. 14, 3–8. London: Imago, 1948.

Gaillard, Françoise. "Pulp Story ou Balzac médiologue." In *Pouvoirs du papier,* 209–21. Cahiers de médiologie 4. Paris: Gallimard, 1997.

Galbraith, John Kenneth. *A Short History of Financial Euphoria.* Knoxville, Tenn.: Whittle Direct Books, 1990.

———. *Money: Whence It Came, Where It Went.* Boston: Houghton Mifflin, 1975.

Gasché, Rodolphe. *Of Minimal Things: Studies on the Notion of Relation.* Stanford, Calif.: Stanford University Press, 1999.

Georgescu-Roegen, Nicholas. *Energy and Economic Myths.* London: Pergamon, 1976.

Giles, Paul. "'Bewildering Entanglement': Melville's Engagement with British Culture." In *Cambridge Companion to Herman Melville,* ed. Robert S. Levine, 224–49. New York: Cambridge University Press, 1998.

Ginsburg, Michal Peled. *Economies of Change: Form and Transformation in the Nineteenth-Century Novel.* Stanford, Calif.: Stanford University Press, 1996.

Ginzburg, Louis. *The Legends of the Jews,* vol. 3. Trans. Paul Radin. Philadelphia: Jewish Publication Society of America, 1911.

Giroud, Vincent, ed. *R. L. S.: A Centenary Exhibition at the Beinecke Rare Book and Manuscript Library Commemorating the Death of Robert Louis Stevenson.* New Haven, Conn.: Yale University Press, 1994.

Gordon, Andrew and Bernhard Klein. "Introduction." In *Literature, Mapping, and the Politics of Early Modern Britain,* ed. Andrew Gordon and Bernhard Klein, 1–12. Cambridge: Cambridge University Press, 2001.

Goux, Jean-Joseph. *The Coiners of Language.* Trans. Jennifer Curtiss Gage. Norman: Oklahoma University Press, 1994.

Guillory, John. *Cultural Capital: The Problem of Literary Canon Formation.* Chicago: University of Chicago Press, 1993.

Gunn, Thom. "Hardy and the Ballads." *Agenda* 10, 2–3 (Spring–Summer 1972): 19–46.

Hamacher, Werner. *Entferntes Verstehen: Studien zu Philosophie und Literatur von Kant bis Celan.* Frankfurt am Main: Surhkamp, 1998.

———. *Pleroma—Reading in Hegel.* Trans. Nicholas Walker and Simon Jarvis. Stanford, Calif.: Stanford University Press, 1998.

Hardy, Thomas. *Jude the Obscure.* New York: Norton, 1999.

———. *The Life and Death of the Mayor of Casterbridge: A Story of a Man of Character.* New York: Penguin, 1985.

———. *The Life and Work of Thomas Hardy.* Ed. Michael Millgate. Athens: University of Georgia Press, 1985.

———. *The Return of the Native.* New York: Penguin, 1985

———. *Tess of the D'Urbervilles: A Pure Woman.* New York: Penguin, 1978.

Hart, Henry H. *Marco Polo: Venetian Adventurer.* Norman: Oklahoma University Press, 1967.

Hayes, Kevin. *Poe and the Printed Word.* New York: Oxford University Press, 2000.

Hayles, N. Katherine. *How We Became Posthuman: Virtual Bodies in Cybernetics, Literature, and Informatics.* Chicago: University of Chicago Press, 1999.

Hazlitt, William. "Godwin." *Essays.* London: Dent, 1960.

Headrick, Daniel. *The Invisible Weapon: Telecommunications and International Politics, 1851–1945.* New York: Oxford University Press, 1991.

———. *The Tools of Empire: Technology and European Imperialism in the Nineteenth Century.* New York: Oxford University Press, 1981.

Hegel, Georg Wilhelm Friedrich. *Phänomenologie des Geistes.* Frankfurt am Main: Suhrkamp, 1970.

———. *Phenomenology of Spirit.* Trans. A. V. Miller. Oxford: Oxford University Press, 1977.

———. *Vorlesungen über die Ästhetik.* 2 vols. Frankfurt am Main: Suhrkamp, 1970.

Heidegger, Martin. *Aristoteles, Metaphysik, Theta. 1–3. Von Wesen und Wirklichkeit der Kraft.* Gesamtausgabe, vol. 33. Frankfurt am Main: Klostermann, 1981.

———. *Aristotle's Metaphysics Theta 1–3: On the Essence and Actuality of Force.* Trans. Walter Brogan and Peter Warnek. Bloomington: Indiana University Press, 1995.

———. *Holzwege.* Frankfurt am Main: Klostermann, 1963.

———. *The Question Concerning Technology and Other Essays.* Trans. William Lovett. New York: Harper and Row, 1977.

———. *Der Satz vom Grund.* Neske: Pfullingen, 1957.

———. *Sein und Zeit.* 1927. Tübingen: Niemeyer, 1993.

Heilbroner, Robert. *Behind the Veil of Economics: Essays in the Worldly Philosophy.* New York: W.W. Norton, 1988.

Helgerson, Richard. "The Folly of Maps and Modernity." In *Literature, Mapping, and the Politics of Early Modern Britain,* ed. Andrew Gordon and Bernhard Klein, 241–62. Cambridge: Cambridge University Press, 2001.

Herbertz, Richard. *Die Lehre vom Unbewußten im System des Leibniz.* Halle: Max Niemeyer, 1905.

Hesse, Mary B. *Forces and Fields: The Concept of Action at a Distance in the History of Physics.* New York: Philosophical Library, 1961.

Holloway, John, and Joan Black, eds. *Later English Broadsides and Ballads.* London: Routledge and Kegan Paul, 1975.

Honneth, Axel. *Unsichtbarkeit. Stationen einer Theorie der Intersubjektivität*. Frankfurt am Main: Suhrkamp, 2003.

Hornung, Erik. *Idea into Image: Essays on Ancient Egyptian Thought*. Trans. Elizabeth Bredeck. Princeton, N.J.: Timken Publishers/Princeton University Press, 1992.

Hou, Ching-Lang. *Monnaies d'offrand et la notion de trésorerie dans la réligion chinoise*. Paris: Presses Universitaires de France, 1975.

House, Humphry. *The Dickens World*. London: Oxford University Press, 1941.

Howe, Irving. *Thomas Hardy*, 2nd ed. London: Macmillan, 1985.

Hunter, Dard. *Chinese Ceremonial Paper; a Monograph Relating to the Fabrication of Paper and Tin Foil and the Use of Paper in Chinese Rites and Religious Ceremonies*. Chillicothe, Ohio: Mountain House Press, 1937.

———. *Papermaking: The History of an Ancient Craft*. New York: Knopf, 1943.

Jackson-Houlston, C. M. *Ballads, Songs and Snatches: The Appropriation of Folk Song and Popular Culture in British Nineteenth-Century Realist Prose*. Aldershot: Ashgate, 1999.

Jacobs, Carol. *The Dissimulating Harmony: The Image of Interpretation in Nietzsche, Rilke, Artaud, and Benjamin*. Baltimore: Johns Hopkins University Press, 1978.

James, Henry. *The Golden Bowl*. New York: Penguin, 1987.

Jensen, Hendrik. *Essai sur l'origine de la gravure en bois et en taillerdouce*. Paris: F. Schoelle, 1808.

Jaworski, Philippe. *Melville, le désert et l'empire*. Paris: Presses de l'École Normale Supérieure, 1986.

Jevons, W. Stanley. *Money and the Mechanism of Exchange*. New York: Garland, 1983.

Johns, Adrian. *The Nature of the Book: Print and Knowledge in the Making*. Chicago: University of Chicago Press, 1998.

Johnson, Barbara. "The Frame of Reference: Poe, Lacan, Derrida." In *The Purloined Poe: Lacan, Derrida and Reading*, ed. John P. Muller and William J. Richardson, 213–51. Baltimore: Johns Hopkins University Press, 1988.

Johnstone, Charles. *Chrysal; Or the Lives of a Guinea*. 3 vols. London: Samuel Richards and Co., 1822.

Jolly, Roslyn. "Robert Louis Stevenson and Samoan History: Crossing the Roman Wall." In *Crossing Cultures: Essays on Literature and the Culture of the Asia-Pacific*, ed. Bruce Bennett, Jeff Doyle, and Satendra Nandan, 113–30. London: Skoob, 1996.

Jordan, Louis. *John Hull: The Mint and the Economics of Massachusetts Coinage*. Fort Myers, Fl.: C4 Publications, the Colonial Coin Collectors Club, 2002.

Kafka, Franz. *Der Prozess*. Frankfurt am Main: Fischer Taschenbuch Verlag, 1979.

———. *The Trial*. Trans. Willa and Edwin Muir and revised by E. M. Butler . New York: Schocken, 1974.

Kant, Immanuel. *Grounding for the Metaphysics of Morals*. Trans. James W. Ellington. Indianapolis: Hackett, 1993.

———. *Werke in Zehn Bänden*, 10 vols. Darmstadt: Wissenschaftliche Buchgesellschaft, 1983.

Keach, William. *Arbitrary Power: Romanticism, Language, Politics*. Princeton, N.J.: Princeton University Press, 2004.

Kelly, George Armstrong. *Hegel's Retreat from Eleusis: Studies in Political Thought*. Princeton, N.J.: Princeton University Press, 1978.

Kibbie, Ann Louise. "Monstrous Generation: The Birth of Capital in Defoe's *Moll Flanders* and *Roxana*." *PMLA* 110, 5 (October 1995): 1023–34.

King, Jeannette. *Tragedy in the Victorian Novel: Theory and Practice in the Novels of George Eliot, Thomas Hardy and Henry James*. New York: Cambridge University Press, 1978.

Kirtley, Bacil F. "The Devious Genealogy of the 'Bottle-Imp' Plot." *American Notes and Queries* 9 (1971): 67–70.

Kittler, Friedrich. *Aufschreibesysteme 1800/1900.* Munich: Fink, 1989.

———. *Draculas Vermächtnis. Technische Schriften.* Leipzig: Reclam, 1993.

Klancher, Jon. *The Making of English Reading Audiences, 1790–1832.* Madison: University of Wisconsin Press, 1987.

Kracauer, Siegfried. "On the Writings of Walter Benjamin." In *The Mass Ornament: Weimar Essays.* Trans. Thomas Y. Levin. Cambridge, Mass.: Harvard University Press, 1995.

Kristeller, Paul. *Kupferstich und Holzschnitt in vier Jahrhunderten.* 2nd ed. Berlin: Bruno Cassirer, 1911.

Lacan, Jacques. "Seminar on 'The Purloined Letter.'" Trans. Geoffrey Mehlman. In *The Purloined Poe: Lacan, Derrida and Reading,* ed. John P. Muller and William J. Richardson, 28–54. Baltimore: Johns Hopkins University Press, 1988.

Lacoue-Labarthe and Jean-Luc Nancy. *L'absolu littéraire: théorie de la littérature du romantisme allemand.* Paris: Seuil, 1978.

Landow, George P. *Hypertext 2.0; Being a Revised, Amplified Edition of Hypertext: The Convergence of Contemporary Critical Theory and Technology.* Baltimore: Johns Hopkins University Press, 1997.

Lawrence, D. H. *Studies in Classic American Literature.* New York: Penguin, 1977.

Leibniz, Gottfried Wilhelm. *Discourse on Metaphysics: Philosophical Essays.* Trans. Roger Arien and Daniel Garber. Indianapolis: Hackett, 1989.

———. *Die Philosophische Schriften von Gottfried Wilhelm Leibniz.* 7 vols. Ed. C. J. Gerhardt. Berlin: Weidmann, 1875–90.

Lester, Richard A. *Monetary Experiments.* Princeton, N.J.: Princeton University Press, 1939.

Locke, John. *An Essay Concerning Human Understanding.* 1689. Oxford: Oxford University Press, 1975.

Lothe, Jakob. "Variants on Genre: *The Return of the Native, The Mayor of Casterbridge, The Hand of Ethelberta.*" In *The Cambridge Companion to Thomas Hardy,* ed. Dale Kramer, 112–29. New York: Cambridge University Press, 1999.

Lowe, E. J. *Locke on Human Understanding.* London: Routledge, 1995.

Lukács, Georg. "Einleitung." In Georg Wilhelm Friedrich Hegel, *Ästhetik,* vol. 2, 587–624 Frankfurt am Main: Europäische Verlagsanstalt, 1955.

———. *Die Seele und Die Formen: Essays.* Neuwied: Hermann Luchterhand, 1971.

———. *Soul and Form.* Trans. Anna Bostock. Cambridge, Mass.: MIT Press, 1974.

———. *Die Theorie des Romans. Ein geschichtsphilosophischer Versuch über die Formen der großen Epik.* Berlin: Paul Cassirer, 1920.

———. *The Theory of the Novel: A Historico-Philosophical Essay on the Forms of Great Epic Literature.* Trans. Anna Bostock. Cambridge, Mass.: MIT Press, 1971.

Mack, Maynard. *The Garden and the City: Retirement and Politics in the Later Poetry of Pope, 1731–1743.* Toronto: University of Toronto Press, 1972.

Marcuse, Herbert. *Reason and Revolution: Hegel and the Rise of Social Theory.* 2nd ed. New York: Humanities Press, 1954.

Martin, Gérard and Michel Petit-Conil. *Le papier.* Paris: Presses Universitaires de France, 1964.

Martin, Henri-Jean. *Histoire et pouvoirs de l'écrit.* Paris: Perrin, 1988.

Marx, Karl. *Capital: A Critique of Political Economy.* Trans. Samuel More and Edward Aveling. New York: Random House, 1906.

———. *A Contribution to the Critique of Politcal Economy.* Trans. S. W. Ryazanskaya. New York: International Publishers, 1970.

————. *Das Kapital: Kritik der politischen Ökonomie*. Frankfurt am Main: Ullstein, 1969.

Marx, Karl. *Zur Kritik des Politischen Ökonomie. Werke*, vol. 13. Berlin: Dietz, 1961.

Massumi, Brian. *Parables for the Virtual : Movement, Affect, Sensation*. Durham, N.C.: Duke University Press, 2002.

Mauss, Marcel. *The Gift: The Form and Reason for Exchange in Archaic Societies*. Trans. W. D. Halls. New York: Norton, 1990.

————. *Sociologie et anthropologie*. Paris: Presses Universitaires de France, 1968.

Maxwell, James Clerk. "On Faraday's 'Electronic State.'" In *The Scientific Papers of James Clerk Maxwell*, vol. 1. New York: Dover, 1966.

Maxwell, Richard. *The Mysteries of Paris and London*. Charlottesville: University of Virginia Press, 1998.

Mayhew, Henry. *London Labour and the London Poor: The Condition and Earnings of Those That Will Work, Cannot Work, and Will Not Work*. 4 vols. London: Charles Griffin, 1864.

McCleary, James. *Le pays Stevenson*. Courtry: Christian de Bartillat, 1995.

McFaul, John. *The Politics of Jacksonian Finance*. Ithaca, N.Y.: Cornell University Press, 1972.

McGill, Meredith. *American Literature and the Culture of Reprinting, 1834–1853*. Philadelphia: University of Pennsylvania Press, 2003.

McLaughlin, Kevin. "The Coming of Paper: Aesthetic Value from Ruskin to Benjamin." *Modern Language Notes* 114, 5 (December 1999): 962–90.

————. "The Financial Imp: Ethics and Finance in Nineteenth-Century Fiction." *Novel: A Forum on Fiction* 29, 2 (Winter 1996): 165–83.

————. "Just Fooling: Paper, Money, Poe." *Differences: A Journal of Feminist Cultural Studies* 11,1 (Spring 1999): 38–67.

————. "Losing One's Place: Displacement and Domesticity in Dickens's *Bleak House*." *MLN* 108 (1993): 875–90.

————. *Writing in Parts: Imitation and Exchange in Nineteenth-Century Literature*. Stanford, Calif.: Stanford University Press, 1995.

McLynn, Frank. *Robert Louis Stevenson: A Biography*. London: Hutchinson, 1993.

McWilliams, Wilson Carey. *The Idea of Fraternity in America*. Berkeley: University of California Press, 1973.

Meier, Thomas Keith. *Defoe and the Defense of Commerce*. Victoria, British Columbia: University of Victoria Press, 1987.

Meisel, Perry. *The Myth of the Modern: a Study in British Literature and Criticism After 1850*. New Haven, Conn.: Yale University Press, 1987.

Melville, Herman. "Bartleby the Scrivener." In *Billy Budd and Other Stories*, 3–46. New York: Penguin, 1986.

————. *The Confidence-Man: His Masquerades*. Oxford: Oxford University Press, 1989.

————. "The Paradise of Bachelors and the Tartarus of Maids." In *Billy Budd and Other Stories*, 259–86. New York: Penguin, 1986.

————. *The Writings of Herman Melville: The Piazza Tales and Other Prose Pieces, 1839–1860*. Ed. Harrison Hayford, Alma A. MacDougall, and G. Thomas Tanselle. Evanston, Ill.: Northwestern University Press, 1987.

Mercier, Louis Sébastien. *Le nouveau paris, 1789–94*. Paris: Mercure de France, 1994.

Meyerson, Emile. *De l'explication dans les sciences*. Paris: Payot, 1928.

————. *Du cheminement de la pensée*. 3 vols. Paris: Félix Alcan, 1931.

————. *Essais*. Paris: Vrin, 1936.

————. *Explanation in the Sciences.* Trans. Mary-Alice and David A. Sipfle. Dordrecht: Kluwer, 1991.

————. *Identité et réalité.* Paris: Félix Alcan, 1908.

Michaels, Walter Benn. *The Gold Standard and the Logic of Naturalism: American Literature at the Turn of the Century.* Berkeley: University of California Press, 1988.

Miller, D. A. *The Novel and the Police.* Berkeley: University of California Press, 1988.

Miller, J. Hillis. "Interpretation in Dickens's *Bleak House.*" In *Victorian Subjects,* 179–99. New York: Harvester Wheatsheaf, 1990.

Mirowski, Philip. *More Heat Than Light: Economics as Social Physics; Physics as Nature's Economics.* Cambridge: Cambridge University Press, 1989.

Mitchell, W. C. A. *History of the Greenbacks.* Chicago: University of Chicago Press, 1903.

Montero, George. "Melville, 'Timothy Quicksand,' and the Dead-Letter Office." *Studies in Short Fiction* 9 (Spring, 1972): 198–201.

Moore, Thomas. *Memoirs, Journal, and Correspondence,* vol. 7. London: Longman, Brown, Green, and Longmans, 1856.

Morris, Henry. *Nicolas Louis Robert and His Endless Wire Papermaking Machine.* Newtown, Pa.: Bird and Bull Press, 2000.

————. *Two Essays on Paper History and Related Matters.* North Hills, Pa.: Bird and Bull Press, 1976.

Morus, Iwan Rhys. "Currents from the Underworld: Electricity and the Technology of Display in Early Victorian England." *Isis* 84, 1 (1993): 50–69.

————. "The Electric Ariel: Telegraphy and Commercial Culture in Early Victorian England." *Victorian Studies* 39, 3 (Spring 1996): 339–78.

Moses, Michael Valdez. *The Novel and the Globalization of Culture.* New York: Oxford University Press, 1995.

Mossman, Philip L. *Money of the American Colonies and Confederation: A Numismatic, Economic and Historical Correlation.* New York: American Numismatic Society, 1993.

Murray, John. *Practical Remarks on Modern Paper.* North Hills, Pa.: Bird and Bull Press, 1981.

Newman, Eric P. *The Early Paper Money of America.* Racine, Wis.: Whitman Publishing, 1967.

————. "The Successful British Counterfeiting of American Paper Money During the American Revolution." *British Numismatic Journal* 29 (1958): 174–87.

Nicholson, Colin. *Writing and the Rise of Finance: Capital Satires of the Early Eighteenth Century.* Cambridge: Cambridge University Press, 1994.

Nietzsche, Friedrich. *The Birth of Tragedy and the Genealogy of Morals.* Trans. Francis Golffing. New York: Doubleday, 1956.

Novak, Maximillian. E. *Economics and the Fiction of Daniel Defoe.* Berkeley: University of California Press, 1962.

O'Donnell, James J. *Avators of the Word: From Papyrus to Cyberspace.* Cambridge, Mass.: Harvard University Press, 1998.

Parker, Hershel, "The 'Sequel' in 'Bartleby.'" In *Bartleby and the Inscrutable: A Collection of Commentary,* ed. M. Thomas Inge, 159–65. Hamden, Conn.: Archon Books, 1979.

Parker, Hershel, "Dead Letters and Melville's Bartleby." *Resources for American Literary Study* 4 (Spring 1974): 90–99.

Paton, H. J. *The Categorical Imperative: A Study in Kant's Moral Philosophy.* London: Hutchinson, 1965.

Phillips, Henry Jr. *Historical Sketches of the Paper Currency of the American Colonies, Prior to the Adoption of the Federal Constitution.* 2 vols. Roxbury, Mass.: W. Eliot Woodward, 1865–66.

Plotz, John. *The Crowd: British Literature and Public Politics.* Berkeley: University of California Press, 2000.

Pocock, J. G. A. "Introduction." Edmund Burke, *Reflections on the Revolution in France,* vii–xlviii. Indianapolis: Hackett, 1987.

———. *The Machiavellian Moment: Florentine Political Thought and the Atlantic Republican Tradition.* Princeton, N.J.: Princeton University Press, 1975.

———. *Virtue, Commerce and History: Chiefly in the Eighteenth Century.* Cambridge: Cambridge University Press, 1985.

Poe, Edgar Allan. *Complete Works.* 17 vols. Ed. Janes A. Harrison. New York: AMS Press, 1965.

———. *Essays and Reviews.* Ed. G. R. Thompson. New York: Literary Classics of the United States, 1984.

———. *The Great Short Works of Edgar Allan Poe.* New York: Harper and Row, 1970.

———. *The Narrative of Arthur Gordon Pym of Nantucket.* New York: Penguin, 1986.

———. *Tales of Mystery and Imagination.* Everyman. London: J.M. Dent, 1993.

Pollin, Burton R. "Poe's 'Murders in the Rue Morgue': The Ingenious Web Unravelled." In *Studies in the American Renaissance, 1977,* ed. Joel Myerson, 235–59. Boston: Twayne Publishers, 1978.

Pollin, Burtin R. and J. A. Greenwood. "Stevenson on Poe: Unpublished Annotations of Numerous Poe Texts and a Stevenson Letter." *English Literature in Transition* 37, 3 (1974): 317–49.

Polo, Marco. *The Book of Ser Marco Polo the Venetian Concerning the Kingdom and Marvels of the East.* 2 vols. Trans. Henry Yule. London: John Murray, 1926.

Pope, Alexander. *Epistle to Allen Lord Bathurst. Epistles to Several Persons (Moral Essays).* Ed. F. W. Bateson. Twickenham ed. London: Methuen, 1951.

Popper, Karl. *The Open Society and Its Enemies.* Rev. edit. Princeton, N.J.: Princeton University Press, 1950.

Potter, William. *Humble Proposal to the Honorable Councell for Trade.* London: Edward Husband, 1651.

Pound, Ezra. *ABC of Economics.* London: Faber and Faber, 1933.

Proust, Marcel. *A la recherche du temps perdu.* 4 vols. Paris: Gallimard, 1954.

———. "Journées de lecture," *Contre Sainte-Beuve.* Paris: Gallimard, 1971.

———. *On Reading Ruskin.* Trans. Jean Autet and William Burford, ed. Richard Macksey. New Haven, Conn.: Yale University Press, 1987.

———. *Time Regained.* Trans. Andreas Mayer and Terence Kilmartin, revised by D. J. Enright. London: Chatto and Windus, 1992.

———. *Within a Budding Grove.* Trans. C. K. Scott Moncrieff. New York: Random House, 1981.

Rachman, Stephen. "'Es lässt sich nicht schreiben': Plagiarism and 'The Man of the Crowd.'" In *The American Face of Edgar Allan Poe,* ed. Shawn Rosenheim and Stephen Rachman, 48–87. Baltimore: Johns Hopkins University Press, 1995.

Rang, Florens Christian. *Shakespeare der Christ: eine Deutung der Sonette.* Heidelberg: Lambert Schneider, 1954.

Ritter, Joachim. *Hegel und die französische Revolution.* Frankfurt am Main: Suhrkamp, 1965.

Ritter, Joachim, ed. *Historisches Wörterbuch der Philosophie.* 8 vols. Basel: Schwabe and Co., 1974.

Roger Bozetto, "L'île dont le trésor est une aventure." *Europe* 770 (March 1994): 62–73.

Ross, W. D. *The Right and the Good.* Oxford: Oxford University Press, 1930.

Rothbard, Murray N. *The Panic of 1819: Reactions and Policies.* New York: Columbia University Press, 1962.

Rotman, Brian. *Ad infinitum—the Ghost in Turing's Machine: Taking God out of Mathematics and Putting the Body Back In: An Essay in Corporeal Semiotics.* Stanford: Stanford University Press, 1993.

Ruskin, John. *Unto This Last and Other Writings.* New York: Penguin, 1985.

———. *The Works of John Ruskin.* Ed. E. T. Cook and Alexander Wedderburn. London: George Allen, 1903.

Saenger, Paul. *Space Between Words: The Origins of Silent Reading.* Stanford, Calif.: Stanford University Press, 1997.

Saltz, Laura. "'(Horrible to Relate)': Recovering the Body of Marie Rogêt." In *The American Face of Edgar Allan Poe,* ed. Shawn Rosenheim and Stephen Rachman, 237–67. Baltimore: Johns Hopkins University Press, 1995.

Sandler, S. Gerald. "Poe's Indebtedness to Locke's *Essay Concerning Human Understanding.*" *Boston University Studies in English* 5 (1961): 107–21.

Schiffman, Robyn. L. "Wax-Work, Clock-Work, and Puppet-Shews: Bleak House and the Uncanny." *Dickens Studies Annual* 30 (2001): 159–71.

Schiller, Friedrich. *Die Räuber. Werke,* vol. 3. Weimar: Hermann Böhlhaus Nachfolger, 1953.

———. *Works.* Vol. 2. Boston: Household, 1884.

Schlanger, Judith. *Les métaphores de l'organisme.* Paris: Vrin, 1971.

Schlott, Adelheid. *Schrift und Schreiber im Alten Ägypten.* Munich: C.H. Beck, 1989.

Schmalenbach, Hermann. *Leibniz.* Munich: Drei Masken Verlag, 1921.

Schneewind, J. B. *Backgrounds of English Victorian Literature.* New York: Random House, 1970.

Sharp, James R. *The Jacksonians Versus the Banks: Politics in the States after the Panic of 1837.* New York: Columbia University Press, 1970.

Shell, Marc. *Art and Money.* Chicago: University of Chicago Press, 1995.

———. *The Economy of Literature.* Baltimore: Johns Hopkins University Press, 1978.

———. *Money, Language, and Thought: Literary and Philosophic Economics from the Medieval to the Modern Era.* Berkeley: University of California Press, 1982.

Shepard, Leslie. *The Broadside Ballad: A Study in Origins and Meaning.* London: Herbert Jenkins, 1962.

———. *John Pitts: Ballad Printer of Seven Dials, London 1765–1844.* London: Priveat Libraries Association, 1969.

Siskin, Clifford. *The Work of Writing: Literature and Social Change in Britain, 1700–1830.* Baltimore: Johns Hopkins University Press, 1998.

Slater, Michael. *The Composition and Monthly Publication of Nicholas Nickleby.* Menston: Scholar Press, 1973.

Smith, Adam. *The Wealth of Nations, Books I-III.* New York: Penguin, 1986.

Smith, Barbara Herrnstein. *Contingencies of Value: Alternative Perspectives for Critical Theory.* Cambridge, Mass.: Harvard University Press, 1988.

Smith, Vanessa. *Literary Culture and the Pacific.* Cambridge: Cambridge University Press, 1998.

Spilka, Mark. *Dickens and Kafka: A Mutual Interpretation.* Bloomington: Indiana University Press, 1963.

Stevenson. Robert Louis. *Dr. Jekyll and Mr. Hyde and Other Stories.* New York: Penguin, 1979.

———. *The Dynamiter*. London: Longman, Green, and Co., 1885.

———. *In the South Seas*. New York: Penguin, 1998.

———. *New Arabian Nights*. London: Chatto and Windus, 1882.

———. *Selected Writings of Robert Louis Stevenson*. New York: Random House, 1947.

———. *South Sea Tales*. Oxford: Oxford University Press, 1996.

———. *Treasure Island*. New York: Penguin, 1999.

———. *Virginibus Puerisque and Familiar Studies of Men and Books*. London: J.M. Dent, 1948.

———. *The Works of Robert Louis Stevenson*. 25 vols. London: Chatto and Windus, 1911–25.

Suchoff, David. *Critical Theory and the Novel: Mass Society and Cultural Criticism in Dickens, Melville and Kafka*. Madison: University of Wisconsin Press. 1994.

Sussman, Henry. "The Deconstructor as Politician: Melville's *Confidence-Man*." *Glyph* 4 (1978): 32–56.

Swann, Charles. "Ruskin's *The Stones of Venice* and Hardy's *The Dynasts*—A Possible Debt." *Notes and Queries* 39 (June, 1992): 187–88.

Szondi, Peter. *Poetik und Geschitsphilosophie*, vol. 1. Frankfurt am Main: Suhrkamp, 1974.

Tagg, John. "Evidence, Truth and Order: Photographic Records and the Growth of the State." In *The Photography Reader*, ed. Liz Wells, 256–60. London: Routledge, 2003.

Tallack, Douglas. *The Nineteenth-Century American Short Story: Language, Form and Ideology*. London: Routledge, 1993.

Tambling, Jeremy. "Carlyle in Prison: Reading *Latter-Day Pamphlets*." *Dickens Studies Annual* 26 (1998): 311–33.

———. *Lost in the American City: Dickens, James and Kafka*. New York: Palgrave, 2001.

Tocqueville, Alexis de. *Democracy in America*. Trans. Henry Reeve. New York: Vintage, 1945.

Trübners Deutsches Wörterbuch. Berlin: Walter de Gruyter, 1939.

The New Oxford Annotated English Bible, with the Apocrypha. Expanded ed. New York: Oxford University Press, 1977.

Thiel, Detlef. "Schrift, Gedächtnis, Gedächtniskunst: Zur Instrumentalisierung des Graphischen bei Francis Bacon." In *Ars memorativa. Zur kulturgeschichtlichen Bedeutung der Gedächtniskunst 1400–1750*, ed. Jörg Jochen Berns and Wolfgang Neuber, 170–205. Tübingen: Max Niemeyer, 1993.

Thiers, A. *Histoire de Law*. Paris: Michel Lévy, 1858.

Tholen, Georg Christoph. *Die Zäsur der Medien: Kulturphilosophische Konturen*. Frankfurt am Main: Suhrkamp, 2002.

Trithemus, Johannes. *In Praise of Scribes (De Laude Scriptorum)*. Trans. Roland Behrendt. Lawrence, Kan.: Coronado Press, 1974.

Turing, A. M. "On Computable Numbers, with an Application to the *Entscheidungsprobleme*." *Proceedings of the London Mathematical Society* 2, 42 (1936–37): 230–65.

Vaihinger, H. *Commentar zu Kants* Kritik der Reinen Vernunft. 2 vols. Stuttgart: Spemann, 1881–92.

Vatin, Françoise. *Le travail: économie et physique*. Paris: Presses Universitaires de France, 1993.

Vernon, John. *Money and Fiction: Literary Realism in the Nineteenth and Early Twentieth Centuries*. Ithaca, N.Y.: Cornell University Press, 1984.

Vicinus, Martha. *Broadsides of the Industrial North*. Newcastle upon Tyne: Frank Graham, 1975.

Virilio, Paul. *La machine de vision*. Paris: Galilée, 1988.

* add Thompson, Gary and Eric Carl Link, *Neutral Ground: New Traditionalism and the American Romance Controversy.* Baton Rouge: Louisiana State UP, 1999.

Wagenbach, Klaus. *Franz Kafka. Eine Biographie seiner Jugend*. 1883–1912. Bern: Francke, 1958.

Walsh, Susan. "Bodies of Capital: *Great Expectations* and the Climacteric Economy." *Victorian Studies* 37, 1 (1993): 73–98.

Warburton, William. *The Divine Legation of Moses Demonstrated*. 2 vols. London: Thomas Tegg and Son, 1837.

Warminski, Andrzej. *Readings in Interpretation*. Minneapolis: University of Minnesota Press, 1987.

Warner, Michael. "The Mass Public and the Mass Subject." In *The Phantom Public Sphere*, ed. Bruce Robbins, 234–56. Minneapolis: University of Minnesota Press, 1993.

Wasserman, E. R. *Pope's Epistle to Bathurst*. Baltimore: Johns Hopkins University Press, 1960.

Watson, Harold F. *Coasts of Treasure Island*. San Antonio: Naylor, 1969.

Watt, Ian. *The Rise of the Novel: Studies in Defoe, Richardson, and Fielding*. Berkeley: University of California Press, 1957.

Wolfreys, Julian, ed. *The Mayor of Casterbridge: Contemporary Critical Essays*. Houndmills, Basingstoke: Macmillan, 2000.

Weber, Samuel. "Benjamin's Style." In *Columbia Encyclopedia of Aesthetics*. Ed. Michael Kelly. New York: Columbia University Press, 1998.

———. "Genealogy of Modernity: History, Myth and Allegory in Benjamin's *Origin of the German Mourning Play*." *Modern Language Notes* 106, 3 (April 1991): 465–500.

———. *Mass Medauras: Form, Technics, Media*. Standford, Calif.: Stanford University Press, 1996.

———. "Reading—'To the Very End of the World.'" *Modern Language Notes* 111, 5 (December 1996): 819–34.

———. "Un-Übersetzbarkeit: Zu Benjamins 'Aufgabe des Übersetzers.'" In *Die Sprache der Anderen*, ed. Anselm Haverkamp, 121–46. Frankfurt am Main: Fischer Zeitschriften, 1997.

———. *Unwrapping Balzac: A Reading of "La peau de chagrin"*. Toronto: University of Toronto Press, 1979.

———. "Virtuailität der Medien." In *Konfigurationen. Zwischen Kunst und Medien*, ed. Sigrid Schade and Hans Christoph Tholen, 35–49. Munich: Wilhelm Fink Verlag, 1999.

Webster, Peletiah. *Political Essays*. Philadelphia: J. Crukshank, 1791.

Weil, Eric. *Hegel et l'état*. Paris: J. Vrin, 1950.

Wellek, René. *Immanuel Kant in England, 1793–1838*. Princeton, N.J.: Princeton University Press, 1931.

West, Gillian. "*Bleak House*: Esther's Illness." *English Studies* 73, 1 (February 1992): 30–34.

Whalen, Terence. *Edgar Allan Poe and the Masses: The Political Economy of Literature in Antebellum America*. Princeton, N.J.: Princeton University Press, 1999.

Widdig, Bernd. *Culture and Inflation in Weimar Germany*. Berkeley: University of California Press, 2001.

Wienold, G. "Kanon und Hierarchiebildung in Sprache und Literatur." In *Kanon und Zensor*, ed. Aleida Assmann and Jan Assmann. Munich: Fink, 1987.

Williams, L. Pearce. *The Origins of Field Theory*. Lanham, Md.: University Press of America, 1980.

Winfield, Christine. "Factual Sources of Two Episodes in *The Mayor of Casterbridge*." *Nineteenth-Century Fiction* 25 (1970): 224–31.

Winkler, Norbert. *Nikolaus von Kues: Zur Einführung.* Hamburg: Junius Verlag, 2001.

Winship, Michael. "The Transatlantic Book Trade and Anglo-American Literary Culture in the Nineteenth Century." In *Reciprocal Influences: Literary Production, Distribution, and Consumption in America,* ed. Steven Fink and Susan S. Williams, 98–122. Columbus: Ohio State University Press, 1999.

Woodmansee, Martha and Mark Osteen, eds. *The New Economic Criticism : Studies at the Intersection of Literature and Economics.* London: Routledge, 1999.

Wordsworth, William. "Preface to Lyrical Ballads." In *The Selected Poetry and Prose of Wordsworth.* Ed. Geoffrey F. Hartman. New York: New American Library, 1970.

Wright, T. R. *Hardy and His Readers.* Basingstoke: Palgrave, 2003.

———. *The Religion of Humanity: The Impact of Comtean Positivism on Victorian Britain.* New York: Cambridge University Press, 1986.

Yolton, John W. *Locke and the Compass of Human Understanding: A Selective Commentary on the "Essay".* Cambridge: Cambridge University Press, 1970.

Zboray, Ronald. *A Fictive People: Antebellum Economic Development and the American Reading Public.* New York: Oxford University Press, 1993.

Index